The Group Basis of Politics

A Study in Basing-Point Legislation

The Group Basis of Politics

A Study in Basing-Point Legislation

By Earl Latham

1 9 6 5
OCTAGON BOOKS, INC.
NEW YORK

Copyright 1952, by Cornell University

Reprinted *1965*
by special arrangement with Cornell University Press

OCTAGON BOOKS, INC.
175 FIFTH AVENUE
NEW YORK, N. Y. 10010

LIBRARY OF CONGRESS CATALOG CARD NUMBER: 65-16775

328.73
L352

Printed in U.S.A. by
NOBLE OFFSET PRINTERS, INC.
NEW YORK 3, N. Y.

To Margaret

12-13-66 OCTAGON 6.30

Preface

This book is a study of the struggle in the Eightieth and Eighty-first Congresses to enact legislation dealing with the basing-point system of quoting delivered prices, which has been widely practiced in industries producing fungible goods, bulky in character, and normally delivered by railroad. The struggle to enact such legislation did not end with these sessions, but the principal alignments were marked out at this time, and the chief arguments for and against were stated.

The validity of basing-point systems under the antitrust laws was thrown into doubt by the Cement Case of 1948, in which the Supreme Court held that the Cement Institute and members of the cement industry had employed the multiple basing-point system of quoting delivered prices in unlawful ways. In this account, the evolution of the bill (S. 1008) which the Eighty-first Congress adopted, and which the President vetoed, is given close attention. Much can be learned from analysis of the mechanism and the procedures by and through which statutes become law, and the legislative history is, accordingly, given prominence. But Congress is imperfectly understood if it is regarded merely as a bill-bearing and resolution-breeding institution. It is an official group functioning in an environment of groups, official and unofficial. The influence of "lobbies" in the legislative process is often pointed out. But even the recognition of the influence of "lobbies," although more realistic than earlier legalistic explanations of legislative behavior, is still an incomplete view of the entire process by which measures become law—that is, become the rules by which society is governed. For if unofficial groups appear to pressure official groups to their desire, and move them to objects which they would not—without this pressure—approach, it may be that the vectors which appear in Congress are merely local lines of force within a larger field. It becomes necessary then to place the legislative process within the larger context of the group struggle of which it is a part. Certain propositions which seek to do this are set out in the first chapter.

Portions of the book have appeared elsewhere as special studies. Acknowledgment is made to the editors of the *Yale Law Journal* for permission to reprint the material which appears in Chapter Two. This was originally given as a paper at the Chicago meeting of the American Political Science Association in December 1948. Acknowledgment is also made to the editors of *Law and Contemporary Problems* for permission to reprint the material in Chapters Three and Four. Special acknowledgment is made to George Goodwin, Jr., for research and editorial assistance and to John C. Wahlke for critical suggestions. Mrs. Barbara Bond supplied patient and efficient stenographic assistance.

This study appears under the auspices of the Joseph B. Eastman Foundation at Amherst College.

EARL LATHAM

Amherst, Massachusetts
May 1951

Contents

The Group Basis of Politics

A Study in Basing-Point Legislation

Chapter One

Group Conflict

and the Political Process

The chief social values cherished by individuals in modern society are realized through groups.[1] The number is countless, and the variety of these social groupings is abundant and complex. No aspect of the life of the individual is untouched by them. Modern man is literally conducted from the cradle to the grave by groups, for he is born in a family, goes to school in organized classes, goes to church, perhaps, plays with boyhood gangs, joins fraternities, works for a corporation, belongs to various associations, cultural, civic, professional and social, and is carried off to his immortal reward by a business enterpriser with the solemnity appropriate to such ceremonies. Some of these groupings are simple in structure, unicellular so to speak, as when the boys in Grade Four feel a community of interest, a conscious-

[1] "The whole structure of modern society is associational. . . ." William Yandell Elliott, *The Pragmatic Revolt in Politics* (New York: Macmillan Co., 1928), p. 434. The view expressed by Elliott is also asserted by John Dewey in *The Public and Its Problems* (Chicago: Gateway Books, 1946. Dewey, however, denies the usefulness of the concept "society" as a generalizing idea, because he says it is devoid of meaning. To pose problems of relationship between the individual and "society" is as meaningless, he feels, as to make a problem out of the relation of the letters of an alphabet to the alphabet. *Ibid.,* p. 69.

ness of kind, that serves to distinguish them from the boys in Grade Five. Both are groups.[2] In complex forms, such as the Cominform and the wartime Combined Chiefs of Staff, these groupings may be intricate meshes of associated, federated, combined, consolidated, merged, or amalgamated units and subunits of organization, fitted together to perform the divided and assigned parts of some common purpose to which the components are dedicated. Many organized groups operate out of the direct public gaze, like religious organizations, which tend to have a low degree of visibility. Others, like many trade union organizations, have a high degree of visibility, to the point where the average newspaper reader may easily see the selfishness of the prominent labor leader but not the selfishness of employer groups who comprise the other half of the collective bargaining relationship. The high visibility of national groups diverts the eye from the great number which stand at the elbow of the citizen of every small town, for groups abound, and may be examined close and afar.[3]

The Group Idea in Social Science

The literature of many disciplines agrees, as it does in little else, on the central importance of groups to an under-

---

[2] Much modern research in social psychology has centered upon interpersonal reactions in these "unicellular" or primary groups. Critics of this research have mentioned the difficulties involved in extending similar investigations into more complex multicellular forms of group organization. See Oliver Garceau, "Research in the Political Process," 45 *American Political Science Review* 69 ff. (March 1951).

[3] In the small town of Amherst, Mass., there are, not counting student organizations and the official groups in the town government, "well more than one hundred Clubs, Lodges, Leagues, Guilds, Tribes, Granges, Circles, Unions, Chapters, Councils, Societies, Associations, Auxiliaries, Brotherhoods, and Fellowships. Their specialties or special interests, to name a few, include cards, cameras, stamps, gardens, churches, teachers, speakers, voters, horses, business, service, golf,

standing of men in their relations with one another. The science of sociology, for example, devotes itself to the study of groups and groupings in society, the forms of group structure and behavior, the role and the relation of the individual to the group, the development of functional norms of behavior, the tendency of informal groups to divide into a leadership and a led, the relation of subgroups to the prime, and so on.[4] But the sociologists are not alone. The instrumentalist philosophy of John Dewey rejects the abstract individual as a fictional character, and asserts that the

nature, eating, fishing, gunning, parents, grandparents, ancestors, needlework, temperance, travel, and kindergarten." William L. Doran, 31 *University of Massachusetts Alumni Bulletin* 4 (December 1948).

[4] See, for example, Talcott Parsons, *The Structure of Social Action: A Study in Social Theory with Special Reference to a Group of Recent European Writers* (New York and London: McGraw-Hill, 1937); Max Weber, *The Theory of Social and Economic Organization,* ed. by Talcott Parsons (New York: Oxford University Press, 1947), especially the concept of the "corporate group," p. 145 ff.; Vilfredo Pareto, *The Mind and Society,* tr. by A. Bongiorno and A. Livingston, 4 vols. (New York: Harcourt, Brace and Co., 1938); Gaetano Mosca, *The Ruling Class* (New York and London: McGraw-Hill, 1939). The concepts of the elite and the mass which are developed by Pareto and Mosca are concepts of group action. For political applications of sociological methods, see the works of the following, in addition to Pareto and Mosca: Robert Michels, *Political Parties: A Sociological Study of the Oligarchic Tendencies of Modern Democracy* (New York: Hearst's International Library Co., 1915); Robert MacIver, *The Modern State* (Oxford: Clarendon Press, 1926); *The Web of Government* (New York: Macmillan Co., 1947); and Karl Mannheim, *Man and Society in an Age of Reconstruction* (New York: Harcourt, Brace and Co., 1948). Michels defines an elite as an equivalent of officialdom; Mosca, of a ruling class broader than officialdom. Some of these sociological insights into the structure and processes of politics are not new. For example, John Adams foreshadowed the view that society fundamentally divides into elite and mass when he said: "It already appears, that there must be in every society of men, superiors and inferiors, because God has laid in the Constitution and course of nature, the foundations of the distinction." Charles Francis Adams (ed.), *The Life and Works of John Adams* (Boston: Charles C. Little and James Brown, 1851), IV, 427.

individual has meaning only in his relations with others.[5] The psychologists, by different routes, come to the same conclusion. The Gestalt school argues that the basic forms of knowing are comprehensive collectivities, general thought forms and patterns, not atomistic particulars. Modern psychoanalytical theory as represented by Dr. Karen Horney rejects the earlier Freudian assumption that the singular person can be understood apart from his culture, and asserts, instead, that what were formerly regarded as innate elements of the personality are, rather, induced traits originating in the culture, the result of interpersonal, that is, group or social, influences.[6] The concept of the group has been indispensable to those who have worked in the combined fields of cultural anthropology and psychology.[7] The concept of the group is basic to certain approaches to

---

[5] John Dewey, *Human Nature and Conduct: An Introduction to Social Psychology* (New York: H. Holt and Co., 1922). See also Dewey's *The Public and Its Problems*.

[6] Karen Horney, *The Neurotic Personality of Our Time* (New York: W. W. Norton, 1937); *New Ways in Psychoanalysis* (New York: W. W. Norton, 1939). For example, Sigmund Freud, *The Interpretation of Dreams,* tr. by Dr. A. A. Brill (New York: Modern Library Edition, 1950), describes and explains the Oedipus complex without limiting it to any culture (pp. 160–162, 269–270). But what becomes of the Oedipus complex in a society like that of the Marquesas or the Trobriand Islands, where, anthropologists assert, it does not exist? Modern research suggests that this fundamental pattern in human behavior is a culture trait. For a discussion of this point, see Abram Kardiner, *The Individual and His Society* (New York: Columbia University Press, 1947), p. 479 ff.

[7] Well known are the works of Bronislaw Malinowski, *Argonauts of the Western Pacific* (New York: E. P. Dutton, 1922); Ruth Benedict, *Patterns of Culture* (Boston: Houghton Mifflin, 1934); *The Chrysanthemum and the Sword* (Boston: Houghton Mifflin, 1946); Kardiner, *The Individual and His Society,* and Ralph Linton, *The Cultural Background of Personality* (New York: Appleton-Century Co., 1945). A comparison of culture patterns is made by David Riesman in an interesting chapter on "Americans and Kwakiutls" in *The Lonely Crowd* (New Haven: Yale University Press, 1950), pp. 271–282.

jurisprudence,[8] and it has been helpful in bringing to economics a knowledge of the human institutions through which men dig coal, make soap and battleships, create credit, and allocate the resources of production. Commons, Veblen, Clark, Andrews, and other pioneers in the empirical study of such economic group forms as banks, corporations, granges, unions, co-operatives, railroads, brokerage houses, and exchanges did much to rectify the notion that some objective law, heedless of men, somehow filled each purse to the exact limit justified by the contribution of its owner to the total of the goods and services of society. The economic theory of a century ago fixed the nature of the economic universe by definition and tended to derive its characteristics by deduction, an economic world inhabited by a multiplicity of individuals in isolation, where combination was a pathological deviation. Such a *defined* (not observed) universe could not fail to work—in the realm of discourse. So far have we come from this view that a whole new vocabulary has been invented to explain the operations of an economic community formed of aggregations, clusters, blocs, and combinations of people and things— not individuals in isolation. Few modern writers on economics would be able to discuss their subject matter without reference to "oligopoly," "imperfect competition," "monopolistic competition," and other group phenomena in the economic community.

The Group Idea in Political Theory

The utilitarians made the same assumptions about the nature of the political community that they made about the nature of the economic community. The liberal philosophy

[8] As in N. S. Timasheff, *An Introduction to the Sociology of Law,* (Cambridge: Harvard University Committee on Research in the Social Sciences, 1939) and Alexander H. Pekelis, *Law and Social Action, Selected Essays,* ed. by Milton R. Konvitz (Ithaca: Cornell University Press, 1950).

of a John Stuart Mill rejected the doctrines of natural law and right that were so familiar to the eighteenth century but retained the feeling that the chief political problems were those that involved the singular individual on the one hand and the "state" on the other. All other and intermediate associations and groupings were dissolved, blanked, and obscured—a kind of sunken hinterland between two dominating mountainous battlements. This exaggerated individualism not only abstracted man from his social environment; it made him more sentient, more responsive to the gentle but compelling dictates of reason, more enlightened about his affairs than the facts justified. The political community had some of the characteristics of an Oxford debating society, policy emerging from endless argument, with reason presiding in the speaker's chair. Such a view was stated by Lord Bryce, who said, "In the ideal democracy, every citizen is intelligent, patriotic, disinterested. His sole wish is to discover the right side in each contested issue and to fix upon the best man among competing candidates." [9]

But utilitarian theories did not entirely dominate the field of political speculations, even in England. On the Continent and to a lesser degree in England, considerable attention was given to the works of the philosophical idealists—the school of Hegel, Fichte, and Treitschke on the Continent, and T. H. Green, Bradley, and Bosanquet later in England. The idealists virtually abolished the individual, by deduction.[10] The utilitarians imagined the political community to be a loose co-existence of singular individuals,

---

[9] This view is also strongly expressed by John Stuart Mill in the famous essay "On Liberty." For a discussion of the relation between Mill's view and the prevailing doctrine of free speech in the United States Supreme Court, see the article by Earl Latham, "The Theory of the Judicial Doctrine of Freedom of Speech," in 12 *Journal of Politics* 637 (November 1950).

[10] For a brief but strong criticism of Hegel, see Bertrand Russell,

like marbles on a plate, held loosely together within the circumference of a common restraint but otherwise complete, unengaged, private, peculiar, and unique. The idealists imagined the political community to be more nearly like beads on a string, of which the separate parts by themselves were incomplete and without meaning, and which existed only to fulfill the pattern of the necklace.

The principal attack, in England at least, upon the political speculations of the philosophic idealists was made by a group of writers professing pluralist doctrines. Figgis, Maitland, G. D. H. Cole, and Laski showed that many of the assumptions of the idealist school were contrary to fact; that the state did not absorb all the loyalties of the individual in the political community, as had been asserted, but that many lesser associations also made claim to the faith, attachment, devotion, and obedience of the individual, such as church, corporation, and trade union, and that these claims were acknowledged by responsive behavior. The state, said the pluralists, is merely one association among a host of associations both as fact and right, which, far from absorbing the entire allegiance of the individual, has to compete with conflicting group loyalties, some of which are invincible. Most people think of themselves first as members of their clubs, lodges, unions, or parishes, and only incidentally as members of the state. The state, therefore, is merely one group among many, without superior right to dominate other associations. In its extreme form (in guild socialism), the pluralist doctrine advocated political communities organized syndically by industries, with common affairs administered by common consent, a loose kind of confederation, or a working alliance.

The pluralists did useful work when they evaporated the misty figment of the state which the idealists had presented

Philosophy and Politics (London: Cambridge University Press, 1947), pp. 16–20.

as a colossus of unity, a monolith, an absolute, a total system swallowing and assimilating all personal beliefs, attachments, obligations, and relations, endowed with some of the attributes of human personality like will, and having an autonomous and independent life and existence apart from the lives and personalities of the members of the political community. But while this spectral personality was exorcised from the state by the pluralists, they materialized the phantasm in other bodies. The state, they said, did not have a "real" personality, separate and apart from the people; it was not a separate corpus possessing human attributes like personality and will. But what was denied to the state was claimed for the other, the nonstate associations, such as churches and trade unions. One would have thought that the arguments that destroyed the rejected real personality of the state should also have destroyed the assumed real personalities of the group associations. Or conversely, if the nonstate associations had real personalities, it was difficult to see why the state should be denied one, since it was also an association. Actually, the effort, by words, to make the state disappear did not succeed because all the pluralist writers found it necessary to invent a normative rule-making apparatus to represent the community interests of the constituent group associations, that is, to perform the functions of the state. What they sought to achieve was a political community based upon a federation of constituent groups to replace the consolidated lump that the idealists had been describing, authoritarian and homogenized.

The important insights of the pluralists were at least two, however. First, they pointed out the undeniable fact of the group basis of society, both in its political and economic communities. Second, they described a few of the virtually infinite number of accommodations between the common and the universal, on the one hand, and the diverse and the particular, on the other, which the principle of federalism makes possible. Federalism is a master design which helps to make political unity out of a multiplicity of dissimilar parts as local as the organizations in the Community Fund and as universal as the United Nations.

The English pluralists typically combined observation and hope. While they described the group basis of society, they then either erected Utopia upon this foundation or employed the insight to rationalize prejudged social and economic reforms. They intermingled wit and fact, and may indeed have been led to the second by the intensity of the first. Some support for this view is supplied by the evidence that writers like Laski, once pluralists, abandoned the doctrine and worked with more authoritarian modes of social reform, ignoring the fact when it seemed no longer to suit the hope. Perhaps for this kind of pluralists, the adjective "philosophic" may be employed as a phrase which combines the characteristics of system, perception, metaphysics, and value judgment, all of which are found in their writings. The philosophic pluralists accepted the group basis of society but failed to investigate its forms, mutations, and permutations in a scientific spirit. It has remained for others to carry forward scientific analyses of group behavior, including a number of writers on politics. The word "pluralists" may properly be applied to these investigators since they deal with the plurality of observed group forms. Unlike the philosophers, however, they are concerned less with prejudged programs of social and economic reform than with the correct investigation of the many phenomena connected with the activities of groups in society. The adjective "analytical" may be used to refer to that species of pluralist who concerns himself with the structure and processes of group forms as they in fact occur. Although analytical pluralism may characterize principal works of sociology, the term is here reserved for political writers, to distinguish them from their philosophic predecessors.

Beginning with Arthur Bentley in 1908 American writers on politics have increasingly accepted the view that the group is the basic political form.[11] Studies have been made of the significance of the group in the enactment of legislation, in the conduct of party activity, in the formulation and execution of public policy, in the process of public administration, and in the protection of civil liberties.[12] The recognition of the importance of groups to a study and

---

[11] Arthur Bentley, *The Process of Government* (Chicago: University of Chicago Press, 1908); Pendleton Herring, *Group Representation before Congress* (Baltimore: Johns Hopkins Press, 1929), *Public Administration and the Public Interest* (New York and London: McGraw-Hill, 1936), and *The Politics of Democracy* (New York: W. W. Norton, 1940); E. E. Schattschneider, *Politics, Pressures, and the Tariff* (New York: Prentice Hall, 1935), and *Party Government* (New York: Farrar and Rinehart, 1942); William Bennett Munro, *The Invisible Government* (New York: Macmillan Co., 1928); Peter Odegard, *Pressure Politics* (New York: Columbia University Press, 1928); Alfred de Grazia, *Public and Republic, Political Representation in America* (New York: Knopf, 1951).

[12] Enactment of legislation: Fred W. Riggs, *Pressures on Congress* (New York: Columbia University Press, 1950); Stephen K. Bailey, *Congress Makes a Law* (New York: Columbia University Press, 1950); Roland Young, *This Is Congress* (New York: Knopf, 1943). Party activity: Peter Odegard and E. A. Helms, *American Politics* (New York: Harper, 1938); Schattschneider, *Party Government;* V. O. Key, *Politics, Parties and Pressure Groups* (New York: Thomas Y. Crowell Co., 1946). Formulation of policy: Stuart Chase, *Democracy under Pressure* (New York: Twentieth Century Fund, 1945); Wesley McCune, *The Farm Bloc* (New York: Doubleday Doran and Co., 1943). Public administration: Avery Leiserson, *Administrative Regulation* (Chicago: University of Chicago Press, 1942); Gabriel Almond, *The American People and Foreign Policy* (New York: Harcourt, Brace and Co., 1950); Robert Dahl, *Congress and Foreign Policy* (New York: Harcourt, Brace and Co., 1950); Herring, *Public Administration and the Public Interest.* Civil liberties: David Riesman, "Civil Liberties in a Period of Transition," *Public Policy,* ed. by Carl J. Friedrich and Edward S. Mason (Cambridge: Harvard University Press, 1942), III, 33 ff.; "Private Attorneys-General: Group Action in the Fight for Civil Liberties," 58 *Yale Law Journal* 574 ff. (1949).

understanding of politics has drawn the attention of political scientists to the considerable amount of work done in the related social science fields on the nature of group organization; and, increasingly, materials which have been developed in these allied fields have been used in political writing and in the class room. Closely relevant to politics are the studies of the structure and process of groups as simple, amorphous, and uncontrived as the street corner gang, as remote as South Pacific islanders, and as near as Middletown.[13] Such studies throw much light upon the contrast between the objective and subjective relationships among people in groups, the difference between the formal and the informal organization which this reflects, the imposed rule and the developed custom, the external and visible structure on the one hand and the internal and invisible network of unconscious, nonlogical personal relationships on the other, the distribution of authority and the distribution of power, the nature of leadership and the relations of leaders and followers, the importance of prestige and status anxieties, and the methods employed to develop and maintain security systems for the protection of the members of the group.[14]

---

[13] William Whyte, *Street Corner Society* (Chicago: University of Chicago Press, 1943); W. Lloyd Warner and Paul S. Lunt, *The Social Life of a Modern Community* (New Haven, Yale University Press, 1941); W. Lloyd Warner and J. O. Low, *The Strike, A Social Analysis* (New Haven: Yale University Press, 1947); W. Lloyd Warner and Leo Srole, *The Social Systems of American Ethnic Groups* (New Haven: Yale University Press, 1945); W. Lloyd Warner, *The Status System of a Modern Community* (New Haven: Yale University Press, 1942); Malinowski, *Argonauts of the Western Pacific;* Robert S. and Helen M. Lynd, *Middletown in Transition* (New York, Harcourt, Brace and Co., 1937); W. Lloyd Warner, *Democracy in Jonesville* (New York: Harper, 1949).

[14] Chester I. Barnard, *Functions of the Executive* (Cambridge: Harvard University Press, 1947); F. J. Roethlisberger and W. J. Dickson, *Management and the Worker* (Cambridge: Harvard University Press, 1939); F. J. Roethlisberger, *Management and Morale* (Cam-

Organized Groups as Structures of Power

The conclusion emerges from an inspection of the literature dealing with the structure and the process of groups
that, insofar as they are organized groups, they are structures of power. They are structures of power because they
concentrate human wit, energy, and muscle for the achieve-
ment of given purposes. They are of the same genus, although a different species, as the state. And so we come by
still another route to the insight which the philosophical
pluralists demonstrated, that the state as an association (or
group) resembles other associations like churches and trade
unions. That which puts both state and nonstate associations in the same category of forms is the common factor
of power. Both are associations of people for the achieve-
ment of ends common to the members, by the application
of the power of the association to the obstacles and hin-
drances which block the goal. The state and other group
forms represent power in different packages. Organized
groups may be regarded as systems of private government
while the organs of the state represent a system of public
government. The ubiquity of power in human relations
and its manifestations in group forms other than the state
are the reason for believing that the subject matter of
politics is power, contrary to the view that its subject mat-

bridge: Harvard University Press, 1942); Elton Mayo, *The Social
Problems of an Industrial Civilization* (Boston: Graduate School of
Business Administration, Harvard University, 1945); Elton Mayo,
The Human Problems of an Industrial Civilization (New York: Mac-
millan Co., 1933); T. North Whitehead, *Leadership in a Free Society*
(Cambridge: Harvard University Press, 1936); Peter Drucker, *The
Concept of the Corporation* (New York: John Day Co., 1946); A. A.
Berle and Gardiner Means, *The Modern Corporation and Private
Property* (New York: Commercial Clearing House, 1932); Herbert
Simon, *Administrative Behavior* (New York: Macmillan Co., 1947);
Herbert Simon, Donald Smithburg, and Victor Thompson, *Public
Administration* (New York: Knopf, 1950); Sebastian de Grazia, *The
Political Community* (Chicago: University of Chicago Press, 1948).

ter is the state, which is only one of the engines through which power is exercised.[15] Private government is not only a legitimate but a much neglected subject of inquiry by political science.

The course of the discussion to this point may be summarized as a doctrine of the politics of plural forms. To use the phrase of John Dewey, the "doctrine of plural forms is a statement of fact: that there exist a plurality of social groupings, good, bad, and indifferent." [16] These groupings have no "real" personality; there is no derivative entity in group organization which is not people but somehow possesses human attributes. For social groupings *are* people in connected relationships; the connected relationships do not exist apart from the people. To recognize the group basis of society and, by inclusion, the group basis of the political and other communities, is not to lose sight of the individual. The groups exist for the individuals to whom they belong. Groups are devices by which the individual fulfills personal values and felt needs. To view the individual as the centerpiece of all group forms is to avoid the error of regarding society as a congeries of discrete and disconnected human particles. The individual is not alone but is in constant relationship with others. To repeat the first observation made at the beginning of this chapter, the whole structure of society is associational; it is neither disjected nor congealed; it is not a multiplicity of discontinuous persons nor a solid fusion of dissolved components.

---

[15] For a study of the political structure and process of an institution of private government, see Oliver Garceau, *The Political Life of the American Medical Association* (Cambridge: Harvard University Press, 1941); A. R. Danielian, *The A.T. and T.* (New York: Vanguard Press, 1939). For three recent general works on the subject of power as the focus of politics, see Bertrand Russell, *Power* (New York: W. W. Norton, 1938); Charles Merriam, *Political Power* (New York: McGraw-Hill, 1934); and Bertrand de Jouvenel, *Power* (London: Hutchinson and Co., 1947).

[16] *The Public and Its Problems*, p. 73.

To say that the structure of the political community is associational is not to elevate the social groups above the state, nor really to put them in a relationship of parity, as the philosophical pluralists did. In civil polities, some association does in fact represent the consensus by which the groups exist in mutual relations. This is the state. It establishes the norms of permissible behavior in group relations and enforces these norms. The fact that men have other group loyalties than the one they bear to the state does not in itself prescribe any limits to the activity of the state. The state is not necessarily confined to a few police functions at the margins where the intersecting and overlapping groups touch each other, nor is it limited to the role of referee in the group conflict. It is established to promote normative goals, as custodian of the consensus, and to help formulate those goals, as well as to police the agreed rules. In the exercise of its normative functions, it may require the abolishment of groups or a radical revision of their internal structure.

Organized groups, then, are structures of power; they are forms of private government different from forms of public government principally in that public governments possess the characteristic of officiality, which will be more fully discussed below.[17] Through usage, the word "govern-

---

[17] See p. 33 ff. It is useful to distinguish groups in three senses or phases of development: incipient, conscious, and organized. The indispensable ingredient of "groupness" is consciousness of common interest and active assistance, mutually sustained, to advance and promote this interest. Where the interest exists but is not recognized by the members of the putative association, the group may be said to be incipient. Thus, all dwellers in the Caribbean may actually possess certain interests in common—economic resources, strategic position, native populations in a colonial status, exposure to the hazards of weather, and so on—which may produce a consciousness of community, as similar predisposing factors produced the Indonesian Republic. A conscious group is one in which the community sense exists but which has not become organized. An organized group is a conscious group which has established an objective and formal apparatus

ment" has come to be associated almost exclusively with the formal official apparatus of presidents, kings, duces, fuehrers, commissars, rajahs, sachems, sagamores, legislators, councilors, commissioners, mayors, governors, ministers plenipotentiary, ambassadors, judges, and other public office holders. But who has not heard of "office politics," "faculty politics," "union politics," and so on? These phrases are more than metaphor. They bespeak the general understanding that the phenomena of power appear in unofficial groups as well as in the formal structures of official agencies of the public government. We may therefore add to the subjects which are proper to politic inquiry the activities of corporation managers, trade union leaders, bishops, colonels, trade association executives, boards of directors, trustees of colleges, and other such functionaries. The vocabulary of power in public governments is a key to the understanding of the structure and processes of systems of private government also. It is in the literature of administration, perhaps, that the most notable advance has been made in recognizing the single identity of the problems of power in its public and private manifestations, one

---

to promote the common interest. Habitual co-operation of the members of a group is possible without an elaborate apparatus. Mannheim in *Man and Society in an Age of Reconstruction* (p. 51 ff.) distinguishes between substantial and functional rationality. The first is conscious, contrived, directed action which makes use of deliberate means to produce known ends, efficiently besought. Functional rationality may be likened to what is here called habitual co-operation. Where the objective and formal apparatus of the organized group appears in its mature manifestations, it exhibits the same general form and pattern. Max Weber in *Essays in Sociology* (tr. by H. H. Gerth and C. Wright Mills; New York: Oxford University Press, 1946, 196 ff.) discusses the phenomenon of bureaucracy, which is not limited to the institutions and behavior of public government but is universal among organized group structures. The three principal characteristics of bureaucracy are a fixed distribution of functions, a fixed distribution of authority, and a predictable procedure. By these terms, it is clear that private organizations have their bureaucracies as well as Washington and Whitehall.

test of the truth of which is the extent to which the public bureaucracy and the private have exchanged knowledge about the ways in which the management of organizations can most efficiently and effectively be carried on.[18] But this knowledge is not modern. John Wise, the liberal Ipswich theologian of the late seventeenth century, wrote tracts on the *government* of the Congregationalist churches in New England, which he wanted to keep democratic, against certain bureaucratic tendencies that appeared in his day.[19] He viewed the church as an ecclesiastical polity and discussed its organization in political terms which were virtually interchangeable with the vocabulary employed for similar speculation about forms of public government.[20]

---

[18] To name only a few of these writers, there are James Mooney and Alan Reiley, *Principles of Organization* (New York: Harper, 1939); Henri Fayol, *Industrial and General Administration,* tr. by J. A. Coubrough (London: Pitman and Sons, 1930); Luther Gulick and L. Urwick, *Papers on the Science of Administration* (New York: Institute of Public Administration, Columbia University, 1937); Lyndall Urwick, *The Elements of Administration* (London: Pitman and Sons, 1943); Mary Niles, *Middle Management* (New York: Harper, 1941).

[19] John Wise in *A Vindication of the Government of New England Churches* (Boston: Congregational Board of Publication, 1860).

[20] The problem dealt with by John Wise involved a few thousands. The same kind of problem today involves millions. For example, in 1947 the Federal Council of Churches of Christ in America listed twenty-five different denominations and claimed a membership of almost 29,000,000 people. The total population of the United States did not reach this figure until just before the Civil War. The form of organization is a loose confederation of the following constituent bodies: National Baptist Convention, Northern Baptist Convention, Church of the Brethren, General Council of Congregational Christian Churches, Czech-Moravian Brethren, International Convention of Disciples of Christ, Evangelical and Reformed Church, Evangelical United Brethren Church, Five Years Meeting of the Friends of America, the Methodist Church, African Methodist Episcopal Church, African Methodist Episcopal Zion Church, Colored Methodist Episcopal Church in America, Moravian Church, Presbyterian Church in the U.S.A., Presbyterian Church in the U.S., Protestant Episcopal Church, Reformed Church in America, Russian Orthodox Church of North

The Politics of Economics

It has been pointed out, and repeated, that the structure of society is associational. Groups are basic. It has also been pointed out that organized groups are structures of power and therefore within the scope of political inquiry. What is true of society is true of the communities of which the society is composed: the religious community, the political community (the state), and the economic community. If we consider the economic community more closely, it is to be seen that it is principally a complex of associations, each of which is a structure of power. Two of the principal group forms in the economic community are the trade union and the corporation.

Union organizations are obvious structures of power. The form of organization in most general use is the presidential form, in which the electorate (union members) choose their local officers (commonly a president, vice-president, secretary, and treasurer) while delegates from the local unions in a national convention choose the national officers—president, vice-president, secretary, treasurer, and members of the executive council. Some of the national unions, like the United Mine Workers of America, are unitary in form, but others are federations. The American Federation of Labor and the Congress of Industrial Organizations are both extensive federations of constituent national and international unions. In 1949 the organized

America, Seventh Day Baptist General Conference, Syrian Antiochian Orthodox Church of North America, Ukrainian Orthodox Church of America, United Church of Canada, United Lutheran Church (Consultive), United Presbyterian Church. In addition, there were numerous local and state councils of churches in America, designed to advance interchurch co-operation locally. *Yearbook of American Churches,* ed. by Benson Y. Landis (Lebanon: Sowers Printing Co., 1947), p. 91. For a discussion of the lobbying activities of church groups, see Luke Eugene Ebersole, *Church Lobbying in the Nation's Capital* (New York: Macmillan Co., 1951).

labor movement had an estimated membership of 16,000,-000 workers, with approximately 8,000,000 in the American Federation of Labor, 6,000,000 in the Congress of Industrial Organizations, and 2,000,000 in independent unions not affiliated with either of the major confederations.

The unions are aggressive institutions, established to improve the standards of living of their memberships, which means, usually, higher wages, lower hours, and improved working conditions. These objectives are normally achieved by collective bargaining, which is another name for negotiation between representatives of the unions and representatives of the companies. Agreements proceeding from these negotiations are reduced to writing and form a protocol of the matters on which disputes were resolved. Agreement with the union proposals is not always secured by negotiation, however, and the union then applies force to the employer to induce an immediate settlement or a favorable disposition. The principal form of force is the diminishment of the employer's income or expectation of income by stopping the production in his plant, by seeking to persuade others from doing business with him, and by preventing other workers from assisting the employer to start his production going. Unions sometimes utilize direct forms of power in action to achieve their purposes, and, although the grosser forms of coercion are prohibited by law (the state operating as a normative agency), the final solvent of labor controversies is trial by battle. Others have pointed out that labor controversy is often like military warfare, and the vocabulary of military conflict is at many points interchangeable with that of labor relations. Thus, the word "strike" may mean a work stoppage or an air attack; "sabotage," a word first used by French workers to denote passive resistance,[21] also means obstructing the enemy's po-

---

[21] The parallel between military and union activity was recognized by Thorstein Veblen. For a discussion of the derivation of the word

tential by covert violence; "pickets" may refer to the men who advertise a strike or to military guards. The entire ideology of the trade union movement reflects the aggressive design to apply force to win "concessions."

The use of force is likely to be more conspicuous in the early stages of the development of union organization. In mature unions the use of force is always present as a possibility and therefore constitutes a form of pressure even when not directly employed. But although it is not directly employed and the union negotiates regular agreements with the management, the political nature of this more peaceful mode of doing union business is not altered. Politics merely takes more settled and sophisticated forms. It was said that the union agreements are protocols of understanding. From another aspect they may be regarded as the rules by which plant operations shall be conducted in areas of interest to the worker and his union. The formulation of rules to guide future conduct is the essential task of legislation; it *is* legislation, and differs from the product of Congress in no substantive respect. Indeed when Congress or a state legislature determines that the minimum wage in an industry shall be forty or seventy-five cents an hour, it is doing nothing substantively different from that which is done by union and management representatives in the automobile industry when they decide what the minimum rate shall be. Where unions share with management the task of writing the rules for the plant, the worker through his representatives has succeeded in partitioning the power of the plant management to direct the enterprise and has appropriated a portion of that power to himself. Union strife, among the many examples of group tension in society, is perhaps the clearest instance in which the chief

"sabotage" see his book, *The Engineers and the Price System* (New York: Viking Press, 1935), portions of which are reprinted in *Veblen*, ed. by Max Lerner (New York: Viking Press, 1948), p. 431 ff.

parties-in-interest publicly and knowingly, without cover
or reservation, contend for power.

In the structures of private government on both the
management and the labor sides, the persistent problems
of politics, made familiar in the history of public governments, are to be encountered and observed. One of these
is the problem of political responsibility, holding the holders of power responsible for their use and administration
of that power. In some national and international trade
unions, the small presidential clique manages to maintain
itself in power by control of the apparatus of communication and representation. The Taft-Hartley Act recognizes
this as a problem and forces a measure of internal democracy from the outside. Thus, the National Labor Relations
Board has been required to hold elections whenever the
question of a union shop has been proposed to the workers,
the object of the election being to make sure that the union
shop represented the free and uncoerced choice of the
workers. The union shop elections were a very expensive
procedure which even its original sponsor, Senator Robert
Taft of Ohio, came to agree was useless. The votes in favor
of union shops were overwhelming, and the suspicion that
reluctant workers were being coerced to adopt the union
shop by union bureaucracies was proved to be unfounded.
There are union organizations that have a strong authoritarian aspect, just as there are churches with a strong authoritarian aspect, both Protestant and Catholic, and the
problem of holding the officers of these unions accountable
to the union electorate is sometimes a difficult one.

To turn from trade unions to corporations, it is by now a
commonplace to point out that the chief form of business
enterprise is the corporation, least extensive in agriculture,
although not negligible there, and most extensive in bank-
ing and utilities. The corporation accumulates human
power, concentrates it, and applies it to given ends by a

division of labor within a known and determinate system of controls (authorities) and according to settled procedures, which are constantly in a process of revision and improvement. It is a scale model of public government. In some instances the model is larger and more powerful than the original. According to the evidence of the Temporary National Economic Committee in 1941, if the American Telephone and Telegraph Company with its stockholders and workers had been admitted to the Union as the forty-ninth state, it would have been bigger, that is, it would have been entitled to more representatives, than any state in the Rocky Mountain area from Canada to Mexico, except Colorado. And it would have been richer (that is, it would have had more assets than the assessed valuation of the states) than any state from the Atlantic to the Pacific below the Mason-Dixon line, and richer than most states above it. Comparable (but, of course, not identical) judgments could be made about other of the billion dollar corporations that have grown out of the American economy.

In all of the corporations of the business world, large and small, the problem of political accountability is present in the relation between the owners (the stockholders) and the managers. The divorce of ownership and management has in many places made it possible for a managerial elite to control the technical apparatus of communication and representation to perpetuate themselves, like certain union bosses. At the annual elections which all stockholders are theoretically permitted to attend, generally few turn up except the managers, the directors, and a sprinkling of publicity seekers who embarrass the smooth tenor of the meeting in order to get their names in the newspapers. The proceedings are in the control of the officeholders, who often bear a resemblance to the operators of party machines in municipal elections, capable of delivering the vote. The officeholders maintain their power through the indifference or ignorance of the electorate whose power they wield.

On occasion there is a showdown fight for power between influential stockholders or between a faction of stockholders and the managers that exhibits all the characteristics of a political party campaign. The uncommitted stockholders are the voting constituency whose support is wooed by rival factions in the traditional manner of political parties. There are the familiar platforms, speeches, advertising circulars, promises of improvement, attacks upon the rascals in office, determined resolutions to make a house cleaning, charges, countercharges, recriminations, reprisals, and raids for votes. The voting is ordinarily done by proxy and the showdown occurs with the election of officers. The leaders of the contending parties cast blocks of proxies for their "party," and the counting of the ballots determines the issue. Usually these fights are obscure affairs in which the press has little interest, but it sometimes happens that such a conflict bursts into the public prints with all the drama of an election campaign. Notable instances have been the fight for control of Standard Oil of Indiana by John D. Rockefeller, Jr., against Colonel Robert Stewart after the Teapot Dome scandal, and the unsuccessful effort to oust Sewell Avery from Montgomery Ward in 1947.

These are only two of the primary group forms of organization in the economic community. There are, of course, others, such as partnerships, co-operatives, unincorporated associations, and the like. Upon the basic structure of these relatively simple forms of enterprise there has grown a superstructure of combinations and associations, bureaus, guilds, institutes, and conferences, they being confederations or alliances of the primary economic groups, performing central services for the constituent members. For Herbert Spencer, the pluralizing of society, the multiplication of group forms, was an inevitable characteristic of an industrial polity. Believing that the "same law of organization pervades the society in general and in detail," he stated as fact what he hoped as wish, that "there is entire congruity between the representative constitutions of . . . private combinations, and that representative constitution of the public combination . . . proper to the industrial type." [22] William Graham Sumner, who also interested himself in the politics of industrial groups, took a different view when he asserted, "Industry may be republican; it can never be democratic, so long as men differ in productive power and in industrial virtue." [23] Far from a congruence between the representative constitutions of private combinations and the representative constitution of the public combination proper to an industrial society, Sumner believed that industrial groups properly contradicted the prevailing American *mythos* about democracy, which he regarded as fanciful and unscientific. Corporations (called joint stock companies), he observed, "which are in form republican are drifting over into oligarchies or monarchies because one or a few get greater efficiency of control and greater vigor of administration." [24] The choice of words like "republican," "democratic," "oligarchies," and "monarchies" is significant. Beneath the conceptions of both

---

[22] Herbert Spencer, *The Principles of Sociology* (New York: D. Appleton and Co., 1897), II(2), 613.

[23] *Essays of William Graham Sumner,* ed. Albert G. Keller and Maurice R. Davie (New Haven: Yale University Press, 1934), II, 165.

[24] *Ibid.* A more recent writer has said of corporations: "It is in no sense a figure of speech to refer to a company like the American Tobacco Company, and to each of its counterparts, large and small, as a private government. A business is a *government* because within the law it is authorized and organized to make rules for the conduct of its affairs. It is a *private* government because the rules it makes within the law are final and are not reviewable by any public body." Beardsley Ruml, *Tomorrow's Business* (New York: Farrar and Rinehart, 1945), p. 51. Chapter IV of Ruml's book, titled "The Structure of a Business," discusses such political questions as the location of centers of power in business enterprises. *Ibid,* p. 69 ff. For an evaluation of Ruml, see Pekelis, *Law and Social Action.*

Spencer and of Sumner lies the assumption that the business community is a structure of power, organized into systems not fundamentally different from systems of public government, subject to the same laws of growth and decay, and capable of description in the same terms.

This is an important insight which has been periodically lost and recovered in American history. One of the basic assumptions about the distribution of power in a democratic society is that this power must be diffused among the generality; it must exist in small portions possessed by the many, and not concentrated in the hands of the few. Where the small increments of power pass from the members of the multitude into the hands of the few, it constitutes a threat to the security of the democracy. Rousseau, it may be recalled, even went so far as to assert that the "sovereignty" of the people cannot be represented.

In American history great concentrations of private power have often invited apprehension, as in the famous fight over the second Bank of the United States. A partisan of Jackson, George Bancroft, remarked in a letter to a newspaper, "Political influence is steadily tending to the summit level of property; and this political influence of wealth must be balanced by the political power of numbers." [25] There is an important similarity between the formal assumptions that theory makes about political democracy and about a free enterprise economy. Both postulate a multiplicity of small components. Private power must be diffuse. Spencer optimistically believed that the multiplication of free associations—that is, their infinite diffusion—would diminish the range within which public government would have to operate. The logic of this view is that where private power is not diffuse, but is concentrated to a degree which Ban-

---

[25] *Jackson versus Biddle, The Struggle over the Second Bank of the United States,* ed. by George Rogers Taylor (Boston: D. C. Heath and Co., 1949), p. 35.

croft's "numbers" will feel to be intolerable, the important economic decisions will pass from private persons to public functionaries representing the protestant multitude. Or, as many said in the debate in the Eighty-first Congress over basing-point legislation, private monopoly begets governmental regulation.

Almost sixty years after the passage of the Sherman Act of 1890 Senator Joseph O'Mahoney of Wyoming said, "Our great dilemma now is to establish the rules under which the American ideal of popular sovereignty in an order of both economic freedom and political freedom can be maintained." [26] Like Spencer, O'Mahoney believes that the political values of industry and the state should be congruent; but like Sumner (although not sharing his complacency) he feels that they are not. Between the affirmations of O'Mahoney and Spencer, more than half a century apart, we have had mergers, combinations, amalgamations, federations, alliances, agreements, monopolies, a great growth of plant and technology, an absolute expansion of the economy, and an absolute increase in the number of enterprisers. Concentrations of economic power have enlarged, even though their proportionate share of the industry, in some cases (United States Steel Corporation, for example), has diminished. In other industries—automobiles, typewriters, cigarettes—control of the industry has passed into the hands of a very few firms. For some modern critics, these developments have raised in new form the conflict stated by Bancroft between the influence of wealth and the political power of numbers.

One identifying characteristic of the "representative constitution of the public combination" in America is federalism. Between this and the "representative constitutions

---

[26] *Hearings before a Subcommittee of the House Committee on the Judiciary on Study of Monopoly Power,* 81st Cong. 1st Sess., No. 14, Part 1, p. 98.

of private combinations" there is a real congruence, not quite in the sense intended by Spencer perhaps but in accord with a dominant American political technique. Federation is a method of reconciling the conflicting values of unity and diversity, of developing a consensus of accepted purposes which retains the rich variegation of local modifications, mutations, and multiformities. One indication of the extent to which the federalizing of the economic community has proceeded is the number, range, and variety of associations described in a publication of the Department of Commerce titled, *National Associations of the United States*.[27] As of 1949 the Department of Commerce counted approximately 1,500 national trade associations and an additional 300 "national associations either consisting of businessmen organized for special purposes or having a large proportion of businessmen as members." [28] In addition, there were an estimated 2,000 state and 8,000 local trade associations. The majority of the national associations had a membership of less than 200 firms each, and the bulk of the representation was (and still is) provided by small business groups. In the main these associations supply useful central research and informational and public relations services and do not constitute controls in the sectors of the economy in which they appear. The Sherman Act has undoubtedly had much to do with the noncoercive character of these associations.

Although federations abound in the structure of the economic community, American capitalism, viewed generally, is obviously less integrated than other systems of private government, like ecclesiastical and military hierarchies, with which it may be compared. There are multiple centers of decision unstratified in any formal or systematic

---

[27] Jay Judkins, *National Associations of the United States* (Washington: U.S. Department of Commerce, 1949).

[28] *Ibid.*, p. viii.

arrangement. There is no central leadership, no single group of administrative organs for planning and executing a unified policy, no master bureaucratic control for co-ordinating the motions of the myriad parts of the economy.

There are sectors of the economy, however, where a form of self-regulation is practiced, and there are others where concerns behave in a way that may be called "corespective," to use the phrase of Schumpeter,[29] rather than competitive. The three firms that dominate the automobile industry supply an example. "Corespective" behavior represents an effort to produce a predictable measure of stability by parallel but noncollusive actions. At a still higher level of co-ordination and integration, there are examples of price leadership which, without explicit sanctions, may produce a considerable measure of responsive behavior in those who follow it. The steel industry is an illustration. Beyond these are the combinations which unlawfully restrain trade. The Cement Institute was such a form of private government, as will be described in the next chapter.

The Dynamics of Plural Forms

So far we have been concerned with the nature of the structure of society and its principal communities, and the composition and classification of the group forms which are basic to both. They have been held still, so to speak, while they were being viewed. But they do not in fact hold still; they are in a state of constant motion, and it is through this motion and its interactions that these groups generate the rules by which the community is to be governed and that public policy is formulated. It is necessary now to consider the impulses which animate the group motion and produce these penetrating and far-reaching results, to observe what

---

[29] Joseph A. Schumpeter, *Capitalism, Socialism, and Democracy* (New York: Harper, 1947), p. 90 n.

has been called "interactions in series between individual and governmental institutions."[30]

Groups organize for the self-expression and security of the members that comprise them. Even where the group is a benevolent, philanthropic association devoted to the improvement of the material and spiritual fortunes of people outside its membership—a temperance or a missionary organization, for example—the work toward this goal, the activity of the organization, is a means through which the members express themselves. Satisfaction in the fulfillment of the received purposes of the group is an important element in keeping groups intact, as Barnard has said.[31] Indeed, if these satisfactions are not fulfilled, the group suffers loss of morale, energy, and dedication.[32] For this reason military organizations and the civil authorities to which they are responsible seek to inculcate in the soldier some sense of the general purposes for which force by arms is being employed, so as to identify the soldier's personal purpose with that of the community he serves. The soldier then fulfills his own purposes in combat, as well as those of other groups in the country whose uniform he wears.

At the same time security is an object of every group organization, even if understood only in its elemental sense of the survival of the group itself in order to carry forward its mission. At the very least, the interest of security means the maintenance of the existence of the group. In different groups one or the other of these impulses—self-expression or security—will predominate. In a chain gang the factor of self-expression would seem to be irrelevant to the maintenance of the gang, but the security of the members can be

---

[30] Oliver Garceau, "Research in the Political Process," *op. cit.*, p. 80.

[31] Barnard, *Functions of the Executive*.

[32] George C. Homans, *The Human Group* (New York: Harcourt, Brace and Co., 1950), pp. 422–423.

a strong spur. If they fail to work together, they run the risk of punishment, often severe. The consideration of personal and collective security from punishment therefore keeps the members of the gang from revolt. These two factors then—self-expression and security—are the axes of policy along the course of which the group will move.

Self-expression and security, ideology and interest, are sought by the group members through control of the physical and social environment which surrounds each group, and in the midst of which it dwells. It is an elemental fact that environments are potentially dangerous to every group, even as homes are potentially dangerous to the members of the household, as the statistics of accidents in the home will attest. The military battalion runs the risk of defeat, injury, and death. The church, new or old, runs the risk of losing its members to competing claims of interest and devotion. The businessman runs the risk of losing his profit or his customer to his rival. The philanthropic organization devoted to good works often regards other agencies in the same field with a venomous eye. Councils of social agencies in large cities are often notorious for the rancor with which the struggle for prestige and recognition (that is, self-expression and security) is conducted one with the other. Every group, large and small, must come to terms with its environment if it is to endure and to prosper.

There are three modes by which this is done. First, the environment may be made safe and predictable by putting restraints upon it. Jurisdictional fights between unions may be explained in this way. Jurisdictional fights are battles in which each claimant union seeks to make an environment for itself in the area of dispute which does not include its rival. On the employer side, the Mohawk Valley Formula was a pattern of actions in a planned sequence by which employers, if they followed it, could break union movements.[33] The objective of this formula was to discredit the union and its leadership and to enlist the support of the townspeople on the side of the plant. This was a concerted plan to make an environment unfavorable to the success of the union. One overcomes the hostility in the environment most directly by destroying the influence that creates the hostility.

Second, the environment may be made safe and predictable by neutralizing it. In the propaganda war of giant world powers, the effort is ceaseless to neutralize the effects of propaganda with counterpropaganda so as to render the international environment favorable or at least not hostile, that is, neutral. The Atlantic and Pacific Tea Company bought a great deal of advertising space in newspapers all over the country to counteract the expectedly unfavorable impressions created by a Department of Justice action against it under the antitrust laws. The object, among others, was to make the customer-inhabited environment of the business enterprise favorable if possible, at the least neutral on the merits of the charges against it.

Third, the environment may be made safe and predictable, and therefore secure, by conciliating it and making it friendly. Even where there is no manifest hostile influence, a credit of good will may be accumulated by deeds and words which reflect favorably upon the doer. Concessions to potentially hostile elements may work sometimes, and again they may not. In the struggle of free nations with the dictatorships, appeasement did not succeed in producing that conciliation which was hoped for it. Politicians are constantly at work making friends and growing votes by performing favors of one kind or another. Friendliness toward

---

[33] *Decisions and Orders of the National Labor Relations Board,* Vol. II: 1936–1937 (Washington: Government Printing Office, 1937), pp. 664–666. The account of the Mohawk Valley Formula appears in a complaint case involving Remington-Rand, Inc., which is reported at p. 626.

the manufacturers of soap and their products is generated on the radio by endless broadcasts of simple tales of never-ending strife and frustration. During the Second World War institutional advertising by business enterprises was a means of cultivating and keeping good will for the products advertised even though there was no market for them because of the wartime restrictions on production.

All of these are methods by which the environment of groups is made safe and predictable, and therefore secure. And because the relations of people are myriad and shifting, subject to cycles of deterioration and decay, because the environment itself changes with each passing hour, there is a ceaseless struggle on the part of groups to dominate, neutralize, or conciliate that part of their environment that presses in upon them most closely. In this struggle there is an observable balance of influence in favor of organized groups in their dealings with the unorganized, and in favor of the best and most efficiently organized in their dealings with the less efficiently organized. Or, to put it another way, organization represents concentrated power, and concentrated power can exercise a predominating influence when it encounters power which is diffuse and not concentrated, and therefore weaker.

The classic struggle of farmers against business enterprise is a case in point, the latter being more efficiently organized and able (before the farmer became "class conscious") to gain advantages which the farmer thought exorbitant, under conditions which the farmer found offensive. The strong nations tend to take advantage of the weak, and imperial powers, of their colonies. But organization begets counterorganization. The farmer organizes in the American Farm Bureau Federation, or the National Grange, and uses his influence with legislatures to write rules to his advantage. In some states of the Middle West, for example, legislation even prescribes the terms of contracts for the sale of farm equipment. But the organized farmer pays little attention to the tenant and the share-cropper, and they in turn experience an impulse to organize for their advantage. The history of the development of farmers' organizations is instructive in this connection because the whole program of farm subsidies which has evolved since the 1920's is an effort on the part of the farmer (organized) to make himself independent of the vicissitudes of the business economy, that is, to take the farmer out of the environment which he can control only imperfectly and to insulate him against economic adversity.

In this constant struggle of groups to come to terms with their environments, one other phenomenon of group politics may be noted. Simple groups tend to become more complex. And the more complex they become the greater is the tendency to centralize their control. Mention has already been made of this tendency. The structure of the business community in 1950 is different from that of 1860 in that relatively simple forms of business organization have become complex—have gone through federations, mergers, combinations, reorganizations, amalgamations, and consolidations in an effort to rationalize the complexity and to integrate elements of the economy in comprehensive structures. Monopolies, combinations, cartels, large integrated enterprises are characteristics of a mature phase of the evolution of group forms in an industrial economy. The same phenomenon has appeared in the growth of trade unions.[34] "Big business" and "big unions" are both characteristic of the American economy in the middle of the twentieth century. The tendency of simple forms of organization to become complex by combination and to develop centralized bureaucracies to cope with this complexity is

[34] Florence Peterson, *American Labor Unions* (New York: Harper, 1945) is a useful account of the growth and structure of American labor unions.

also amply illustrated in the history of federal administration, for this tendency is to be observed among official groups as well as among the groups like the CIO and the American Legion, which dwell outside the domain of public government.

The struggle of groups to survive in their environments and to carry forward the aims and interests of the members, if entirely uninhibited, would produce violence and war. Social disapproval of most of the forms of direct action reduces this struggle to an effort to write the rules by which groups live with each other and according to which they will compete for existence and advantage. Thus, in the development of mature institutions of collective bargaining out of the raw material of unorganized workers, the time comes when violence, disorder, and force are put to one side as the normal aspect of labor relations and the conduct of negotiations occupies the energies of the leaders. In the relations of nations to each other, a persistent effort has been made to substitute diplomacy and the rule of law for war as the arbiter of the differences among national groups. As groups come to put away gross forms of coercion in their dealings with each other, by equal degree the area widens within which the behaviors of each are subject to codification by rules. The struggle for advantage, for benefits to the group, for the self-expression and security of their members tends then to concentrate upon the writing of these rules to the advantage of the parties-in-interest. These rules take the form of statutes, administrative orders and decrees, rules and interpretations, and court judgments.

The Concept of Officiality

We come then to the apparatus of the state which, through its manifold offices—legislatures, councils, agencies, departments, courts, and other forums—maintains a system of instrumentalities for the writing and enforcement of the formal rules by which society is governed. But all of these instrumentalities are themselves groups, and they possess a sense of group belonging and identification which is very strong. In what respect are these groups different from the more numerous groups outside the structure of public government? In a political sense they are not different at all, but are the same. They exhibit all the internal social and political characteristics of group forms in that infinite universe of plural forms outside the state apparatus. But there *are* differences in behavior which may be observed. The Bureau of Internal Revenue collects taxes, that is, it takes a portion of the substance of individuals and corporations. But individuals and corporations do not take a portion of the substance of the Bureau of Internal Revenue. The policeman on the corner is permitted to blow a whistle at an automobile driver and stop his travel. But the driver of the automobile is not permitted to blow a whistle at the policeman and stop him from walking up and giving the driver a tag. Why is there this unilateral relationship between some groups and others? How does it happen that a man with a badge may give orders to men without badges while the man without a badge is not permitted to give orders to the man with the badge? The obvious answer of course is that the law permits this. It establishes the difference between the badge wearer and the others. But this does not go far enough. The Eighteenth Amendment was also "law" in the sense that it was on the books. For law to have force there must be something to support the law— popular consent and understanding.[35] In the example of the policeman there is a social understanding that approves the unilateral relation between men with badges and men

---

[35] For an interesting argument in behalf of a new international order based upon a body of international law which rests "fundamentally on its own merits" and not upon the assumption of "some pressure behind it," see Gerhard Niemeyer, *Law without Force* (Princeton: Princeton University Press, 1941).

with boutonnieres. It is a part of the political consensus—
the understood and agreed conditions of life in a civil society—that certain groups will be permitted to act in this
fashion. The groups so privileged collectively make up the
instrumentalities of the state. Such groups are distinguished
from others only in their possession of the characteristic of
officiality. The designation "official" is the sign manifest
that the bearer is authorized by social understanding to
exercise against all groups and individuals certain powers
which they may not exercise against him. The concept of
officiality then is the sum of the technical differences which
are rooted in social understanding as to who does what to
whom. The difference between the public and private
groups is the "officiality" of the former.[36]

What is the function in the group struggle of the complex of official groups? What role do they play in the restless
flux of effort on the part of groups to dominate, neutralize,
or conciliate the environment in which they seek to survive? The principal function of official groups is to provide
various levels of compromise in the writing of the rules,
within the body of agreed principles that forms the consensus upon which the political community rests. In so
performing this function, each of the three principal
branches of government has a special role.

The legislature referees the group struggle, ratifies the
victories of the successful coalitions, and records the terms
of the surrenders, compromises, and conquests in the form
of statutes. Every statute tends to represent compromise
because the process of accommodating conflicts of group

---

[36] This distinction is illustrated by the experience of the Cement Institute in the National Recovery Administration. See below, pp. 71–72.
For further discussion of the distinction, see Louis Jaffe, "Law Making by Private Groups," 51 *Harvard Law Review* 201 (December
1937), in which the author examines the problem of making "official"
the authority of groups "to coerce under the sanction of law dis-
sentient members of the group."

interest is one of deliberation and consent. The legislative vote on any issue tends to represent the composition of strength, i.e., the balance of power, among the contending groups at the moment of voting. What may be called public policy is the equilibrium reached in this struggle at any given moment, and it represents a balance which the contending factions of groups constantly strive to weight in their favor.[37] In this process, it is clear that blocs of groups

[37] John Fischer in "Unwritten Rules of American Politics" 197 *Harper's Magazine* 27 (November 1948) expresses the thesis that Calhoun, who devised the doctrine of the concurrent majority, provided the key to an understanding of American politics today. Fischer asserted that the legislative system, especially as it functions in Congress through committees, was a modern-day institutionalization of Calhoun's concurrent majority, in which no important interest is forced to accept legislation unfavorable to it in the particulars in which its interest is immediately invested. Economic interests and others also, through the groups in which they are organized, according to Fischer, then exercise a minority veto on legislation which concerns them, like the minority veto that Calhoun sought to establish for the protection of the interests of the South.

This view, however, gives too much credit to Calhoun. Far from having the key to the mysteries of American politics, Calhoun was outside the main stream of American political thought and tendency in his own time. Calhoun was closer to Andrei Vishinsky than he was to any American politico of our day. In fact, Calhoun could have written Vishinsky's speech of November 24, 1948, to the United Nations General Assembly's Ad Hoc Political Committee (*New York Times,* November 25, 1948) in which he said: "The veto is a powerful political tool. . . . Perhaps we use it more, but that is because we are in the minority and the veto balances power. If we were in the majority we could make such grandiloquent gestures as offering to waive the veto on this or that."

In the functions which the American legislature performs, it is clear that no minority exercises a *veto* on legislation that affects it. Certainly no veto power is recognized in law. The assumption that there is a minority veto must show that minorities can always exercise it, as they do in the United Nations Security Council, and that no minority is without it. So far as the first is concerned, it may be asked what veto did businessmen interpose against the enactment of the Wagner Act of 1935? How successful have been the bankers in applying a veto to the currency reforms of the last decade? How successful were the

can be defeated. In fact they can be routed. Such groups do not possess a veto on the proposals and acts that affect them.[38] What they do possess when they are defeated is the right to make new combinations of strength if they are able to do so, combinations that will support a new effort to rewrite the rules in their favor. This process is fully in accord with the American culture pattern which rates high in the characteristics of optimism, risk, experimentalism, change, aggressiveness, acquisitiveness, and a colossal faith in man's ability to subdue and bend nature to his desire. The process is dynamic, not static; fluid, not fixed. Today's losers may be tomorrow's winners.

In these adjustments of group interest, the legislature does not play the inert part of cash register, ringing up the additions and withdrawals of strength, a mindless balance pointing and marking the weight and distribution of power among the contending groups. For legislatures are groups also and show a sense of identity and consciousness of kind that unofficial groups must regard if they are to represent their members effectively. In fact, the two houses of the Congress have a conscious identity of special "house" interest and a joint interest against the executive establishment.

---

labor unions in opposing the enactment of the restrictive features of the Taft-Hartley Act? Where were the vetoes in these and many other instances that might be cited? The answer is that they did not exist. Contrariwise, the hypothesis of a minority veto fails to account for the failure of substantial minorities to get a hearing, let alone exercise a veto. Among these are Negroes, small businessmen, share-croppers, Okies, and so on.

[38] Riesman, *The Lonely Crowd*, p. 244 ff. The author says there are "veto groups," each of which "has attained a power to stop things conceivably inimical to its interest and, within far narrower limits, to start things." *Ibid.* The comments made about the Fischer thesis above apply to the Riesman view. A further difficulty in the latter statement is the ambiguity with which the word "veto" is sometimes used, as in the following statement: "Those veto groups are in many political situations strongest whose own memberships are composed of veto groups, especially veto groups of one." *Ibid.*, p. 247.

More will be said below of the struggle of official groups among themselves. At this point it may be noted that the dignity of the Congressman is an expression of his official group interest, and it cannot be invaded lightly. Legislators have to be approached with a certain amount of deference and tact; they may be pressured but some forms of pressure will be regarded as too gross. The most hateful threat is the one that the political action branches of the AFL and the CIO make, namely, that they will encourage a Congressman's constituents to vote against him. This attacks the legislator in his most vulnerable place and the reaction is accordingly great. A Congressman, like men everywhere, comes to his position carrying in his mind a mixture of ideas, principles, prejudices, programs, precepts, beliefs, slogans, and preachments. These represent his adjustment to the dominant group combination among his constituents. If he mistakes the pattern of his support or acts too independently of its desire, he may lose his seat, as some Congressmen have, after only one term.

The function of the bureaucrat in the group struggle is somewhat different from that of the legislator.[39] Administrative agencies of the regulatory kind are established to carry out the terms of the treaties that the legislators have negotiated and ratified. The administrative agency of the regulatory kind is like an army of occupation left in the field to police the rule won by the victorious coalition. Thus the Transportation Act of 1920 substantially augmented the role of the Interstate Commerce Commission by vesting it with authorities acceptable to labor unions,

---

[39] Merle Fainsod has made an important criticism of the failure of A. F. Bentley in his *Process of Government* properly to estimate the significance of official groups (including regulatory agencies) in the group conflict. Bentley especially underestimated their ability to generate "a certain amount of independent power" to change their environments. "Some Reflections on the Nature of the Regulatory Process," *Public Policy*, I, 299.

investors, weak roads and shippers. The Robinson-Patman Act of 1936 gave to the Federal Trade Commission authority to control the price practices of one classification of business groups in favor of another by limiting the power of the chains in favor of the independents. The defeated coalition of groups, however, does not cease to strive to wring interpretations favorable to it from the treaties that verbalize its defeats. Expensive legal talent is employed to squeeze every advantage which wit and verbal magic can twist out of the cold prose of official papers. The regulatory agencies are constantly besought and importuned to interpret their authorities in favor of those for the regulation of whom they were originally granted. Nor do the losing coalitions of groups confine their fight against unfavorable rules to the bureaucrats appointed to administer them. They constantly seek to rewrite the rules in their favor through compliant legislators. Where the balance of power is precarious, the law will remain unsettled until the balance is made stable. This is especially true in the enforcement of the labor relations and antitrust laws.

The function of the judge is not unlike that of the bureaucrat, for the judiciary, like the civilian bureaucracy, is one of the instrumentalities for the administration of the agreed rules. But the responsibility rests with the judge more than with either the legislator or the bureaucrat to develop a more or less homogeneous and objective *system* out of statutes, administrative decrees, and the causes of private clients.[40] It is an agency superior to the bureaucracy

---

[40] Much ingenuity and resourcefulness go into the production of an objective and homogeneous pattern of law. Benjamin Cardozo, *The Nature of the Judicial Process* (New Haven: Yale University Press, 1925), confessed that the function of the judge was creative and original in those many interstices of the law left vacant by the statutes and administrative decrees. James M. Landis, *The Administrative Process* (New Haven: Yale University Press, 1938), expounded the case for judicial self-restraint in the relations between the courts and

in performing this important and fateful task, and it is in this superiority that its distinguishing characteristic lies. All other distinctions (procedural mainly) between the judges and the bureaucrats are derived and secondary, not innate.

The Group Struggle in Officialdom

In the small universe of official groups—small at least by comparison with the infinite group configuration outside the official domain—the same phenomena of struggle for self-expression and security take place that may be witnessed in the various nonstate communities of society. In fact some interesting variants are thrust into the entire political process by the state of rivalry which often characterizes the relations among the official groups. The Founding Fathers made sure that these rivalries would occur by separating the powers of the government. It was their intention to prevent the public powers from being brought to focus in the same public authority and to endow each separated public authority with the capacity to fend off attempts by the others to invate its domain. The object of this, as Mr. Justice Brandeis said in an important case where the rivalry of official groups was at issue, was "not to promote efficiency but to preclude the exercise of arbitrary power. The purpose was not to avoid friction, but *by means of the inevitable friction incident to the distribution of government powers among three departments,* to save the people from autocracy." [41]

the bureaucrats. The judiciary and the regulatory agencies of the quasi-judicial kind have really been rival bureaucracies, with overlapping jurisdictions. The judges have been jealous for a half-century of the threat represented by the bureaucracy to their historic monopoly to say what the law is. The judges, until recent years at least, protected their security against this threat in their environments by dominating the danger and nullifying it on appeal.

[41] Italics supplied. The case is *Myers* v. *United States,* 272 U.S. 52 (1926), which involved an attempt by Congress to exercise the power which presidents supposed they possessed to remove officials at will.

Congress is traditionally suspicious of the President and historically has sought to dominate the executive establishment. The chief executive of any business enterprise is permitted to manage such staff facilities as personnel and budget, but Congress itself sometimes seeks to exercise these powers of the President. When Congress set up the Tennessee Valley Authority, it reserved to itself the authority by concurrent resolution (not subject to the veto) to remove the members of the board of directors.[42] In the Lend-Lease Act of 1941 and the Emergency Price Stabilization Act of 1942, to name only two, Congress wrote language into the statutes reserving to itself the authority to withdraw from the President the powers conveyed by those acts of legislation.[43] Time and again Congress has sought to force the President's subordinates to surrender information deemed by the Presidents to be confidential.[44] Washington refused in 1796 to disclose the instructions he had given to the

---

The jealousy which Congress has displayed toward the Chief Executive is both extensive and historic. The Budget and Accounting Act of 1921 was vetoed by Wilson when it first passed Congress because Congress had reserved the authority to dismiss the Comptroller-General, and Wilson believed this to be unconstitutional, 50 *Cong. Rec.* 8609–8610 (June 4, 1920). Wilson's veto was anticipated by the observation he made in his book, *Congressional Government* (Boston and New York: Houghton Mifflin Co., 1900), pp. 48–49: "It is not often easy to see the true constitutional bearing of strictly legislative action; but it is patent even to the least observant that in the matter of appointments to office, for instance, senators have often outrun their legal rights to give or withhold their assent to appointments, by insisting upon being first consulted concerning nominations as well, and have thus made their constitutional assent dependent upon an unconstitutional control of nominations."

[42] See *Morgan* v. *Tennessee Valley Authority*, 115 F. (2d) 990 (1940), certiorari denied, 312 U.S. 701 (1941), where the court held that the authority of the President to remove such directors for any cause he chose was not limited by the congressional reservation of power.

[43] Emergency Price Control Act of January 30, 1942, 56 Stat. 23, as amended by the Inflation Control Act of October 2, 1942, 56 Stat. 765.

[44] See discussion of this problem in the *New York Times*, September 3, 1948, p. 5, cols. 5–8.

United States Minister respecting the Jay Treaty. Strong presidents like Jackson and Theodore and Franklin Roosevelt have not only refused to yield information demanded by Congress on the ground that it involved the personal relation of the executive and a subordinate, but Calvin Coolidge refused to give Congress in 1924 a list of the companies in which Andrew Mellon, the Secretary of the Treasury, was interested, and Herbert Hoover in 1930 declined to surrender the telegrams and letters leading up to the London Naval Treaty. One of the prime deterrents to the development in the United States of an adequate federal civil service is the manifest hostility, relentless and unceasing, which Congressmen pour out upon officials of the executive establishment. One former official of the federal government said that it was "like being nibbled to death by ducks," and former Secretary of the Interior Krug, when asked whether he would return to Washington to mobilize industry at the start of the Korean War in July 1950 (as he had in the Second World War) replied to the effect that he would seek a painless death by joining the military forces this time.

It has been pointed out that overlapping but different combinations of economic groups are marshaled behind the President and Congress in this historic duel.[45] The rivalry between Congress and the executive establishment would be natural and expected because of the group interest of

---

[45] Wilfred Binkley, *The Powers of the President* (New York: Doubleday, Doran, 1937). Binkley's thesis is that the conservative groups have tended to support Congress and the popular and less conservative groups have tended to support the President. The Whigs and the Republicans in the main have preferred a strong Congress and a weak President, while the Democrats, in the New Freedom, New Deal, and Fair Deal versions, at least, have preferred a strong President and a weak, that is subordinate but not docile, Congress. The alternation of strong and weak presidents and of strong and weak Congresses is the result of the shifts in the balance of power among the multifarious groups that comprise the society.

each of these sets of functionaries, but the struggle is exacerbated by the support that each of the contestants is given by alliances and coalitions of groups whose interests are at stake in the outcome. The leverage in this contest is with Congress. As Woodrow Wilson said, "The legislature is the aggressive spirit. It is the motive power of the government. . . ." [46] Even when, as in the national elections of 1948, Congress and its own particular and unique behavior are made an issue and a new Congress is returned, the new Congress may behave much as the old one did. The presidential power to campaign for a mandate from the people does not necessarily mean, when the President gets one, that Congress will enact it.

The rivalry between the judiciary and the executive has sometimes emerged in spectacular form as in the duel between Jefferson and Marshall and the controversy over the unsuccessful Court Plan submitted by Roosevelt to Congress in 1937, but the most enduring struggle has really taken place below the surface of public events and out of the public gaze in the silent war waged by the judiciary against the regulatory agencies. The chief characteristic of the regulatory agency of the quasi-judicial kind is that it combines in one instrumentality the legislative, the executive, and the judicial powers. It is a device invented by necessity for bringing to a focus the public powers (otherwise separated in the Constitution) for the regulation of conditions to which any single one of the three traditional powers had been found inadequate. Although legislatures in the early days of railroad regulation sought by statute to fix the rates which were determined to be reasonable, it became manifestly impossible for legislatures long to occupy themselves with these concerns, in view of the complexity of the subject and the volume of administrative business that rate-making entailed. So the regulatory agen-

---

[46] *Congressional Government,* p. 36.

cies were given authority within defined limits of jurisdiction to fix rates—the legislative function. They were also given the authority to determine whether the fixed rates were violated, proceeding upon complaint by aggrieved persons. This was the judicial function. The executive function was performed in many ways—the prosecution before the courts of complaints of wrongdoing, the policing of remedial orders made by the quasi-judicial agency, and the performance of many administrative functions unconnected with the quasi-judicial process. To repeat, the quasi-judicial agency was a device for bringing to a focus the public powers that the theory of the Constitution sought to keep separate.

The judges persisted in looking at the work of these agencies with split vision—trifocal in character. They persisted in separating the powers that necessity and the legislatures had put together. By looking at the agencies through the prism which divided agency work into the three primary colors, the judges failed to develop an adequate theory of bureaucracy. Many anomalies resulted. At first the courts regarded rate making as legislative in nature and not for the judges. Said the Supreme Court in the celebrated case of *Munn* v. *Illinois* in 1876, "For protection against abuses by legislatures the people must resort to the polls, not to the courts. . . ." [47] Eventually, however, the judges came to regard the reasonableness of rates not as a question to be decided at the polls but as one to be decided in the courtrooms, that is, a judicial question, although they continued to describe the rate-making process of quasi-judicial agencies as legislative in nature.[48] The entire logomachy of words and definitions contained in the law of jurisdictional facts, quasi-jurisdictional facts, historical

---

[47] 94 U.S. 113.

[48] See *Federal Power Commission* v. *Hope Natural Gas Company*, 320 U.S. 591, 64 S.Ct. 281 (1944).

facts, constitutional facts, and evidentiary facts developed out of the concern of the judges to keep within their hands the determination of the kinds of question that historically had been decided by the judges. This is understandable, perhaps, but the judges, having the last word on questions of jurisdiction, tended to decide the close votes in their favor, and many that were not in their favor at all, moving some of the legal profession to urge that the judges retain authority in the matter in which they were expert—to wit, the law—and yield to administrative bodies the authority to decide matters in which they were expert—questions of valuation, for example.[49]

Except where the simulacra of the judicial process were on display, the judges tolerated a great range of unreviewed discretion in executive agencies. Thus due process is not judicial process [50] but may embrace many forms of executive self-help including the forced sale of property distrained by Treasury agents, the enforcement of fraud orders in the Post Office Department, the control and deportation of aliens by the Department of Justice, the enforcement of the customs laws, and the regulation of public lands by the Department of the Interior. But where the executive process appeared to rival the judicial, the judges were stern and adamant. The Administrative Procedure Act of 1946 perpetuates the internal separation of powers within the executive agencies and thus institutionalizes and sanctifies by legislative enactment the rule that the judges enforced by themselves.[51]

It might be mentioned that even within the structure of official agencies in one branch of the federal government competition of group interests takes place. Mention has

---

[49] One such critic was James M. Landis, *The Administrative Process.*

[50] *Murray's Lessee* v. *Hoboken Land and Improvement Company,* 12 Howard 272 (1856).

[51] Administrative Procedure Act of 1946, Pub. No. 404, 79th Cong., 2d Sess. C. 324, June 11, 1946.

been made of the consciousness of a separate group interest as between the two houses of Congress. Although the Senate shares with the President some measure of the national authority to conduct foreign relations, the House of Representatives sometimes seeks to share the Senate's power. The House of Representatives Foreign Affairs Committee works in behalf of this goal, and the modern problems of foreign relations are such that there is work for all, and to spare.[52] The competition among the official groups in the executive establishment is long-standing and notorious. The long contest over unification of the military services and the rebellion of the Navy in 1949 against the curtailments enforced against it in favor of the Army and the Air Force by the Secretary of Defense are in point. The rivalry among the Corps of Engineers, the Bureau of Reclamation of the Department of the Interior, and the Department of Agriculture has complicated and made more expensive the control and development of water resources. The Office of Strategic Services, which performed valuable intelligence and counterespionage work during the Second World War, was partitioned and divided among the State, War, and Navy Departments after the close of military hostilities, these agencies being strong and suspicious claimants to the jurisdiction exercised by the OSS. Examples from the ad-

---

[52] Robert A. Dahl has written: "Where for a century and a half the House had little or no responsibility for foreign affairs, today, three significant tools of foreign policy require its consent. In the first place, parts of foreign policy have come to rest upon *legislation*. Equally important is the recent development of foreign loans and grants, which place upon the House the responsibiliy for *authorizations* and *appropriations*. Finally, the use of *executive agreements* as a substitute for the treaty process has also brought the House into the determination of foreign policy, for in a large number of cases the executive has considered it necessary or desirable to have Congressional support, in the form of a joint resolution, for an executive agreement." By permission of the publisher, from *Congress and Foreign Policy*, by Robert A. Dahl, Harcourt, Brace and Company, 1950, pp. 132–133.

46

ministrative record of the federal government could be multiplied. Nor are the states immune from the effects of rivalry among the official groups in the public government. State departments of health are often in conflict with state departments of industry over matters that fall within the jurisdictions of both, as for example the prevention and control of diseases induced by industrial callings and occupations. In states with unintegrated state administrations —where the chief administrative officers are elected by voters—the attorney general may frequently be at odds with the governor whose office he covets.

To carry analysis a step further, the subgroups of single official groups may be in competition with each other. In both the Senate and the House of Representatives separately, the committees of these bodies frequently contest for jurisdiction over bills, parts of which fall within the competence of more than one committee. In the Senate struggle in 1948–1950 over the repeal of the discriminatory tax on oleomargarine, for example, it became a matter of vital importance whether the Senate Committee on Agriculture got hold of the repealer or the Senate Committee on Finance, for the first was dominated by the farm groups that were opposed to the repealer while the second was not. The Legislative Reorganization Act of 1946 split jurisdiction on antitrust matters between the Senate Judiciary Committee and the Senate Committee on Interstate and Foreign Commerce, with amendments to the Clayton Act under the jurisdiction of the Judiciary Committee and amendments to the Federal Trade Commission Act under the jurisdiction of the Committee on Interstate and Foreign Commerce. The vital position held by committees in the legislative processes of Congress intensifies the effort of partisans in the group struggle to get their favored view before the committee with the power of life and death over legislation.

Group tension and conflict exist within the structure of bureaus and divisions of single agencies and departments in the family of official executive groups. Thus within the Department of Agriculture in the 1930's, there was a right-left axis along which some of the bureaus tended to line. In the middle period of the New Deal, the Farm Security Administration, speaking for the small farmer, the tenant, and the sharecropper, advocated a generous lending policy and locked in strife with the Farm Credit Administration, the Soil Conservation Service, and the Agricultural Adjustment Administration over the question of conversion to a defense policy, one of the issues of which was a proposal to establish an integrated and unified set of field services for the Department of Agriculture. In this contest the Farm Credit Administration won over the Farm Security Administration. Within the War Department the Corps of Engineers is so powerfully entrenched, with civilian support among Congressmen interested in rivers and harbors improvements and behind them business groups in the "improved" localities, that it was able to defy the expressed command of the Commander-in-Chief in wartime in a dispute between the Corps and the Bureau of Reclamation over the building of dams in the Central Valley of California.[53]

The struggle of subgroups within a department—the rivalry of bureaus with each other—is to be found in still lower levels of administration. Divisions within bureaus may and often are in contest with each other. Management improvement divisions or units of organization may and do run rival to finance and accounting divisions, and the personnel division or office is often the butt of bitter humor

---

[53] Commission on Organization of the Executive Branch of the Federal Government, *Task Force Report on Organization and Policy in the Field of Natural Resources* (Washington: Government Printing Office, 1949), Appendix 7, "The Kings River Project in the Basin of the Great Central Valley—A Case Study," pp. 149–182.

from all the others. Group spirit with its attendant feelings of belonging and not belonging and of acceptance of those within the group and hostility to those outside, the fastidious sense of jurisdiction which these group feelings engender and represent, the desire for status and prestige, the wish to be admired and to feel of account—all of these characteristics of the behavior of people in groups are to be found where people are in groups, in public government and in private enterprise, in school, college, and fraternity, in the bank wiring room of the Western Electric Plant in Hawthorne, Illinois, and in the Acropolis in an earlier and more classic time.

Official Groups and the Political Process

The group struggle, therefore, is apparent in the universe of unofficial groups and it is apparent in the universe of official groups. But these are not separate universes. They are one. Official groups are inhabitants of one pluralistic world. That world is an aggregation, a collection, an assemblage, a throng, a moving multitude of human clusters, a consociation of groups, a plurality of collectivities, an intersecting series of social organisms, adhering, interpenetrating, overlapping—a single universe of groups which combine, break, federate, and form coalitions and constellations of power in a flux of restless alterations.[54] Official

---

[54] The noted Polish sociologist of the late nineteenth century, Ludwig Gumplowicz, reflected the prevailing concepts of the day by writing a Darwinlike sociology of politics. Groups, which are basic in politics, are in a state of constant warfare. Indeed the state itself originated in conquest, being the early fruit of the victory of one class over another. This view has properly been criticized as an unverified conclusion about the past, deduced from an incomplete inspection of the present. See, for example, Edward Sait, *Political Institutions* (New York: Appleton-Century, 1938), p. 132 n. Gumplowicz accurately described the group basis of politics but conceived of the conflict in somewhat mechanical terms, viewing the course of the social process as a sequence of helpless inevitabilities, the product

groups, because of their officiality, have a leverage in many group situations which makes them valuable allies and stern foes. Before 1937, for example, business groups could combine with courts (i.e., judicial groups) to defeat combinations of other official groups such as presidents, Congressmen, and administrators.[55] Thus the ruination of the

---

of blind forces. It was for another Darwinian to find increasing perfectibility in the group struggle in politics, as Spencer had found it in economics and social life. Walter Bagehot, writing in 1873, felt justified in saying of nations (which he defined as "hereditary co-operative" groups) that: "The majority of the 'groups' which win and conquer are better than the majority of those which fail and perish, and thus the first world grew better and was improved." *Physics and Politics* (New York: D. Appleton and Co., 1873), p. 218. One need not view the constant struggle of groups for security and advantage as either completely mechanistic or tending toward perfectibility.

[55] The leverage possessed by the courts in this pattern of power was a force composed of identifiable but somewhat intangible ingredients: the cult of the Constitution and the companion myths about the judiciary. The Constitution, regarded as symbol rather than as instrument, as a norm of right behavior and the sum of limitations upon officeholders, as a restraint rather than as a grant, was, until 1937 at least, one of the strongest and most widely cherished symbols in the American political tradition. See W. Y. Elliott, "The Constitution as a Social Myth" in Conyers Read (ed.), *The Constitution Reconsidered* (New York: Columbia University Press, 1938), p. 209 ff. The companion myths about the judiciary presented the judges as a group of wise men, detached, above the storms of partisan controversy, impervious to the passions of men, moving by inexorable reasoning to conclusions of right judgment from a foundation of right principles, holding the balance of law and will steady with the aid of an objective rule. This view was held in the face of the somewhat puckish insistence of Justice Holmes that the judges were human and therefore fallible, that they were naïve and could use a touch of Mephistopheles. In fact however, the United States Supreme Court, was and is a political institution, not a trafficker in votes and election campaigns, to be sure, but one of the principal holders of the public power, favorably located to influence the balance among the shifting weights of interest and desire among the myriad groups that form the society. Walton G. Hamilton and G. D. Braden, "The Special Competence of the Supreme Court," 50 *Yale Law Journal* 1319 (1941); Earl Latham, "The Supreme Court as a Political Institution," 31 *Minnesota Law Review* 205 (1947).

first New Deal in the years 1935–1937. Even before the advent of the New Deal, the combination of business groups and judges had wrought havoc in labor relations with the abuse of the injunction and had mystified and confused the law of rate regulation hopelessly, inasmuch as the judges required the rate makers to take heed of the factor of reproduction cost new less depreciation, without ever telling them how much heed. The threat of a combination of the executive and the legislature in 1937 (even though the legislature refused to "combine") forced the working alliance of business and judicial groups asunder when the judges consulted their security as an undominated institution, in accord with the historic tradition, and yielded to the executive and the legislature in their interpretation of the nature of their powers under the Constitution. It is of note that this change of view by the Supreme Court was not produced by filling the Court with New Deal judges. The change occurred in 1937, before any new judges had been appointed. Since that time, however, the composition of the Court has been more radically and thoroughly changed than at any comparable period in history, and the law has been revised in substantial particulars. If the new judges now reflect more closely the aspirations of the new groups that came to power in 1933—the farmer, the small businessman, the industrial worker, the consumer, the aged, the buyers and holders of securities, and so on—they also reveal the uncertainty of a society which has lost its old guides and has not yet found new ones.

Since 1937 a new alliance has been formed between Congressmen and economic minorities, an alliance which sometimes circumvents the judges. It was such a combination that temporarily set aside the Supreme Court decision which brought insurance companies under the antitrust laws by reversing sixty years of precedent.[56] It was such a

---

[56] *Southeastern Underwriters Association* v. *U. S.*, 322 U.S. 533

combination that sought to put tidelands oil under the control of the states after the Supreme Court had held that title to such tidelands oil did not rest with the states.[57] Before 1937 it was one of the axioms of legal practice and constitutional interpretation that the pronouncements of the Supreme Court were final and binding, even when they were palpably wrong.[58] Much less has been heard of the

(1944). This case held that the far-flung operations of insurance companies, spreading the risks of coverage over the peoples of many states, were in interstate commerce or closely enough connected with interstate commerce to be subject to the regulatory powers of the federal government under the antitrust laws. This was a departure from the view established in *Paul* v. *Virginia,* 8 Wallace 168 (1869), which had held that the contracts of insurance were local contracts (and therefore intrastate), deriving their force from local law. It was said by Mr. Justice Black for the majority that all of the precedents were irrelevant because they had dealt with the question whether state statutes regulating insurance companies were an invasion of the commerce power of Congress, even though Congress had not acted. Congress immediately acted after the Supreme Court decision, and in 1944 the McCarran Act exempted insurance companies from any federal statutes not specifically referring to insurance companies, except the Sherman Act and three others. In *Prudential Insurance Company* v. *Benjamin,* 328 U.S. 408 (1946) and *Robertson* v. *California,* 328 U.S. 440 (1946), state statutes affecting insurance companies were upheld.

[57] *United States* v. *California,* 322 U.S. 19 (1947); *United States* v. *Louisiana,* 339 U.S. 699 (1950); *United States* v. *Texas,* 339 U.S. 707 (1950). Those disagreeing with the Supreme Court decision in the tidelands oil cases can draw comfort from the remarks of Mr. Justice Frankfurter in *United States* v. *Texas,* cited above. The opinion is not an actual dissent, and is not labeled so, but the justice washed his hands of the entire controversy, with the outcome of which he disagreed. Said Frankfurter: "Time has not made the reasoning of *United States* v. *California* . . . more persuasive but the issue there decided is no longer open for me. . . . I must leave it to those who deem the reasoning of that decision right to define its scope and apply it, particularly to the historically very different situation of Texas" (pp. 723–724).

[58] In the case of *Pollock* v. *Farmers Loan and Trust Company,* 157 U.S. 429 (1895), the Supreme Court nullified a congressional tax on incomes by declaring such a tax to be direct and therefore subject to apportionment, although for one hundred years the Court had

finality of Supreme Court pronouncements since 1937, although the traditional respect for the independence of the judges is strong, and the advocates of legislation to reverse the judges proceed with some caution toward their goals. In any event, the judges, including the members of the Supreme Court, would seem more clearly since the New Deal to perform the function which they performed before the New Deal, namely, that of serving as one more level of official compromise in the never-ending march and counter-march, thrust and parry, among economic groups, enforcement agencies, legislators, and executive functionaries. If the Supreme Court is not now looked upon by economic groups with the same friendly eye as heretofore, it is because the judges for the first time in the history of the Court are less conservative than Congressmen.

---

held the opposite, namely, that such a tax was not direct and therefore not subject to apportionment. On June 26, 1909, President Taft said of a bill to re-enact an income tax: "While I am generally in favor of the power of the government to levy such a tax, the truth is that the Supreme Court has decided that such a tax is unconstitutional, and this bill proposes to resubmit the question to the Supreme Court. I am opposed to this method of securing an income tax or the power to pass one. I think . . . the best thing to do is to accept the opinion of the court and submit to the people the question of a constitutional amendment." Henry F. Pringle, *The Life and Times of William Howard Taft* (New York: Farrar and Rinehart, 1939), I, 433. In the movements since 1937 to have Congress reverse, modify, or limit the application of Supreme Court decisions, the pronouncements of the Court about constitutional power are left intact, but questions of constitutionality are not in 1951 as critical as they were thought to be in 1935. The principal business of the Supreme Court in reviewing the constitutionality of statutes concerns the states, not the federal government. Indeed it may be queried whether there are many substantive limits that the judges will enforce against the federal government.

Chapter Two

The Cement Institute:

A Political Analysis

The preceding chapter has set out certain general political propositions that the evidence of political life seems to support. The statement of these propositions is essentially a sociological theory of politics. Such a theory regards groups as the basic political form. As was explained, however, this does not lose sight of the individual, since the groups exist to fulfill the desires of the individual, to minister to his wants, and to maintain his values and his security. It is now necessary to turn to some specific events in which the fundamental conflict of groups to write the rules of the society in their favor may be seen. The story is the struggle over the effort in the Eighty-first Congress by Senator O'Mahoney of Wyoming, Senator O'Conor of Maryland, and others to secure the adoption of a bill dealing with the problem of basing-point pricing in industry, and the counterefforts of Senators Long of Louisiana, Douglas, of Illinois, and Kefauver of Tennessee to defeat this design.

The Cement Case

The movement was touched off by a decision of the United States Supreme Court in April 1948 in the case of the *Federal Trade Commission* v. *Cement Institute*.[1] Although expressed in the language of the lawyers and the judges, which sometimes obscures the sense it professes, the Cement Case of 1948 dealt with the central problem of politics—the organization, administration, and control of power—in this instance, the power of a structure of private government. At issue were the legality of a system of basing-point prices maintained by the Cement Institute and the order of the Federal Trade Commission which required the Cement Institute to cease and desist from conspiring to eliminate competition through private price controls in the marketing of cement.[2] Struggles over prices are a good

---

[1] 333 U.S. 683 (1948), by certiorari from the Seventh Circuit Court of Appeals, *Cement Institute* v. *FTC* 157 F. (2d) 533.

[2] The structure, incidence, and regulation of basing points are dealt with in a fairly voluminous literature which includes the following: Temporary National Economic Committee, *Investigation of Concentration of Economic Power*, Monograph No. 33, "Geographical Differentials in Prices of Building Materials" (Washington: Government Printing Office, 1940); Monograph No. 38, "A Study of the Construction and Enforcement of the Federal Anti-Trust Laws" (1941); Monograph No. 42, "The Basing Point Problem" (1941); *Final Report and Recommendations* (Washington: Government Printing Office, 1941); "United States versus Economic Concentration and Monopoly," *A Staff Report to the Monopoly Subcommittee of the Committee on Small Business, House of Representatives*, (Washington: Government Printing Office, 1947); New England Council, Supplement to the *New England News Letter*, "The Basing Point Decisions and the New England Economy," October 1948; Address of Commissioner Lowell B. Mason before the Twentieth Boston Conference on Distribution, October 26, 1948, reported in the *Boston Herald*, October 27, 1948; Statement of Corwin Edwards on "Basing Point Systems," delivered at a Technical Seminar sponsored by the Department of Commerce for State Planning and Developing Agencies, Washington, D.C., August 4, 1948; Statement by Corwin D. Edwards on "How Business Is Affected by the Recent Basing Point Decisions," delivered at a meeting of the Chicago Association of Commerce and Industry, October 6, 1948; Federal Trade Commission, *Notice to the Staff, Commission Policy toward Geographic Pricing Practices*, October 12 and 21, 1948; Federal Reserve Bank of Philadelphia, "F.O.B.," *Business Review*, September 1948; "Proceedings

example of the "politics of economics," for they are struggles for security and advantage, and for the power that is at stake when prices move up or down.

In the Cement Case, prices had been determined by formulas which left customers with no price basis for choosing between one producer as against another. Price control was central to the maintenance of what may be described as a security system, operated for the benefit of the members of the Cement Institute. Although uniformity of delivered prices is theoretically consistent with a condition of free competition, or with a condition of monopoly,[3] the Federal Trade Commission found that restraint of interstate trade was both the object and the necessary result of the Cement Institute conspiracy. As one of the Institute's trustees had put it in a moment of friendly candor to a colleague in the cement industry, "The truth is of course—and there can be no serious, respectable discussion of our case unless this is acknowledged—that ours is an industry above all others that cannot stand free competition, that must systematically restrain competition or be ruined. . . ."[4] The Federal Trade Commission proved to the satisfaction of the Supreme Court that the Cement Institute did "systematically restrain competition."

In political terms, the Cement Institute was a private

---

of the Annual Convention of the American Economic Association" (papers on and discussion of monopoly, basing points, and antitrust regulation) *American Economic Review*, December 1947; *Hearings before a Subcommittee of the Committee on Interstate and Foreign Commerce on Senate Resolution 241*, 80th Cong., 2d Sess. (1948) (hereinafter cited as *Hearings on S. Res. 241*); Fritz Machlup, *The Basing-Point System* (Philadelphia: Blakiston Co., 1949); Symposium on "Delivered Pricing" in *Law and Contemporary Problems*, Spring 1950.

[3] *In the matter of the Cement Institute, et al.*, 37 *Federal Trade Commission Decisions* 87, at p. 251. Subsequent citations to the FTC decision in the Cement Case will appear as 37 *FTC*.

[4] 37 *FTC*, p. 144.

government, organized to protect an economic security system. Many official groups exist or have existed to divert the force of such private governments away from socially unacceptable objects. Among these groups are the Federal Trade Commission, the lower federal courts and the Supreme Court, the Departments of Commerce and Justice, the Temporary National Economic Committee, the House Select Committee on Small Business, the two branches of Congress, and the White House. Although possessed of the advantage of officiality, these agencies have sometimes suffered from grave weakness in dealing with organized structures like the Cement Institute. The latter possess unity of command and community of purpose and interest. The official groups have often been in strife with each other, making it difficult to deploy their strength in full vigor against the concentrations of monopoly power organized in the many systems of private government that inhabit the economy. Congress has frequently failed to give the Antitrust Division of the Department of Justice sufficient appropriations; judges have countermanded Commission orders; committees have made solemn recommendations which have gone unheeded by Congressmen and Presidents. More than ten years passed before the Commission and the Supreme Court succeeded in combining their forces to declare the cement combination unlawful.[5]

---

[5] Although counsel for the cement industry sought to argue that they had not had a fair hearing in the Federal Trade Commission because it was "prejudiced and biased against the Portland cement industry generally" and because it had prejudged the issues, the Seventh Circuit Court of Appeals (which decided against the Commission) rejected this argument. To the proposal that the Supreme Court should hold against the Commission, Mr. Justice Black said that there was a special reason "why courts should not lightly modify the Commission's orders made in efforts to safeguard a competitive economy." *Federal Trade Commission* v. *Cement Institute,* 333 U.S. 683 (1948), 68 S.Ct. 793, 815. The Commission, he said, is a body of "men trained to combat monopolistic practices." And further, "In the present pro-

In the political process, the Cement Case of 1948 was one stage in the struggle of a combination of enterprisers to dominate and exploit its environment for the security and advantage of its members. The Supreme Court decision represented the temporary victory of official power over a centrally organized system of private government, but the struggle did not end with the Supreme Court decision. In

---

ceeding, the Commission has exhibited the familiarity with the competitive problems before it which Congress originally anticipated the Commission would achieve from its experience." 68 S.Ct. 793, 816. Black also cited the statement of the Senate Committee on Interstate Commerce which (in discussing the Commission's power to aid courts in drafting antitrust decrees) attributed to the Commission "special expert experience and training in matters regarding which neither the Department of Justice nor the courts can be expected to be proficient." 68 S.Ct. 793, 816 n. In sum, the Supreme Court accepted the findings of the Federal Trade Commission as the reliable product of an expert body, established, trained, and trusted to investigate and find the facts.

The integrity of the Commission was also attacked by cement industry lawyers on the ground that the "findings [i.e., of the Commission] do not reflect any aspect of the truth inconsistent with the purpose of the Commission." Breck McAllister and Murray Quigg, "The Art of Selecting and Exploiting Half Truths," 58 *Yale Law Journal* 1069 (1949). But these findings were accepted by the Supreme Court (Justice Burton dissenting), and it was pointed out that the Commission's hearings were not *ex parte*. Said the Supreme Court, "Members of the cement industry were legally authorized participants. They produced evidence—volumes of it. They were free to point out to the Commission by testimony, by cross examination of witnesses, and by arguments, conditions of the trade practises under attack which they thought kept these practises within the range of legally permissible business activities." 68 S.Ct. 793, 803. The respondents in the Cement Case not only got a fair hearing, as the Supreme Court held, but got it in proceedings that lasted three years, in which were amassed 49,000 pages of oral testimony and 50,000 exhibits. Even in the Seventh Circuit Court of Appeals, the findings of the Federal Trade Commission bore up very well. For a similar appraisal of the Circuit Court's action on the Commission's findings, see Sergei S. Zlinkoff and Robert C. Barnard, "Basing Points and Quantity Discounts: The Supreme Court and a Competitive Economy, 1947 Term," 48 *Columbia Law Review* 985, 999 n. 55 (1948).

fact, the Supreme Court decision may be regarded most clearly as only one level of compromise in a never-ending series of compromises and adaptations, armistices, and adjustments. Immediately after the Cement Case, the cement and steel industries began to rally fresh groups to their support to revise or overrule the Supreme Court decision, and did succeed in getting congressional relief, only to have victory snatched ultimately by a presidential veto.

The Roots of Conflict

The controversy between government officials and spokesmen for industry over the economic effects and the legality of basing-point systems for making prices may be dated from the year 1921, when the Federal Trade Commission issued a complaint, or 1924, when it issued a cease and desist order to the United States Steel Corporation requiring it to abandon the basing-point pricing method known as "Pittsburgh plus." [6] Under this system, the price of steel quoted by the Corporation anywhere in the United States was a delivered price containing transportation charges estimated as though the steel products were shipped from Pittsburgh, whether they were or not. Pittsburgh was regarded as a "basing point," and the price at Pittsburgh was under the control of the producer. The freight charges added were those fixed by the Interstate Commerce Commission for the transportation of heavy goods from Pittsburgh to the point of destination. It is obvious that a buyer in Chicago who purchases steel which is manufactured in Gary, Indiana, and pays the freight on it as though it were delivered from Pittsburgh has been paying more than he should if the freight were figured from the actual source of supply. This overage is called "phantom freight," and one consequence of this system of pricing is to induce users of

[6] *In the matter of the United States Steel Corporation,* 8 *FTC* 1 (1924), at p. 3.

steel to locate their plants near the basing point, in this case, near Pittsburgh.

The Federal Trade Commission regarded "Pittsburgh plus" as as discriminatory method of pricing. The Commission believed that when a single company charges the same delivered price to customers wherever located, a superficial equality of treatment of all customers actually conceals a hidden form of discrimination. If the producer is located in Pittsburgh, say, and his price to the customer in Chicago is the same as his price to the customer in Pittsburgh, the producer has absorbed the freight cost between Pittsburgh and Chicago. But if he absorbs the freight cost, the net (delivered price minus freight) will be different for the Chicago and the Pittsburgh customers. It will clearly be considerably less for the Chicago customer. The latter will not be able to enjoy this mill differential if he is required to accept the delivered price. In the normal operation of a basing-point delivered price system, he would be so constrained. If he should offer to pay the low mill net and undertake to haul his purchase from Pittsburgh to Chicago in his own trucks or other conveyances, he would be refused by the Pittsburgh producer. It is because the delivered price system creates a different mill net for near and remote customers that the Federal Trade Commission has said a price discrimination against the nearby customers exists. If the mill net charged to the Chicago customer is the "true" price, the Pittsburgh customer has been overcharged. If the mill net charged to the Pittsburgh customer is the "true" price, the Chicago customer has been favored at the expense of the Pittsburgh customer. In some cases, it could be argued that the Pittsburgh customer has been "taxed" by the producer to maintain the subsidy granted to the Chicago customer.

What happens when all producers in the same industry use the same basing point? This occurs when one company acts as price leader and other companies in the industry use the price quoted at the leader's mill as the basing point for estimating bids to potential buyers. When this happens, all quote exactly the same price to all customers. This is so because all producers know the basing-point price and all can add to it the freight cost as fixed by schedules of the Interstate Commerce Commission. A customer in Butte who asks for bids from eighty producers located throughout the country will receive exactly the same bid from all of them, figured down to four decimal places, if they quote delivered prices figured from the same basing point. In this circumstance the producers near the customer will reap phantom freight and the distant producers will be required to absorb freight. A system of prices so structured has been referred to as an "umbrella," the implication being "that it holds up a price level under which mills of all degrees of efficiency or obsolescence find shelter."[7]

This system of price leadership has been defended on the ground that it permits producers in the same industry to compete all over the United States with each other. The effect is therefore to augment competition, not to diminish it. Under such a system producers in the East are permitted to compete in St. Louis or Kansas City on equal terms with producers in the Mississippi Valley. The fact that Kansas City producers may be near to the buyers gives them no advantage which cannot be enjoyed by producers in Philadelphia. In return, Kansas City producers are permitted by a basing-point system to compete in Philadelphia for the customers of the Philadelphia producer. This system of pricing is not uncommon. According to the Federal Trade Commission, in 1940 the basing-point system was widespread, being practiced (as of that date) in iron and steel, bathtubs, pig iron, cement, coffee, copper, lumber, asphalt shingles and roofing, gasoline, lead, metal lath, soap, stoves,

---

[7] TNEC Monograph No. 42, "The Basing Point Problem," p. 3.

newsprint paper, zinc, gypsum plaster, bolts and nuts, cast-iron pipe, range boilers, paper and paper products, salt, sugar, corn derivatives, industrial alcohol, and linseed oil and fertilizers,[8] to name some of the industries.

Against the argument that the basing-point system augments and increases competition, it has been said that its effect is socially and economically wasteful, because it encourages crosshauling. Why should a Kansas City producer sell his goods to the Philadelphia customer while the Philadelphia producer sells the same product at the same price to the Kansas City customer? If the Kansas City producer sold to the Kansas City customer and the Philadelphia producer sold to the Philadelphia customer, two unnecessary hauls across half the country would be saved. The unnecessary burden on the railroads could tax transportation facilities during times of national emergency, such as a defense or war effort. On the other hand, the abolishment of basing-point systems of quoting delivered prices would fundamentally change the prevailing practice in large and important sectors of the economy. The advocates of such change look upon it with equanimity, regarding it as a matter of decades and not a year or a few months, and in any case not likely to be more severe than many other economic changes which businessmen support. A more recent rationalization urges that the probable dispersal of industry in an era of atomic warfare alone would justify the abandonment of the basing-point system of quoting delivered prices, regardless of other considerations. Of course this argument was not available in 1924 when the Federal Trade Commission moved against Pittsburgh plus. But then, as now, critics of the basing-point system have insisted that it is wasteful and uneconomic, and that not the least of its uneconomic effects is that it encourages auxiliary enterprises to locate in areas which a free price system would render economically untenable.

[8] TNEC, *Final Report and Recommendations*, p. 19.

At the time the Federal Trade Commission put the United States Steel Corporation under order to cease and desist from continuing Pittsburgh plus, the Supreme Court decided two cases that tended to discourage further efforts on the part of the Commission to control pricing practices thought to be offensive to the law either as unlawful price discriminations (and therefore unfair trade practices) or as instruments tending to create monopoly in interstate enterprise. The cases were *Cement Manufacturers Protective Association* v. *United States*[9] and *Maple Flooring Manufacturers Association* v. *United States*.[10] Both cases, decided in the 1924–1925 term, extended the approval of the courts to the exchange of statistical and other information among producers of cement and flooring through trade associations organized for the purpose. Certain kinds of information, especially schedules of railroad rates, are essential to the successful operation of basing-point systems of quoting delivered prices. In fact, as will be seen below, accurate rate information is the pivot on which the whole system revolves.[11] Without it, producers are unable to quote the same price to all customers, thereby eliminating price competition. Neither collusion nor monopoly was proved in the Cement and Maple Flooring cases. The Court in the Cement Case of 1925 had before it evidence of identical bids, but it believed this to be a possible sign of competition rather than its reverse. In any event it did not appear after these two cases that there was much point in pushing complaints against basing-point pricing systems through the courts in an attempt to prove violation of the antitrust laws.[12]

The zeal of the Federal Trade Commission to regulate

---

[9] 268 U.S. 588 (1925).   [10] 268 U.S. 563 (1925).

[11] See below, pp. 76–77, 86–87.

[12] Leverett S. Lyon, Myron W. Watkins, and Victor Abramson, *Government and Economic Life* (Washington: Brookings Institution, 1939), I, 303.

pricing practices through cease and desist orders abated in 1925 for a reason other than the Court decisions. A fundamental change in the point of view of the Commission was wrought by President Coolidge when he appointed William E. Humphrey as one of the commissioners. The appointment of Humphrey was representative of a fundamental shift in the balance of groups operating in the environment of the Federal Trade Commission, which up to 1925 reflected the philosophy of its progressive origin. As Pendleton Herring has said of Humphrey's appointment:

The shifting of political fortunes had brought a combination of groups into control whose leaders expressed theories very different from the Wilsonian principles of the New Freedom. Big business had become more than respectable. . . . The effect of Humphrey's appointment was more far-reaching than any decision of the Supreme Court. It gave a radically altered policy and viewpoint to the commission.[13]

The advent of Humphrey meant that embarrassing investigations were dropped, a more lenient regulatory policy was followed, and the "self-regulation" of industry through trade practice conferences was encouraged.[14]

With the election of Franklin Roosevelt as President of the United States in 1932, a still newer combination of groups came into control whose leaders, to paraphrase Herring, "expressed theories very different" from the business philosophy of the middle twenties. One of President Roosevelt's early acts was the removal of Humphrey from his post in the Federal Trade Commission, a step which resulted in a well-known Supreme Court decision adverse to the asserted presidential power.[15] Despite the supposed hostility of Roosevelt toward business groups, the early

---

[13] By permission from p. 126 of *Public Administration and the Public Interest,* by Pendleton Herring. Copyright 1936, McGraw-Hill Book Company, Inc.   [14] *Ibid.,* p. 129.

[15] *Humphrey's Executor (Rathbun)* v. *U. S.,* 295 U.S. 602 (1935).

philosophy of the New Deal toward antitrust regulation was one of friendly relaxation. Indeed, industry was encouraged to regulate itself co-operatively with the government through the medium of the codes of fair competition authorized by the National Industrial Recovery Act. After the Supreme Court declared the National Industrial Recovery Act unconstitutional in 1935, however, the policy of the administration toward the antitrust laws became more rigorous, culminating in the extensive investigations of the Temporary National Economic Committee.[16]

To turn back to the Commission order of 1924, even a critic of the Federal Trade Commission has said, "It has been generally accepted since that date that the Pittsburgh-Plus system was an unfair and improper means of pricing steel." [17] The Commission order forbade the steel company to price its steel products at any other point than the place of production or shipment. The steel company then told the Federal Trade Commission that it would comply with the order "so far as practicable." [18] The Pittsburgh-plus system was abandoned, and the steel company changed to a multiple basing-point delivered price system. Pittsburgh alone was no longer the only basing point; instead many basing points were established around the country. The principle of the multiple basing-point system of quoting delivered prices is not different from that underlying the single basing-point system; and the same arguments apply for and against such systems. The Commission made no attempt to enforce its order for over fourteen years. As has been suggested, the views of the Supreme Court and the

---

[16] For an account of the work of the TNEC, see David Lynch, *The Concentration of Economic Power* (New York: Columbia University Press, 1946).

[17] *Study of Federal Trade Commission Pricing Policies, Interim Report,* 81st Cong., 1st Sess., Sen. Doc. No. 27, I (1949), p. 36. Subsequent citations will appear as Sen. Doc. No. 27.

[18] *Ibid.*

domination of the Humphrey philosophy in the Federal Trade Commission undoubtedly had much to do with the passive attitude of the Commission.

It was Congress that precipitated action in the steel case when it amended the Federal Trade Commission Act in 1938.[19] Before the Wheeler-Lea amendment, orders of the Commission were not final unless the respondent complied or the Commission petitioned a circuit court of appeals to enforce its edict. The Wheeler-Lea amendment made orders of the Federal Trade Commission final if the respondent to Commission proceedings failed to petition a circuit court of appeals to review them. In short, the Commission was relieved of the need to carry its cases affirmatively into the courts to enforce its orders, and the burden instead was shifted to the respondents to resist them. Orders not actively contested by respondents were legal obligations that respondents could be required to obey. With the enactment of the Wheeler-Lea amendment, the steel company petitioned a circuit court of appeals in Philadelphia for a review of the 1924 order. If it had not done so, its failure to contest would have made the 1924 order final and binding. This steel case never came to final court decision, however, but was affirmed by agreement between the Commission and the steel companies in 1948 after the decision of the Supreme Court in the Cement Case of 1948.

As the Federal Trade Commission moved from the policy of soft regulation associated with the views of Commissioner Humphrey through the state of co-operative regulation, which the early New Deal supported, and then once again into the period of strict control, other events moved in the same direction. In 1936 a bill was introduced in the Senate "to prevent uniform delivered prices." [20] The justifying reason adduced in the preamble was the discrimination be-

---

[19] Wheeler-Lea Amendment, 52 Stat. 111.
[20] Sen. Doc. No. 27, p. 37.

lieved to be caused among purchasers "by bearing substantially greater expense of transportation charges on sales to some customers than they bear on sales to other customers." The Federal Trade Commission supported the measure, but it was never reported out of committee. The Robinson-Patman Act of 1936 (an amendment to the Clayton Act) made it an offense for a seller to discriminate among his customers as to price except where the discrimination was based upon differences of cost, was made in good faith, and had no unlawfully adverse effect upon competition.[21] But what is a discrimination in price? Is the "true" price the delivered price or is it the mill net? If it is the mill net, then delivered price systems in which the seller absorbs freight will invariably produce a discrimination in mill net. The original bill contained a definition of price which made it identical with mill net, but opposition to this definition succeeded in having it withdrawn. The Supreme Court was later to interpret this withdrawal as an indication of the refusal of Congress to outlaw all uniform delivered pricing systems as such.[22] The withdrawal of the definition, however, then made it uncertain as to which uniform delivered price systems were to be held lawful and which were to be held unlawful.

In the next year, 1937, the Federal Trade Commission began to test its authority under the Robinson-Patman Act of 1936. A complaint was filed in July 1937 against the Cement Institute and other respondents (cement companies) charging a conspiracy in violation of the antitrust laws to operate a multiple basing-point delivered price system, the intent of which was to restrain interstate commerce.[23] This challenge to the multiple basing-point pricing system in the

---

[21] Act of June 19, 1936, 49 Stat. 1526.

[22] *Corn Products Company* v. *Federal Trade Commission*, 324 U.S. 726 (1945), p. 737.

[23] Federal Trade Commission, Docket No. 3167, July 2, 1937.

cement industry of course constituted a threat to the similar system functioning in the steel industry, for although unlawful conspiracy was alleged in the cement industry, an element not necessarily present in other industries, it seemed as though the multiple basing-point delivered price system—as such—was at stake. Indeed, there were those who were ready to assert that no multiple basing-point delivered price system could be maintained without unlawful co-operation, silent or overt. The Federal Trade Commission later filed a complaint against the Rigid Steel Conduit Company in 1941 alleging collusion as in the Cement Case and, in addition, conscious parallel action which resulted in uniformity of prices at any given destination.[24] Count I of the complaint in the Rigid Steel Case, alleging collusion and conspiracy in the sale of rigid steel conduit, was eventually dismissed; and the case proceeded to the Supreme Court on the second count, charging conscious parallel action.[25] The Supreme Court split four and four on this matter, as will be more fully related below.[26] The theory of the Federal Trade Commission under Count II of its complaint in the Rigid Steel Case was that any basing-point system was an automatic frustration of competition. In this its view was supported by some professional economists [27] and disputed by spokesmen for industry.[28] Besides these two cases the Federal Trade Commission proceeded against basing-point systems in the glucose, corn products, and salt in-

---

[24] Sen. Doc. No. 27, p. 39.

[25] *Triangle Conduit & Cable Co.* v. *Federal Trade Commission,* 168 F. 2d 175 (C.C.A. 7th 1948), *aff'd per curiam sub nom., Clayton Mark & Co.* v. *Federal Trade Commission,* 336 U.S. 956 (1949).

[26] See below, p. 126.

[27] Machlup, *The Basing-Point System.* For an earlier but similar view, see Frank Fetter, *The Masquerade of Monopoly* (New York: Harcourt Brace and Co., 1931).

[28] See the summary of arguments made by representatives of the steel industry in hearings before the TNEC in Lynch, *The Concentration of Economic Power,* pp. 81–82.

dustries, winning victories in the Supreme Court that heightened the apprehensions of practitioners of basing-point systems.[29]

It is not the law of these cases that is of concern here but rather the political process of which they were a part. The most interesting of these cases politically was the Cement Case, which touched off the movement to enact new legislation on the subject of basing-point pricing practices.

The Cement Confederation

As a system of private government, the organization, structure, and institutions of the Cement Institute most closely resembled a confederation. That is to say, it was a union of virtually all the manufacturers of cement in the United States. The constituent corporations were semi-autonomous in the management of their respective enter-prises,[30] limited in their choice of alternative plant policies by their compliance, willing and forced, with the rules administered by the central organization in behalf of all. The members were theoretically free to leave the confederation at any time, but a secessionist or nullification policy

---

[29] See above, pp. 61–62.

[30] The Federal Trade Commission found that managements could make their mills base mills or nonbase mills. The Commission also found that discipline was imposed to keep this semiautonomy within limits so that the pricing system could be maintained. In its own words, "Successful maintenance of the system requires, therefore, that the price leaders, usually the larger chain mills, possess the power to force recalcitrants to adhere to the system and that this power be exercised when necessary." 37 *FTC*, pp. 178–179. These price leaders constituted an inner circle functioning within the formal framework of the Institute. The chastisements involved in the use of punitive bases were in the control of these corporate members of the Institute. For the Commission findings on the use of punitive bases, see *ibid.*, p. 178 ff. The formal Institute, however, also lent its services in matters of discipline. See for example the part played by the Cement Institute in the use of espionage against, and boycott of, imported cement. *Ibid.*, p. 236.

on the part of individual members invited coercion against those who tried it. The principal method of coercion before the Cement Case of 1948 was economic loss.[31] By making the offender's mill an involuntary basing point, all members of the confederation were enabled to sell in the offender's territory at a price ruinous to him. The central organs of the confederation were officers, trustees, committees, divisions, bureaus, and other agents, including field agents.[32] The executive authority was vested in the president, vice-president, and treasurer, and legislative authority was vested in the trustees. Taxes were laid upon the members of the confederation by the central body, and each member had to continue to pay these assessments (dues) for a period of twelve months after resignation from the Institute.[33] These dues were collected as a species of pecuniary penalty for withdrawal and constituted one of the devices for maintaining the confederation intact.

Like the federal union in the United States, the Cement confederation came into existence as a form of private government only after inferior forms had been tried and failed to produce the degree of control desired. One of its predecessors and, later, one of the largest constituent subgroups within the Institute was the Portland Cement Association, called from 1902 (when it was organized) until 1916 the American Portland Cement Manufacturers.[34] Another predecessor organization, the Cement Manufacturers Protective Association, through the compilation and publication of statistics about cement manufacturing and distribution sought obliquely to control and make uniform cement prices. The Protective Association lasted from 1916 to 1924, when it was made the subject of a Justice Department prosecution.[35] The Cement Institute was organized in

---

[31] *Ibid.,* p. 179.   [32] *Ibid.,* p. 125.   [33] *Ibid.,* p. 126.

[34] *Ibid.,* p. 143.

[35] This was the case of the *Cement Manufacturers' Protective As-*

1929 as a device for the more efficient control of the industry in private hands after the two previous arrangements had failed. As the articles of association said, one of the purposes of the Institute was "to adopt and promulgate a code of ethics for the *government* of the members." [36] It was also one of the declared purposes of the Institute "to establish and maintain all such lawful trade customs and usages for the protection of the members as the Institute may deem advisable." [37] The multiple basing-point delivered price system was one of the "customs and usages" to be maintained.

Organized for the private government of the cement industry, the Cement Institute in 1933 was given virtually official status as part of the apparatus of public government when the Trade Practice Committee of the Cement Institute became the Code Authority for the cement industry under the National Industrial Recovery Administration.[38]

---

sociation v. *U. S.*, 268 U.S. 588 (1925), previously mentioned. In this case, the Supreme Court held that the Department of Justice had not proved the existence of a combination in restraint of interstate commerce. Identical delivered price quotations were thought by the judges to be compatible with a condition of free competition. The Association maintained a reporting service that distributed "information . . . with reference to production, price of cement in actual closed specific job contracts and of transportation costs from chief points of production. . . ." 268 U.S. 588, at p. 602.

[36] 37 *FTC*, p. 157. Emphasis supplied.   [37] *Ibid.*

[38] *Ibid.*, p. 159. As one writer has put it, "The Code of Fair Competition now took over where the Code of Ethics had left off, but the enforcement power of the Government was obviously stronger than that of an informal cartel that had to rely on ethics and moral suasion (i.e., intimidation) backed by the financial strength of the leaders." Machlup, *The Basing-Point System*, pp. 78–79. The evidence is that the Institute used the official status with which the Act had endowed it to improve the system of control over the industry. See for example, 37 *FTC*, p. 168 (as to land grant rates); p. 197 (as to truckers); p. 219 (as to limitations on increase of productive capacity). For working purposes the Cement Institute was the federal government in the cement industry, although this does not mean that it had its way in all things. For example, the Board of Trustees of the In-

When the NIRA was declared unconstitutional in the Schecter Case in 1935, the members of the Trade Practice Committee for a period of seven months thereafter continued to administer some of the provisions of the NRA Cement Code.[39] This is an interesting example of the purely technical character of the distinction between "official" and "unofficial," "public" and "private." During the whole of the NRA period, the multiple basing-point delivered price system continued to prevail despite objection to it in the Consumers Advisory Board [40] and despite the efforts of state and federal agencies to purchase cement f.o.b.[41]

Certain physical and geographical characteristics of the cement industry made the confederation form of organization the favored one, as against mere working agreements, alliances, *ad hoc* understandings, or outright monopoly.

---

stitute was authorized under the Code to formulate a plan for the sharing of the available business. Although "substantially all members of the industry desired a proration plan" none could be agreed upon, and no plan or method was ever approved by the NRA. *Ibid.*, p. 215. The Code Authority disseminated destination prices to members of the Institute although, according to a finding of the Federal Trade Commission, the Code did not specifically provide for such dissemination. *Ibid.*, p. 168. The Commission said that the result of this practice "was to facilitate greatly the efforts of respondents to make identical bids to the Government." *Ibid.*

[39] Only four companies saw fit to resign from the Institute right after the National Industrial Recovery Act was declared unconstitutional, and a motion to dissolve in May 1936 was able to muster only three votes. McAllister and Quigg, *op. cit.*, p. 1071. In December 1935, the Cement Institute issued a "Compendium of Established Terms and Marketing Methods" which codified the established rules and trade practices of the industry. They bore a close resemblance to the rules that had been established under the Code of Ethics and the Code of Fair Competition. Machlup, *The Basing-Point System*, p. 79. The Federal Trade Commission found that after the NRA, the trade practice committee of the Cement Institute served as the means for circulating "arbitrary prices" to Institute members. This was a phase of the struggle by the Institute and its members against imported cement. 37 *FTC*, p. 236. See below, p. 88.

[40] 37 *FTC*, p. 153.   [41] *Ibid.*, p. 160.

There were approximately eighty manufacturers of cement in the United States operating a total of about 150 mills.[42] Since cement is bulky, the cost of transporting it from the point of manufacture to the point of use constitutes a substantial part of the delivered cost. The high relative cost of transportation has contributed to the extension of the manufacture of cement throughout the United States. Cement is manufactured in thirty-five states because the raw materials and fuel for its production are not concentrated in any one area.[43] In the cement industry monopoly cannot be created by preclusive control of a short supply of a natural resource, geographically concentrated. The twin factors of high hauling cost and general distribution of raw materials and fuels therefore have made it relatively easy for numerous cement manufacturers to set up business. Their local positions make it costly to attempt to dislodge them except through a ruinous kind of competition. Federation is a well-tried political instrumentality for producing unity of purpose within a complex of entrenched local institutions, each of which maintains its autonomy and independence of action in all matters except those that involve the general security.

Although the number of producers was not small and the distribution of plants was widespread, there nevertheless existed within the cement industry a considerable concentration of power. Five producers controlled one-third of the output in the cement industry and this group of five was able to reach every part of the United States except the West Coast.[44] These five, and five more, controlled more than one-half of the productive capacity of the industry. The productive capacity was roughly divided, therefore, half to ten producers and half to the remaining seventy producers.

The Select Committee on Small Business of the House of

---

[42] *Ibid.,* p. 141.   [43] *Ibid.,* p. 140.   [44] *Ibid.,* p. 142.

Representatives found in 1947 that there was a regional concentration of power as well as a national one. In 1947 the five largest producers of cement in the country were Universal Atlas, a subsidiary of the United States Steel Corporation; Lehigh Portland Cement Company; International Cement Corporation (Lone Star); Alpha Portland Cement Company; and Pennsylvania Dixie Cement Corporation.[45] In each of the twelve producing districts, the percentage of capacity held by the five largest companies within the district was higher than the percentage held by the five largest companies in the country as a whole. In two of the districts, the five largest companies held over 80 per cent of the capacity; in two others they held 70 to 80 per cent of the capacity. The Select Committee also found that in "one producing district, the largest five producers, within the district, held 94% of the capacity, and in 8 of the 12 districts there were fewer than 10 producers altogether in the area." [46]

Cement has been manufactured in the United States for a period of only about seventy years, having been imported before that time.[47] With the appearance of the industry in the United States the movement for control of it soon followed. Three principal control devices have been utilized for the purpose of producing uniformity of price: patent control, dissemination of price and cost data, and the administration of a formulary price system through the Cement Institute. The use of these principal methods of control corresponds with fairly well defined periods in the history of the industry. The patent control period lasted from 1900 to 1911.[48] Two employees of the Atlas Portland

---

[45] "United States versus Economic Concentration and Monopoly," A Staff Report to the Monopoly Subcommittee of the Committee on Small Business, House of Representatives (Washington: Government Printing Office, 1947), p. 125.

[46] *Ibid.*   [47] 37 *FTC,* p. 140.

[48] Patent control was attempted by the Association of Licensed Ce-

Cement Company, the Messrs. Hurry and Seaman, secured a patent on a method of burning powdered coal in rotary cement kilns.[49] From this beginning developed a system of price manipulation through licensing agreements, which collapsed in 1911 after a court decision adverse to the validity of the Hurry and Seaman patents. The next principal method of control was the dissemination of statistical information through the Cement Manufacturers Protective Association. The Association was organized in 1916 for the purpose of disseminating information regarding specific job contracts. Although a lower court found [50] that the spread of such information tended to limit production and to create uniformity of price and that there was, therefore, a restraint of commerce within the principles of *American Column and Lumber Company* v. *United States*,[51] the Supreme Court held that there was no violation of the antitrust laws.[52] There was no evidence of any concerted action except with respect to the dissemination of information. Although the Cement Manufacturers Protective Association eventually was given a clean bill of health by the Supreme Court, it became inactive.

The third and most effective system of control was the multiple basing-point delivered price system which the

---

ment Manufacturers. Preceding this in November 1906, the North American Portland Cement Company was created with an exclusive license to the Hurry and Seaman patent, and authority to sublicense. In 1903 the Atlas Portland Cement Company sued for infringement; this suit led to the settlement which set up the North American Company, which led to the Association of Licensed Cement Manufacturers. The patent-control period, therefore, may be dated from the event that led to all these consecutive developments, namely, 1900, the year that Hurry and Seaman secured the patent.

[49] 37 *FTC*, p. 153.

[50] *U. S.* v. *Cement Manufacturers Protective Association*, 294 Fed. 390.

[51] 257 U.S. 377 (1921).

[52] *Cement Manufacturers Protective Association* v. *U. S.*, 268 U.S. 588 (1925).

Cement Institute administered for a period of some twenty years. Under this system, sixty basing points were established in the United States, each with its base price for cement. In calculating the delivered price for cement for any customer, the seller had first to decide which basing point governed. This was done by adding to the price maintained at all basing points near the customer, the all-rail freight charge from each of the basing points to the customer. The smallest sum of these factors (basing-point price plus rail charge) was the price at which any producer would sell to the customer. Every seller of cement in the United States would sell to a given customer, therefore, at the same price.

In order to enable any seller to make this simple arithmetical calculation it was necessary for all of them to know the location of the basing points, the basing-point prices, and the freight rates.[53] The information as to freight rates was supplied by the freight bureau of the Cement Institute in the form of freight rate books.[54] These rates are fixed by

[53] 37 *FTC*, p. 103.

[54] The Commission made a finding that "the rate books published by the Institute were intended . . . to provide common freight rate factors for pricing purposes, avoid differences in delivered price quotations resulting from errors in rate calculations or failure to keep abreast of rate changes, and thus enable the corporate respondents to quote identical delivered prices for cement at all destinations; and they were in fact used for that purpose." *Ibid.*, p. 163. The freight rate books were regarded by the Commission as deficient in information that a genuine rate service would be expected to supply. The all-rail freight rates contained in the books were used to calculate delivered prices even though shipment was made by water transportation or by motor truck at rates different from those on which the price was calculated. *Ibid.*, pp. 166–167. The allegation was made by the defense in the Cement Case that the books were designed to supply manufacturers with accurate information about freight costs. But the Commission found that the rate books contained rates from points where no shipments of cement originated, and failed to contain rates from all producing points. *Ibid.*, p. 166. The value to the manufacturer in calculating actual freight costs was therefore small. The value of the freight rate books for the Institute and its members in maintaining

the Interstate Commerce Commission and by state regulatory bodies and are distressingly complex. Control of the location of basing points and of the basing-point prices was in the hands of members of the Institute, but control of the basic freight rates was not. In cases of conflict between the published rates of the ICC and those set out in the freight rate books distributed by the Institute the members of the industry were disciplined to conform to the Institute's figures.[55] When the Interstate Commerce Commission, for example, changed a rate, the members of the cement industry continued to calculate their delivered prices at the old freight rates until they were told by the Institute that they could calculate them at the new rates.[56] This was clearly an instance of the substitution of private authority for that of public authority in an area where the latter was presumed to possess overriding control. It is an especially good example of what Beardsley Ruml describes as the rule-making function of private business groups.

In the case of *Cement Manufacturers Protective Association* v. *United States* in 1925, the Supreme Court held that the distribution of freight information was a species of research activity only, in the absence of evidence of collusion to fix prices by this device. The Federal Trade Commission in the Cement Case of 1948 found that the freight rate books were an instrument of control and constituted evidence of collusion to fix prices.[57] The success of the security system in fixing the delivered prices of cement was very great. The Federal Trade Commission was able to cite many instances of identical bids on cement, similar to each other in ten-thousandths and even millionths of a dollar.[58]

their private price control system was very great. This is also the view of Machlup, *The Basing-Point System*, p. 18.

[55] Members of the Institute used the freight rates in the book in calculating prices, even though these book rates were at variance with official rates, and did not use new official rates until such new rates had been cleared with the Institute Rate Bureau. 37 *FTC*, p. 165.

[56] *Ibid.*, p 109.   [57] *Ibid.*, p. 109.   [58] *Ibid.*, p. 177.

Security by Force

The linchpin of control, the buttress of this security system, therefore, was the multiple basing-point delivered price. But as in the execution of its programs and policies by public government, the system of private government represented by the Cement Institute had to devise and administer numerous corollary, supporting, and protective activities to maintain the central point of control intact and viable. The Cement Institute lived in an environment of groups potentially hostile to it and to the basing-point system. Security in this environment made it necessary, therefore, to neutralize outside pressures that threatened the system. Divisionist influences had to be fought off so that the members of the confederation might continue to exist in domestic tranquillity and noncompetitive amity. Among the troublesome groups in the universe in which the Cement Institute dwelt were truckers, dealers, customers, foreign importers, and state and federal agencies. Consequently the policies of the cement confederation sought to preserve the pattern of internal order by blocking and counteracting these groups, some of which were merely nonconformist while others were hostile.

a. Truckers. With respect to truckers for example, the danger to the security system was that customers would want to truck their own cement from the plant of the manufacturer to destination. Such a practice if widespread would break the basing-point formula by destroying dependence on the freight rate factor. In fact, if the buyer were permitted to take delivery at the mill and transport by truck, the seller lost control of the delivered price.[59] After an initial period of some ten years after the First World War, during which the cement industry tolerated a certain amount of such buying, the industry, by co-operation, un-

[59] *Ibid.*, p. 191.

derstandings, and agreements among the members, began systematically to discourage the practice. It is interesting that this policy coincided with the appearance of the Cement Institute and is another indication that the Institute was a superior form of private government, much more efficient than the arrangements that had previously existed, for protecting the security system of the cement manufacturers. Various restrictive steps were taken to discourage trucking by customers, including the imposition of penalties in the form of a fifteen-cent-a-barrel charge in addition to the mill base price, a charge paid only by those asking delivery to trucks.[60] There were several regional variations in the use of penalty prices.[61] By 1932 a major part of the cement-manufacturing industry had declined to permit trucking under any circumstances, and most of the rest forced buyers to pay penalty prices for delivery to trucks.[62]

b. Dealers. A second group capable of upsetting the security of the cement manufacturers was the body of dealers who comprise one of the principal classifications of purchasers of cement.[63] Irregularities (in price and otherwise) in the sale of cement by dealers tended to disturb the security system of the cement manufacturers, and various policies were employed to neutralize this dangerous influence. Before 1913 no discounts were given to dealers by Lehigh, one of the principal producers of cement, but for the next eighteen years some form of dealer differential was maintained.[64] Eventually the discount was ten cents a barrel, and the discount proved to be a source of weakness in the security system of the manufacturers. Some dealers in order to get attractive carload business, sold to consumers on a

---

[60] *Ibid.,* p. 192.   [61] *Ibid.,* p. 193.

[62] *Ibid.,* p 198. Although the manufacturers combined to prevent customers from taking delivery f.o.b. trucks, the manufacturers frequently employed trucks for delivery while charging the all-rail freight rate. *Ibid.,* p. 114.

[63] *Ibid.,* p. 141.   [64] *Ibid.,* p. 226.

five-cent margin. They were thus able to quote the manufacturer's product to the consumer at less than the manufacturer's price to the consumer.[65] With the co-operation
of dealers who would cut their differential, some manufacturers shipped cement for the account of such dealers
to outside markets. The price to the customer through the
dealer from the producer was less than the price to the
customer from the producer directly. In this case, however,
the manufacturer and not the dealer reaped the benefit of
the split differential.[66]

The Institute therefore abandoned the trade discount to
dealers but then found it necessary to devise other methods
for controlling the competition between dealers and manufacturers and among dealers. This was done by making the
dealers the exclusive outlets for cement in dealer markets,
with certain exceptions. Manufacturers reserved the right
to sell directly to the federal and state governments, railroads, and certain users employing cement for the manufacture of cement products, but not for resale in bulk.[67]
This rationalization of the market was written into the
Code for the Cement Industry in 1933, but it was set aside
in 1934. Defeated in the attempt to write these restrictions
into law, the Institute reached the same result by declara-
tions of policy to which the customers of cement were expected to adapt themselves. That they did so is shown by
the correspondence gathered by the Federal Trade Commission from the National Federation of Builders' Supply
Associations, Southwestern Lumbermen's Association, Nebraska Lumber Merchants Association, and the Mountain
States Lumber Dealers Association.[68] Arrangements were

---

[65] *Ibid.*, p. 227.   [66] *Ibid*, p. 227.   [67] *Ibid.*, p. 228.

[68] *Ibid.*, p. 230. Representatives of the Institute met with representatives of the dealers in Chicago in 1935 to decide on dealer policies. A
district meeting of the Institute attended by the manager of the Institute agreed upon a method of marketing cement substantially identical with the policy worked out in the Chicago meeting. *Ibid.*, p. 231.

also made to maintain uniform compliance with the new policy by the designation of a "contact" man between the Institute and the National Federation of Builders' Supply Associations to police the new rule and to report violations of it.[69] This is a good example of the manner in which the Cement Institute as a system of private government put into effect a rule of conduct which not only differed from the rule of public authorities but violated it.

The dealer policy of 1935 reserved to the manufacturer the right to make sales to the federal government, but the right was not preclusive. In fact, the dealers were made the exclusive channel for sales to unemployment and relief agencies like the Works Progress Administration, Civilian Conservation Corps, and Federal Emergency Relief Administration. This made it necessary for the federal government to buy through dealers and prevented these agencies from buying directly from the manufacturer. All sales through dealers carried the dealer's markup. The result was a tax imposed upon the people of the country by the Cement Institute for the benefit of the dealers and the maintenance of the cement manufacturers' security system.[70]

c. Customers. A third, and the most numerous, group dwelling in the environment of the cement confederation was the customers. Since their behavior as customers could threaten the security system with disorder, it was thought necessary to organize, classify, and rationalize this behavior. It had to be made safe for and predictable by the confederation. Many stratagems and strokes of policy were employed to accomplish this object. Customers, motivated by the same desire for security and advantage as the Institute and

The president of the Institute appointed a committee to maintain contact with government purchasing agencies and so far as possible further the new dealer policy. *Ibid.*, p. 232.

[69] *Ibid.*, p. 231   [70] *Ibid.*, pp. 232–233.

its members, sought to free themselves from the restrictions of a rigid price system by making long-term contracts with dealers at the price determined at the time of the contract. The purpose of these contracts was to ensure the customer against increases in price decreed by the manufacturers. In effect it was an engagement by dealers to absorb such increases in return for the advantage of a long-term order. A variation of this practice was for customers to order cement from a number of sources for the same job, stock-piling this commodity as an insurance against price increases.[71] The Institute met this subterfuge by collecting and disseminating information about specific job contracts. This information quickly showed which customers were placing orders beyond the needs of specific jobs on hand, both in quantity and length of contract.[72]

The Institute did not leave it to the individual action of its members to control this practice, however. Collective action and the pressure of collective opinion were brought to bear upon members of the Institute to cancel the contracts violating or threatening the security system.[73] In all of this politicking, the Institute took pains to make it appear that the checking and canceling of contracts was a matter of individual action.[74] For example, the Institute supplied daily summaries of contracts and cancellations to the members of the Institute but declined to send such information directly to the field representatives of members of the Institute. The Institute in a letter to one of its members explained this refusal on the ground that it wanted to avoid "the implication that the Cement Institute has any authority in the control of contract obligations." [75]

Customers also sought to avoid exploitation under the price policies of the Cement Institute and its members by resorting to a subterfuge which the latter thought was

---

71 *Ibid.*, p. 202.   73 *Ibid.*, p. 204.   75 *Ibid.*

72 *Ibid.*, p. 203.   74 *Ibid.*, p. 206.

highly "unethical." Customers would order cement to be delivered to a named destination, the price for which was set in accordance with the formula applying to that destination. While the cement was in transit, the customer would then order it diverted to another point. The railroad would deliver to the new destination, the freight charge for which would be less than the freight charge to the ostensible destination. Since the customer actually paid the freight charge to the railroad, the delivered price of the cement to him would be less than the price charged. The manufacturer's mill net would be the same, with the exception that if the cement had been consigned to the second destination without diversion, the manufacturer's mill net would have been higher. By means of understandings and agreements, the Institute sought to prevent purchasers from making diversions in transit.[76]

The practice of diversion was castigated in the Code for the Cement Industry in 1933 as an unfair trade practice. It had previously been asserted to be a venal practice in the Code of Ethics adopted by the cement manufacturers when the Cement Institute was established in 1929. After the expiration of the NIRA, the trustees of the Institute drew up a compendium of established terms and marketing methods which also characterized the diversion of freight as an unfair method of competition. The compendium recommended the use of a standard contract form which required the purchaser to pay the full original price if the freight was diverted in transit. In its effort to regulate the behavior of purchasers of cement, the Cement Institute was able to enlist the co-operation of the railroads. The traffic advisory committee of the Association of American Railroads was induced to recommend to its members that they accept bills of lading stamped with a clause prohibiting diversion. These bills of lading were used by many of the

[76] *Ibid.*, p. 199.

members of the Institute.[77] After 1937 the members of the Institute began to prepay the freight charges for cement. As the Federal Trade Commission concluded, "When freight is prepaid, there can be no diversion of shipments by the consignee to his advantage in price." [78]

d. Official agencies. A fourth group of groups constituting a threat to the security system of the cement manufacturers was the complex of federal and state agencies. There is no evidence that the members of the Cement Institute at any time were impressed by the character of federal and state agencies as organs of government, possessors in some small part of the sovereign power of the people, the supreme political power of an organized community. The evidence tends rather to show that the members of the Cement Institute regarded agencies of the federal and state governments as just another group of individuals, not too scrupulous, seized of certain unfair privileges in dealing with nonofficial groups. They were considered to be a fat source of profit, not entitled to better treatment from the members of the Institute than any other customer, and certainly not entitled to preferences merely because they happened to be serving public policy for the whole nation. The Institute insisted on treating the members of governmental agencies like other customers but complained loudly when the members of the Institute were treated by governmental agencies on the same cold-blooded basis of profit.

For example, as part of its policy to fix high prices and to ration low production,[79] the cement confederation under-

---

[77] *Ibid.,* p 201. [78] *Ibid.,* p. 202.

[79] See the comment on this policy of M. A. Adelman, "Competition and Antitrust Laws," 61 *Harvard Law Review,* 1345–1346 (1948). "For the ten years 1928–37 inclusive, the average percent of capacity utilized was about 45%. Additional cement could at any time have been produced at half, or less than half, of the current price. . . . Under unrestrained competition, the price would have been driven toward the incremental cost, i.e., below average cost, and the industry as a whole forced to suffer losses until the redundant firms and mills

took to discourage the entry of new producers into the cement industry. When the Tennessee Valley Authority was established, it required millions of barrels of cement for construction work. It called for bids on cement and received such bids from members of the Cement Institute, all of them substantially identical. Thereupon TVA made a study to determine the practicability of building and operating its own cement plant. Representations were made to the TVA by members and officers of the Institute, after which the TVA decided to make a joint examination of costs to determine a fair price for cement. It also decided that if the bids received were not reasonable in terms of these findings, it would make some move to build its own plants. The threat, accompanied by an ultimatum, guarded but firm, produced the desired result. A compromise price was agreed upon and TVA purchased its cement.[80]

Although the Institute had no qualms about charging a monopoly price and no scruple about insisting that the TVA "take it or leave it," it was with the sharpest cries of pain and self-pity that it received the TVA ultimatum. In a long, ill-tempered telegram to the Chairman of TVA, one of the trustees of the Institute employed such phrases as "prejudice against business men," "to coerce the companies," "arbitrary power," "immense power," "control of vast government funds," "ruthless declaration," "arbitrary determination," "under threat of dire punishment," and so on.[81] The Cement Institute was not a happy contributor to the reconstruction of the Tennessee Valley.

The somewhat cynical conception of governmental agencies as a group of enterprisers to be overreached if possible

---

were squeezed out. But in point of fact, the respondents' profits before taxes averaged 3.56 percent of their capital assets. *Something*—whether we call it normal trade practises with Judge Major or combination with Mr. Justice Black—prevented competition from being effective. In no other way could profits have been earned."

[80] 37 *FTC*, pp. 223–225.   [81] *Ibid.*, p. 224.

was implicit in the classification and division of customers between manufacturers and dealers, of which note has already been made. When the dealer arrangement was established as an Institute policy, it was thought to be desirable to maintain close liaison with federal purchasing officials to make sure that the Institute view was properly presented. The representatives of the Cement Institute did their work well and persuaded the military men who were in the Procurement Division that it was in the public interest to buy through dealers at a higher price than by direct purchase from manufacturers at a lower price.[82] The secretary of the National Federation of Builders' Supply Associations was jubilant over the victory as he confided in a letter of August 28, 1935:

> There were those who said "it couldn't be done." To them it seemed a hopeless task to buck a Department of the Government which was determined to buy direct. However it has been done and, in my judgment, it is conservative to say that in excess of $50,000,000 of business will be held in dealer channels which . . . would certainly have gone direct.
>
> Instead of disaster which seemed to be certainly headed in our direction, we have been able to gain a signal victory. We have proved to the Government, to manufacturers, and to ourselves that we are alive and willing to fight for our rights. More than 10,000 communications went into Washington, I am informed, either directly to members of Congress or to the Procurement Division. . . .[83]

This "signal victory" helped to swell the cost of government, about which business groups are sometimes solicitous.

In the struggle to overreach government agencies, one situation continued to baffle the Cement Institute. This was the method of making bids for federal purchases of cement to be carried over railroads to which the federal government pays land-grant rates. Land-grant rates are less than ICC

[82] *Ibid.*, p. 233.   [83] *Ibid.*, p. 234.

rates and are not published, but are a matter of business between the carriers and the government. The basing-point delivered price formula employed by the members of the Cement Institute required for its successful operation an exact knowledge of the freight rates between basing points and any point of destination. Since the rates that govern the carrying of federal freight under the land-grant discount are not generally known, one indispensable element of the pricing formula was missing.

Under the Code for the Cement Industry, members of the Cement Institute filed destination prices with the Code Authority, which were then disseminated. It was then possible for each of the member companies to know in advance what each of its fellow members would charge the federal government; uniformity in the bidding could therefore be achieved, even though the bids did not represent the calculation that might have been made had the freight rates been known. After the Codes, the Institute began a systematic search for land-grant rates, a search akin to the espionage activities familiar in foreign relations, with a vigorous underground and a central intelligence headquarters. The Cement Institute sought to piece together information about land-grant rates from a variety of sources—the railroads themselves, previous lettings, and competitors.[84] The search was given up after a year or so, and the problem of land-grant rates continued to be a baffling one.[85]

e. Strangers. New domestic producers and importations of foreign cement constituted a fifth threat to the security system of the cement industry. Attacks were therefore made upon new producers and upon foreign importations of cement. The Code for the Cement Industry in 1933 contained a provision permitting the Institute to petition the President of the United States to prohibit the establishment of new plants, increases in the capacity of existing plants,

---

[84] *Ibid.,* p. 168.　　　　　[85] *Ibid.,* p. 173.

and even the moving of an existing plant from one location to another.[86] Hostility to increases of production that would disturb the security system of the existing members of the Institute led it to protest the granting of loans by the Reconstruction Finance Corporation to units of industries already in a state of excess capacity of production.[87] The strategy of opposition to this "harmful practice," as it was called, of the RFC included the use by private persons of the letterhead of the NRA Code Authority for the Cement Industry,[88] the solicitation of letters of protests, and help to a writer for the *Chicago Herald and Examiner* in the preparation of an article in support of the cement industry, titled, "Wasted Taxes." [89] In view of the Institute's insistence that agencies of the federal government pay the dealers' markup for cement, the Institute had expert knowledge on the subject to share with the newspaper writer. The plant which was the particular object of the Institute's attention was not put into operation, but the Institute was not always so successful in crushing incipient competition.[90]

Different situations called for different methods in repelling new groups threatening the security system and in defeating those who managed to gain entry. The appearance of imported cement in the American market was the signal for concerted attacks upon the dealers and other handlers of it—attacks that utilized the techniques of espionage, encirclement, systematic price undercutting, boycotts, and reprisals.[91]

Security by Propaganda

Like public governments, and like many other systems of private government, the cement confederation maintained a ministry of information and propaganda, a committee on public relations. When the price of cement went up in

---

[86] *Ibid.*, p. 219.   [88] *Ibid.*, p. 220.   [90] *Ibid.*, p. 223.
[87] *Ibid.*, p. 220.   [89] *Ibid.*, p. 223.   [91] *Ibid.*, pp. 235–236.

1933 in the face of continuing depression, there were many protests against the cement industry from both public and private sources.[92] The Institute and its members thereupon engaged in a concerted and systematic campaign of propaganda to allay the criticism and put to sleep the incipient hostility. This was difficult, as some of the members of the Institute admitted, because it was hard to defend the industry without defending its most characteristic policy, viz., that competition should be stifled. A sense of grievance that the industry should be required to defend itself is carried in such comments as the following: a midwestern governor acted in "a rather unfriendly and unjustified manner"; [93] certain editors "who should be friendly feel that we are gouging"; [94] and the "cement business is in public disfavor." To counteract this public disfavor, to neutralize the growing acidity of the environment which it had to keep bland, the Institute put on a campaign with the usual appurtenances of a promotional drive familiar in the advertising world.[95]

One proposed instrument of this campaign is especially noteworthy because it exhibits a cold political calculation of the strength of the opposition to be quieted or appeased. This was a table entitled "Approximate Number of Leaders of Groups to Be Convinced," of which twelve groups were listed.[96] The first five groups covered officialdom and the press, as follows: (1) federal and state officials; (2) newspapers, magazines, and journals, general and economic writers, financial editors and writers; (3) United States Senators and Representatives; (4) state senators and representatives; (5) county commissioners and engineers, mayors and city managers, and city engineers. This proposal assumed, and probably correctly, that the apparatus of the public government and the media of mass communication

[92] *Ibid.*, p. 239 [94] *Ibid.*, p. 241. [96] *Ibid.*, p. 246.
[93] *Ibid.*, p. 240. [95] *Ibid.*, pp. 244–245.

were the first and most important of the centers of potential resistance and hostility that had to be influenced. The experience of underground movements in Europe would seem to confirm the correctness of this calculation.

Behind this first rank of five groups came seven others, representing the principal structures of interest in the immediate business milieu of the cement industry. These were (1) building materials dealers; (2) civic leaders and financiers; (3) contractors; (4) manufacturers of concrete products; (5) civil engineers and architects; (6) co-operating organizations; and (7) other industries, like the steel industry, having the common problem of defending basing points and monopolies. These tables of the organization of the opposition listed the number of leaders to be persuaded over to the side of the cement industry. The entire calculation is of interest politically because it is based on the assumption that the significant political form is the group, and that within the group there is a leadership-followship relation which can be exploited. Capture the leaders and the followers will not be troublesome.[97]

Making Internal Unity

This analysis of the politics of the Cement Institute may be concluded with some brief observations about the devices used by the Institute to create and maintain a community of interest among the members. The elements of governance in private as well as public systems are constraint and consent. Community interest is cultivated by

---

[97] The Institute did not launch this particular campaign. As the chairman of the Institute's marketing research committee said, no "sound defense of our methods of selling cement can be made without the admission that some limitation of competition is necessary in such an industry as cement. This is not a subject which can be presented to the public through advertising, or in any way. It is an argument that has to be made and can be made in special places where it may be calculated to do some good." *Ibid.*, p. 248.

use of the carrot and the cudgel. Consent is a perishable good, and the managers of governmental systems must depend upon its constant renewal. If it is not constantly renewed as a by-product of policies that keep the constituent members content, consent must be manufactured. The private government of the Cement Institute was aware of these problems of rulership and pursued courses pointing to the following objects: belief in the equality of the constituent members; belief in the existence of a community of interest among the members; and the development of a group morality.

a. Equality. The policies of the Cement Institute were designed to confront the customers with an industry in which there was no valid economic basis for choosing one manufacturer as against another. The Institute supported this doctrine of equality by asserting the official line that cement was a fungible product and that there were no substantial qualitative differences. To be sure, there were grades of quality but no differences within these categories.[98] The result of this policy was to destroy brand preferences and quality competition. Competition among the manufacturers took place on the level of social diversion. As the president of the Lone Star said, the scramble for business uses weapons "wrought from influences which have nothing to do with the product or the merits of the manufacturer's proposition." [99] The claim that all Portland cement is the same not only served as an instrument of price control but also served the political purpose of establishing a confederation of constituents of equal rank. Equality of rank in a confederation is not indispensable to its continued existence but it helps. Another aid in maintaining the doctrine of equality was the control of the market that enabled each manufacturer to leave his natural territory and compete in that of others at no disadvantage. Each suffered the

---

[98] *Ibid.,* p 237.   [99] *Ibid.,* p. 238.

loss of priority in his own territory for the supposed advantage of competing in that of others. When this policy put some behind others in the scramble for business, arrangements were made for dividing business among producers in accord with prearranged formulas.[100]

b. Community of interest. Belief in the existence of a community of interest among the members was promoted by the often repeated assertion that the industry could not stand competition. Divided, all stood a chance of loss. United, all stood a chance of gain. The world which the Institute conjured for its members was one in which the cement industry was encircled by a ring of hostile groups. The security of the members consisted in their adherence to each other in a common front against this danger to their well-being. This is a tactic familiar in the foreign policies of public governments and is a well-tested device for maintaining internal controls. The threat of foreign invasion goes far to convince the domestic members of a federation that they must stay together.

c. Group morality. Belief in a community of interest established a foundation for the development of a group morality, a pattern of right and wrong, a structure of values in behavior to ensure survival. This morality was not necessarily the morality in the outgroup universe, since the outgroup universe did not assume the self-preservation of the ingroup as the highest goal, as the Cement Institute did. The internal code of morality then was functionally connected with the preservation of the group. A "code of ethics" was created by the Institute shortly after its establishment in 1929, and this code became the basis of much of the NRA Code for the cement industry. When this occurred, the private code became the public law for the group, theoretically enforceable by public authority as well as by the discipline of the private group. When the NRA

---

[100] *Ibid.*, p. 211.

died, the Institute continued to exert control that was little less effective until the Federal Trade Commission finally caught up with it in the Cement Case of 1948. This setback turned the efforts of the cement industry—and of a host of enterprises similarly situated—toward revision of the troublesome antitrust laws.

The Supreme Court agreed that the Federal Trade Commission had proved the Cement Institute to be an unlawful conspiracy in violation of the antitrust laws. The decision of the Court was not an attack upon basing-point systems as such, nor upon delivered price systems of selling. Chocolate bars and chewing gum, for example, are sold throughout the United States at the same price, and the producers of these goods necessarily absorb freight in so doing. The Supreme Court decision in the Cement Case laid down no rule that necessarily endangered the pricing practices of the manufacturers of such goods.

But inevitably, perhaps, the safety of other delivered price systems was called into question. Basing-point systems could be employed as instruments of control by combinations of producers, as the Cement Case had shown. Theoretically, noncollusive basing-point systems were not affected by the Cement Case, but some economists at least were of the opinion that multiple basing-point delivered price systems could not be maintained without "co-operation" among parties nominally in competition with each other. One of these, Senator Paul Douglas of Illinois, made a strong case against basing-point pricing systems on this ground in debate in the Senate.[101] Even though conspiracy was absent, there was apprehension that the Federal Trade Commission conception of price—mill net—would come to prevail, making all delivered price systems of the basing-point variety violations of the Robinson-Patman Act.

The decision of the Supreme Court did not require all

---

[101] See below, pp. 145 n. 98, 160 n. 3.

sellers to quote prices f.o.b. mill nor did it prohibit the absorption of freight. Its *decision,* as distinguished from its *opinion,* was confined to the narrow issue of the case, namely, whether the Cement Institute and other respondents had collusively, and therefore unlawfully, restrained interstate commerce by stifling competition through the instrumentality of the multiple basing-point delivered price system. But Justice Black went further than this. The Robinson-Patman Act forbids price discriminations between different purchasers unless they are made "in good faith" to meet "an equally low price of a competitor." The Seventh Circuit Court of Appeals, which, by a vote of two to one, had set aside the Commission order, had nevertheless held that the order was valid insofar as it applied to "phantom freight" and invalid insofar as it applied to freight absorption, even systematic freight absorption. These prices were within the "good faith" proviso of the Robinson-Patman Act.[102] Justice Black disagreed, saying that there was no discernible "distinction between the 'good faith' proviso as applied to a situation involving only phantom freight and one involving only freight absorption." [103] Since the case involved a conspiracy to restrain interstate competition, the animadversions of Justice Black about freight absorption and the good faith proviso could also perhaps have been limited to cases of collusion. Justice Burton, in dissent, gave some credence to this view. As he said, "This Court . . . has not here determined the relation, if any, of either of the foregoing statutes [Federal Trade Commission Act and Clayton Act, as amended] to the absorption of freight charges by individuals when not participating in a combination of the kind of charged by the Commission." [104]

---

[102] 157 F. 2d 533.   [103] 333 U.S. 683, 725, 68 S.Ct. 793, 815.
[104] 333 U.S. 683, 733, 68 S.Ct. 793, 819.

Chapter Three

Evolution of
the Myers Bill

The Cement Case of 1948, then, outlawed a more or less obvious form of price fixing by conspiracy to use a basing-point system in forbidden ways. The case aroused an immediate controversy and a din of conflicting counsels was raised. Few cared or dared to attack the principal holding directly. Many said they saw in the dicta a covert menace to free and independent enterprise. It was asserted that the law now required all sellers to quote prices f.o.b. mill and that it inhibited every enterpriser from ever meeting the lower price of a competitor. By December 1948 a former chairman of the Federal Trade Commission was moved to say of this view that he had to agree with Mr. Bumble: "If the law supposes that, the law is a ass, a idiot." [1] The drive

[1] Robert Elliott Freer, "Let's Stop Kicking the Anti-Trust Laws Around," remarks prepared for delivery before the Sales Executives Club of New York, Roosevelt Hotel, New York City, December 7, 1948. *New York Times*, December 8, 1948, p. 49, col. 2. Some currency had been given to this view by another member of the Federal Trade Commission, Lowell B. Mason. See remarks of Lowell B. Mason before the Boston Conference on Distribution, Boston, Mass., October 26, 1948. A statement released to the press in the name of the Federal Trade Commission, however, denied that the law forbade freight absorption or prevented meeting competitors' prices. See FTC, *Notice to the Staff, In Re: Commission Policy Toward Geographic Pricing Practices* (October 12, 1948).

to have Congress take legislative action to "clarify" the law, which was assumedly made unclear by the Cement Case of 1948, began with the creation of the Capehart Committee in the closing months of the Second Session of the Eightieth Congress and ended in temporary stalemate in the closing days of the First Session of the Eighty-first Congress.

Representatives from the great steel state of Pennsylvania acted quickly after the Cement Case of 1948. Both Representative Francis E. Walter and Senator Francis J. Myers introduced bills in the House and Senate, respectively, to provide a moratorium on further proceedings under the decision and to authorize an investigation of its effects.[2] Senator Capehart of Indiana, however, had also introduced a resolution (S. Res. 241) to investigate the impact of the cement decision on consumers and business.[3] Since the Walter, Myers, and Capehart resolutions all provided for substantially the same thing, a conference was arranged between Walter, the majority floor leader (Halleck of Indiana), and the chairman of the House Committee on the Judiciary to clear the brief tangle. Representative Walter in the House agreed not to press his resolution in that body and withdrew in favor of the Senate hearing which had been authorized by the Capehart resolution. If the House and the Senate had run hearings on the same subject at the same time, there would undoubtedly have been unnecessary duplication of witnesses and testimony.[4]

The reaction of the steel industry to the Cement Case

[2] H.R. 2222 and S. 1008, 81st Cong., 1st Sess. (1949); 95 *Cong. Rec.* 8993 (July 6, 1949).

[3] S. Res. 241, 80th Cong., 1st Sess. (1948), introduced by Senator Capehart and referred to the Senate Committee on Interstate and Foreign Commerce, 94 *Cong. Rec.* 6158 (May 18, 1948); reported with amendments (Sen. Rep. No. 1566) and referred to the Committee on Rules and Administration, 94 *Cong. Rec.* 7501 (June 4, 1948); reported back, 94 *Cong. Rec.* 7949 (June 10, 1948); passed Senate as amended, 94 *Cong. Rec.* 7949 (June 10, 1948).

[4] 95 *Cong. Rec.* 7949 (June 10, 1948).

was mixed at first, with opinion divided as to the next steps for steel.[5] The Cement Case had outlawed conspiratorial use of a multiple basing-point system of delivered prices among cement companies. The chairman of United States Steel said that its subsidiary, Universal Atlas Cement Company, would comply with the Court's order. The big question was whether the Court's decision affected the use of basing-point formulas in pricing steel. Some steel men wanted to await the outcome of the Federal Trade Commission's case against the manufacturers of rigid steel conduit,[6] and others wanted to press for congressional legislation immediately to protect the steel industry's pricing system, even though the question of the system's legality was then in the process of litigation. By June 1948 there were strong rumors that the steel industry would press for legislation to protect the basing-point system in steel. It was the opinion of Senator Morse that the steel industry intended not merely to have the existing law "clarified" but to validate the basing-point system in steel, whatever the meaning of the existing law.[7]

The point is of some importance because Senator Capehart repeatedly asserted that the existing law was so confused that clarification was necessary and that businessmen should be informed by Congress that it was legal and proper for them to absorb freight in quoting prices to buyers. This was also the official theory of the O'Mahoney Bill, which was introduced in the First Session of the Eighty-first Congress and which will be discussed more fully below.[8] It is difficult, if not impossible, to ascertain with exactness the intention of the steel industry in this matter, but there is certainly a sense in which it could be argued that the trouble with

---

[5] For a description of these events, see speech of Senator Wayne Morse of Oregon, *ibid.*, pp. 7025–7031 (May 31, 1949).

[6] See p. 126 n. 7.   [7] 95 *Cong. Rec.* 7026 (May 31, 1949).

[8] See below, p. 124 ff

the existing law was not that it was unclear but that it was becoming painfully clear, and that the hope of practitioners of the basing-point system was not to clarify the trend but to reverse it.[9] At least some supporters of the O'Mahoney Bill thought they were making basing-point systems safe.[10]

On July 7, 1948, United States Steel abandoned the basing-point system of delivered prices and changed to f.o.b. mill.[11] Although the steel industry was not required by the

---

[9] For a good statement of the meaning of the law, see Note, 58 *Yale Law Journal* 426 (1949).

[10] See remarks of Representative Crawford of Michigan on the floor of the House: "If the basing point system is done away with, in accordance with the decisions of the Supreme Court, then I think we will have worse conditions from the standpoint of the expansion of monopolies and the destruction of small enterprise. . . ." 95 *Cong. Rec.* 8989 (July 6, 1949). And further, "I see nothing whatsoever in the basing point system which destroys competition." *Ibid.* See also remarks of Representative Walter of Pennsylvania, in which he said that the opponents of the O'Mahoney bill are those who oppose basing-point systems. *Ibid.*, p. 8993. At another place Representative Walter said that the bill did not "re-establish" the basing-point system but failed to answer directly whether it prohibited basing-point systems from being re-established. *Ibid.*, p. 8994. The Department of Justice representative, testifying before the House Judiciary Committee, referred to the bill as basing-point legislation, without rebuke. *Hearings before Subcommittee No. 1 of the House Committee on the Judiciary on S. 1008,* 81st Cong., 1st Sess. 13 (1949), (hereinafter cited as *H. R. Hearings on S. 1008*).

[11] The *Wall Street Journal* quoted an unidentified manufacturer as saying: "The pressure on Congress to pass legislation making freight absorption a legal business practice probably will be terrific as a result of United States Steel's action. For a lot of steel users, it means higher prices; many toes will be pinched. Apparently steel officials felt they couldn't win their price case before the courts, so they're using this means to take it to the people." *Wall Street Journal,* July 8, 1949, p. 1, col. 6. Two months later *Fortune* (September 1948, p. 79) said: "As a general rule business has far more to gain through placing its faith in the slow interpretation of the law by the courts than by political action. The latter is apt to yield more confusion and bitterness. The former, however difficult, can give the kind of continuity that makes industrial democracy possible."

Cement Case to go f.o.b.,[12] and although the steel industry was shown by one witness to have gone on an f.o.b. basis in some instances before the Cement Case,[13] the impression became fairly widespread that the Supreme Court had forced the steel producers to require their customers to pay the freight.[14] It is interesting that, although the steel industry (which was not involved) seemed to feel it necessary to go f.o.b., one of the respondents in the Cement Case, according to its attorney, continued to sell cement priced and delivered at destination.[15] The new policy of United States Steel raised the price of steel several dollars a ton.[16] According to one of the witnesses before the House Small Business Committee in the summer of 1949, the change to f.o.b. pricing actually made the cost to the steel companies

---

[12] See Corwin Edwards, New England Council speech, September 18, 1948: "The Commission has no authority to require business men to sell f.o.b. mill or to impose upon them any other specific pricing practice."

[13] Testimony of Otis Brubaker, United Steelworkers of America, CIO, in *Hearings before a Subcommittee of the Senate Committee on the Judiciary on S. 1008*, 81st Cong., 1st Sess. (1949), p. 20 (hereinafter cited as *Senate Hearings on S. 1008*). The Senate Small Business Committee report, "Changes in Distribution of Steel," accepted by Wherry and Martin, shows the same thing. *Ibid.*, p. 20. See reaction of Senator Myers in *Hearings before a Subcommittee of the Senate Committee on Interstate and Foreign Commerce on S. 236*, 81st Cong., 1st Sess. (1949), p. 221 (hereinafter cited as *Senate Hearings on S. 236*).

[14] See the census of views taken by the National Small Business Men's Association, in *Hearings before a Subcommittee of the Senate Committtee on Interstate and Foreign Commerce on S. Res. 241*, 80th Cong., 2nd Sess. (1948), pp. 30–49 (hereinafter cited as *Senate Hearings on S. Res. 241*), where some of those answering thought that the Supreme Court had specifically forced the steel industry into its action.

[15] Testimony of Edward A. Zimmerman, in *Senate Hearings on S. 236*, p. 247.

[16] Testimony of Otis Brubaker, in *Senate Hearings on S. 236*, p. 195. Mr. Coyle estimated the increase at $9.00 a ton. See note 17, below.

go down $1.00 a ton.[17] A professor of political economy at Johns Hopkins University termed the steel company action an "attempt to deceive the consumers by telling them that freight absorption was unlawful and that delivered prices were, therefore, necessarily higher than before." [18]

Whatever may have been the motivation behind the decision to adopt f.o.b. pricing, the effect upon the customers of steel-producing companies was immediate and enduring. A clamor was raised for legislative action, which the steel companies encouraged by direct solicitation.[19] There is evidence that dissident customers were reluctant to identify themselves because they might be disciplined by their suppliers.[20] One Washington correspondent discovered a public relations firm that had been hired at a compensation of at least $11,000 a month and expenses to get the law amended. According to his account, a "National Competitive Committee" was established with local chapters, and

---

[17] Statement of David Cushman Coyle, in *Hearings before the House Select Committee on Small Business*, 81st Cong., 1st Sess. (1949), p. 97 (hereinafter cited as *Small Business Committee Hearings*).

[18] Statement of Professor Fritz Machlup, *ibid.*, p. 214.

[19] Speech of Senator Wayne Morse, 95 *Cong. Rec.* 7026 (May 31, 1949). The forms of solicitation included suggestions by salesmen to customers that Congress be asked to legalize basing-point practices, statements by company officials to the press, and letters by company officials to customers urging pressure upon Congress. See *ibid.*, p. 11347 (August 12, 1949) for further details about the public relations program. See also letter from Ben Moreell, President, Jones & Laughlin Steel Corporation, July 21, 1948, to shareholders and employees, announcing new pricing policy and need for action by Congress. *Ibid.*, pp. 11356 and 11357 (August 12, 1949). Ernest T. Weir, Chairman of the National Steel Corporation, followed a similar course. *Ibid.*, p. 11357 (August 12, 1949).

[20] *Ibid.*, p. 7164 (May 31, 1949). A garden toolmaker was said to have made a price reduction of one per cent but feared reporting it because of the possibility of the loss of steel allocations. Even larger reductions were made by other manufacturers but fear of trade reprisals prevented them from declaring themselves. *New York Times,* October 14, 1948, p. 45, col. 2.

agents were sent about the country to organize others. The firm is said to have stood ready to perform such a job "as delivering to a client a ready-made nation-wide grass-roots organization." Of this attempt to manufacture pressure, Senator Morse said: "This lobbying effort was one of the best organized, one of the most heavily financed, and one of the most adroitly deceptive that has ever been addressed to the Congress of the United States." [21]

The Capeheart Hearings

With beaters in the states flushing the thickets, witnesses winged their way to Washington, where they gave testimony to the Capehart Committee.[22] The members of the Committee were Hawkes of New Jersey and Brewster of Maine on the Republican side, and Johnson of Colorado and McMahon of Connecticut on the Democratic side, with Capehart of Indiana as chairman. The major work of the Committee was done by the chairman and the general counsel, while the other members participated, presumably, as their busy schedules permitted. The stated purpose of the Senate resolution under which the Committee functioned was to inquire into existing legislation concerning government policy affecting the activities of the Federal Trade Commission and the Interstate Commerce Commission and the impact of these policies as interpreted by the Supreme Court, "with particular relation to the basing-point or freight equalization system of pricing." [23] The Committee was also to study the effect of the continuance or discontinuance of these pricing policies on the consumer and small businessman. In addition, it was charged with the duty of

[21] 95 *Cong. Rec.* 7028.

[22] The title of the Capehart Committee was Subcommittee of the Senate Committee on Interstate and Foreign Commerce on S. Res. 241.

[23] *Study of Federal Trade Commission Pricing Policies, Interim Report,* 81st Cong., 1st Sess., Sen. Doc. No. 27, I (1949), (hereinafter cited as Sen. Doc. No. 27).

exploring the character and extent of industrial concentration in the United States.[24] The resolution establishing the Committee was adopted on June 12, 1948, and on July 30 the Committee resolved to concentrate its first efforts upon the impact upon the economy of the law as recently interpreted and administered by the Federal Trade Commission and the courts. It never did get into the character and extent of industrial concentration in the United States.

In August 1948 the Committee appointed an advisory council to aid it in the inquiry. Under the direction of a chairman, forty-five people were invited and participated in the deliberations of the council. The council met three times and made a final report to the Committee recommending modifications in the law for the relief of the business community. A representative of the National Farmers Union who was a member of the council and who attended all of its meetings found it objectionable because of its composition.[25] Of the original members of the council, he said, there were three executives of the cement industry, whose case had started the entire controversy; representative of one of the respondents in the Glucose Cases of 1945; and three representatives of steel companies who were respondents in a Federal Trade Commission case. There were also seven representatives of customers of the cement and steel industries. Transportation was represented by a rep-

---

[24] The Chairman of the Federal Trade Commission objected that with $15,000 and a deadline of March 15, 1949, nothing like the investigation authorized by S. Res. 241 could be achieved. Statement of Robert E. Freer, Chairman, Federal Trade Commission, to a Subcommittee of the Senate Committee on Interstate and Foreign Commerce on S. Res. 241, 80th Cong. 2nd Sess. I (June 2, 1948), (mimeographed).

[25] Statement of Angus McDonald, in *Small Business Committee Hearings*, p. 75 ff. The Committee was also described by Otis Brubaker of the United Steelworkers as a basing-point business committee, although he did not suggest that it was deliberately "stacked." *Senate Hearings on S. 236*, p. 222.

resentative of the railroads, which benefit under basing-point schemes. There were no representatives of the trucking industry, which does not benefit under basing-point schemes. No representative was known as a strong antimonopolist, nor were there representatives from government departments or agencies concerned with the enforcement of the antitrust laws. Of the labor representatives, one was the head of the Cement Workers Union, and one (United Steelworkers of America) withdrew. Of the farm groups, only two were originally represented—the American Farm Bureau Federation and the National Grange. The National Farmers Union was added at the instigation of Senator Johnson of Colorado.[26] Congressman Patman of Texas repeated the observation of the National Farmers Union representative that "the inclusion of representatives of three great farm organizations can be accounted for only on the theory that their interest in the basing-point problem had not been publicly expressed in recent years and that their devotion to the policies of the antitrust laws was underestimated." [27] None of the farm organization representatives agreed with the majority report of the advisory council.[28]

The center of the Committee's activities, however, was in the Committee itself.[29] Its stated object was to inquire into the impact of the Supreme Court's decision in the Cement Case upon consumers and small businessmen. Even this was an impossible goal, for the time was too short for any reliable indication of effect to make itself apparent. As the friendly Senate Report on the hearing stated: "Al-

---

[26] *Small Business Committee Hearings*, p. 76.

[27] 95 *Cong. Rec.* 8987 (July 6, 1949). Cf. *Small Business Committee Hearings*, p. 80.

[28] *Ibid.*, p. 63. The American Farm Bureau Federation neither approved nor disapproved the majority report. The National Grange and the National Farmers Union representatives wrote minority reports.

[29] The Committee hearings were held on November 9, 10, 11, 12, 16, 17, 18, 19, 29, and 30; December 6, 7, and 8, 1949.

though many business witnesses appeared before the sub-committee and testified as to the harmful effects of required f.o.b. mill selling, it does appear that sufficient time has not yet elapsed to determine the actual effect on the cement, steel, and other industries in which that pricing practice has been adopted." [30] The inability of the Committee to obtain the information which it was established to obtain did not prevent it, however, from compiling a record of some 1,400 pages, most of it representing, to use the language of the Senate Report, "conclusions of witnesses as to what would happen to their respective businesses if f.o.b. mill pricing was required of all industry." [31] Instead, therefore, of amassing testimony upon the effect of the Supreme Court decisions upon the economy, the subcommittee posed a fictitious situation (every enterpriser selling f.o.b. mill) and made a record of responses. There was no documented proof that the existing law actually required anyone to adopt f.o.b. mill pricing.

The witnesses before the Committee represented a great congeries of group interests: steel customers; [32] cane and beet sugar growers and refiners whose products were sold on a delivered price basis; [33] candy and glucose manufacturers,[34] including some under complaint by the Federal Trade Commission; cement customers; [35] building materials manufacturers and dealers; [36] cement producers; [37] steel producers; [38] railroad traffic spokesmen; [39] pulp and paper pro-

---

[30] Sen. Doc. No. 27, p. 35.   [31] *Ibid.*, p. 36.

[32] *Senate Hearings on S. Res. 241*, pp. 255, 71, 259, 282, 285, 305, 323, 743, 786, 1075, 1236.

[33] *Ibid.*, pp. 564, 581, 592, 606, 610, 641.

[34] *Ibid.*, pp. 614, 625, 627, 1046.

[35] *Ibid.*, pp. 647, 657, 667, 672, 676, 1235.

[36] *Ibid.*, pp. 52, 55, 292, 662, 679, 683, 774.

[37] *Ibid.*, pp. 776, 841, 852.

[38] *Ibid.*, p. 262; Pittsburgh Steel Co., *ibid.*, p. 505; Inland Steel Co., *ibid.*, pp. 514, 526, 540, 1259.

[39] *Ibid.*, pp. 896, 1188, 1198.

ducers; [40] some officials of the Department of Justice and the Federal Trade Commission; [41] spokesmen for trade associations in lumber,[42] groceries,[43] and other commodities; small-business-association representatives; [44] and representatives of the Army,[45] Navy,[46] and other federal agencies.[47] A scattered representation from other assorted enterprises appeared [48] and some minor public officials. Three unions were represented, one of which was a small union in the cement industry [49] and another in the railroads.[50] All three were from industries representing basing-point interests or benefiting from basing-point systems. None of the major unions appeared, although telegrams and statements were sent by several locals. None of the principal farm organizations appeared. Big steel and cement producers were notably absent. At one point in the hearings, Senator Capehart threatened to subpoena companies in the steel industry, but the threat turned out to be a request for letters answering the question whether steel companies would return to a freight absorption sales policy "if permitted by Congress so to do." [51] They thought they might.

One of the most interesting and important visitors was Senator Joseph O'Mahoney of Wyoming, who appeared in the company of Robert D. Pike, a spokesman for the Westvaco Chemical Company, Westvaco, Wyoming.[52] Mr. Pike

---

[40] *Ibid.,* pp. 1012, 1034, 1038, 1049, 1055.

[41] *Ibid.,* pp. 96, 111, 127, 142, 694, 790, 1347.

[42] *Ibid.,* pp. 768.   [43] *Ibid.,* pp. 1061, 1162.

[44] *Ibid.,* pp. 29, 1116, 1227, 1240.   [45] *Ibid.,* pp. 85, 923.

[46] *Ibid.,* p. 928.

[47] Reconstruction Finance Corporation, *ibid.,* p. 885; Bureau of Federal Supply, *ibid.,* pp. 917, 921; Agriculture, *ibid.,* p. 933.

[48] *Ibid.,* pp. 64, 277, 296, 356, 534, 561, 631, 762, 875, 901, 912, 980, 996, 1079, 1159, 1172, 1210, 1221, 1254, 1261.

[49] United Cement, Lime and Gypsum Workers, *ibid.,* pp. 19, 1148.

[50] Order of Railway Conductors, *ibid.,* p. 1206; Glass Bottle Blowers Association of the United States and Canada, *ibid.,* p. 971.

[51] *Ibid.,* p. 1374.   [52] *Ibid.,* p. 949.

testified that his firm was interested in developing trona deposits in Wyoming for the purpose of producing soda ash, and that the entire investment would amount to some $25,000,000.[53] He testified that his investment might be endangered if he did not have assurance that he would be permitted to absorb and equalize freight with any competitor any place in the United States.[54] Senator O'Mahoney had long been interested in developing this chemical industry in his state, and his appearance with Mr. Pike is evidence of the zeal with which he sought to advance its interest.

The hearing was a good show, with numerous witnesses to supply a chorus of protest under the directorship and leadership of Senator Capehart. Although he repeatedly asserted that he wanted the facts about the effect upon industry of required f.o.b. pricing (which the law did not "require"), few witnesses were cross-examined except those from the Federal Trade Commission, the Department of Justice, an economist from the University of Washington, and a small-business-group representative, all of whom testified either that the law did not require f.o.b. pricing or that they thought that it would be a good idea if it did. Harmony prevailed in the relations between the subcommittee, its chairman, and all other witnesses. With the skill of a conductor on the podium, Capehart led witness after witness (once their prepared statements were out of the way) through a series of questions that made it appear that enterprisers were confused by the existing law, that they had no place to go in the government for a definitive answer, and that it was necessary for Congress to come to their rescue and write legislation on the subject. He was his own best witness, and he spoke to the record through many voices. He finally worked himself around to the view that the Cement Case of 1948 was a boon to United States Steel,[55] the larger steel companies, and big business,[56] and that he

---

[53] *Ibid.*, p. 955.   [54] *Ibid.*   [55] *Ibid.*, p. 341.   [56] *Ibid.*, p. 347.

106

was defending the little businessman, presumably by "forc-ing" the steel industry to stop f.o.b. pricing.[57] The represent-ative from Inland Steel lent a hand to this piece of dramaturgy by saying that f.o.b. pricing would be to the advantage of the steel industry but that he opposed it be-cause it would stifle competition and lead to monopoly.[58] One of the more imaginative speculations about the conse-quences of required f.o.b. pricing was Capehart's suggestion to a witness that it was injurious to health, because more people would be poisoned by smog created by concentrated industries—concentration being an alleged consequence of required f.o.b. pricing.[59]

In matters of substance, the Capehart hearings produced a potpourri of paradoxes and contradictions. Big business wanted new legislation but small business enterprisers argued their case for them. The normal competitive ad-vantage of low freight cost (nearness to mills) was repre-sented as offensive monopoly. The industry-wide system of uniform delivered prices, which lends itself to the curtail-ment of price competition under conditions of conspiracy or conscious parallelism, was called competition. It was argued that local monopolies would be produced unless a pricing system which produced national monopolies was restored. Although all producers offer the same buyer one price under some forms of the basing-point delivered price

---

[57] *Ibid.*, p. 563. See also *Senate Hearings on S. 236*, p. 224, where Senator Capehart said that he thought "that the big steel industries would welcome a law making it illegal to sell on any other than f.o.b basis." If one assumes with Senator Capehart that the Federal Trade Commission and the courts already required f.o.b pricing, it would appear that the steel companies should have supported the Federal Trade Commission. The record does not indicate such sup-port.

[58] *Senate Hearings on S. Res. 241*, p. 514 ff.

[59] *Ibid.*, p. 510. On this point the colloquy concluded as follows: "Senator Capehart. So we might add health. Mr. Beeson. I would like to add health."

system, the federal government was assumed to be doing the same thing when it sells stamps for three cents everywhere, even though the federal government is one producer charging the same price to every buyer. Speakers for little business asked Congress to "permit" them to employ a system (freight absorption) which works to their disadvantage more often than to their advantage, since, by being small, they often do not have the resources to compete in a national market. In the interest of clarity the Capehart Committee laid the foundation for new legislation that would take years of court action to interpret.

One jarring note in the proceedings was supplied by the persistent off-stage racket of Congressman Wright Patman of Texas, who took a disrespectful view of the entire affair. When a Texas steel producer testified that he was confused by the law on pricing, that the uncertainties of the law should be cleared up, and that Congress should do the clearing,[60] the Senator from Indiana heckled the Congressman from Texas, in absentia. Capehart and the steel man agreed that the steel man knew more about steel than Congressman Patman.[61] The Democratic National Committee made releases of some of Congressman Patman's charges that the subcommittee was a big business committee and that the hearings were a not too covert attack upon the antitrust laws. The rumor got about that the Democratic National Committee itself would make an official statement at the behest of the "high policy makers in the Democratic Party," but Senator McMahon scotched the rumor.[62] Capehart finally took official notice of the activities of Congressman Patman by inserting into the record a release bearing the heading of the Publicity Division of the National Democratic Committee.[63] The release contained the text of Congressman Patman's charges, with many citations from the

---

[60] Statement of Ralph L. Gray, *ibid.,* pp. 540–541.
[61] *Ibid.,* pp. 556–557.   [62] *Ibid.,* pp. 1133–1134.   [63] *Ibid.,* p. 1166 ff.

press, including a *Wall Street Journal* report of an inter-
view with a leading steel company president to the effect
that a multitude of steel customers would get farther than
a few big steel companies in the movement to change the
law.[64] Capehart made an attack upon Patman in the hearing, charging him with making misstatements and with
being unfair. The advisory committee, he said, was not
"stacked"; its members had been selected because of their
knowledge of the subject. Capehart specially mentioned
the union and farm representatives. He was particularly
annoyed by the Patman statement, issued after the election
in November 1948, that "if the Republicans had gained
control of Congress and the Presidency, the anti-trust laws
would have been repealed in 30 days and organized greed
would have been in complete charge of the country." [65]
This piece of political extravagance seemed to produce a
stronger reaction than it deserved. Senator Capehart waved
it in front of a subsequent witness who said appropriate and
soothing things.[66]

The Evolution of S. 236

The election undoubtedly had some influence upon the
plans of those who wanted Congress to write new legislation on the subject of pricing policies.[67] With a change in
the political complexion of the House and the Senate, the
committee memberships were reshuffled and Capehart
lost his chairmanship.[68] Those who assumed that the subcommittee would be making its report to a friendly and

---

[64] *Ibid.,* p. 1167.   [65] *Ibid.,* p. 1171.   [66] *Ibid.,* p. 1242.

[67] See excerpt from *Newsweek,* November 29, 1948, reprinted in
ibid., p. 1257.

[68] Senator Johnson took over Senator Capehart's job as chairman on
January 3, 1949. See *Senate Hearings on S. 236,* p. 223. This did not
mean a change in leadership, however, for the record shows that
Senator Capehart did most of the talking on the subcommittee side
after the reshuffle.

well-disposed Congress were faced with a Congress of unpredictable temper. As events showed, however, the movement to write a new law went far in the new Congress and, indeed, was temporarily halted only by the tireless efforts of a small group of Senators led by Kefauver of Tennessee, Long of Louisiana, and Douglas of Illinois. Even they could not prevent Congress from enacting legislation eventually in the Second Session of the Eighty-first Congress.

Before any report could be made to the Senate on the original Capehart resolution, Senator Capehart and Senator Johnson of Colorado, who succeeded Capehart as chairman of the subcommittee, introduced a bill (S. 236) on January 5, 1949, to make permanent amendments to the Federal Trade Commission Act and the Clayton Act, as amended by the Robinson-Patman Act. The bill was referred to the Committee on Interstate and Foreign Commerce, which proceeded, through the subcommittee headed by Johnson, to hold hearings.[69] At the least, this effort to secure permanent legislation before the investigating committee had reported showed haste and justified the feeling that the sponsors were in an unseemly hurry. The bill of Senator Johnson was understood by Secretary of Commerce Sawyer to have the purpose of "preserving the existing status of regulation as businessmen generally understood it to be prior to the opinion in the Cement Case." [70] It had taken almost eleven years to get the Cement Case decided.[71] While regulation walked with tortoise speed, relief from regulation was to fly on wings.

The proposed bill would have amended the Federal

---

[69] *Senate Hearings on S. 236,* p. 2. The hearings were held for only three days in January and one day in February. The February meeting was held for the purpose of amending S. 236 before transferring jurisdiction over the bill to the Senate Committee on the Judiciary.

[70] *Ibid.,* p. 5.

[71] Secretary Sawyer in no way proposed that the decision in the Cement Case as it related to conspiracy was to be modified. *Ibid.*

Trade Commission Act by outlawing any price-fixing conspiracy or combination. This was surplusage since they were already illegal under the Cement Case and other cases. In the absence of such agreement or conspiracy, no pricing practice was to be deemed an unfair method of competition because the delivered price was uniform on goods of like quality and grade, was similarly uniform within any geographical zone, or absorbed freight charges. Practices tainted with fraud, deception, or coercion were denied the benefit of the amendment. The justifications available to a seller charged with practicing discriminatory pricing under the Robinson-Patman Act were increased. Prices lower than those of a competitor were exempted from the prohibitions of the act where the differential was customary in the general price relationships of the respective products or "otherwise justified by the competitive situation of the two or more sellers." [72] The authority of the Federal Trade Commission to require remedial action to dissipate the effects of a conspiracy was expanded.

Two people from federal agencies who had testified in the Capehart hearings appeared to testify in the brief hearings on S. 236.[73] Some new witnesses appeared to express a point of view different from the standard assertions of confessed confusion, helplessness to choose acceptable pricing courses, and desire for congressional relief.[74] Business groups, of course, were represented, among them being the

---

[72] *Ibid.,* p. 3.

[73] These were Herbert A. Bergson, Assistant Attorney General, Anti-trust Division of the Department of Justice, *ibid.,* p. 74, and Allen C. Phelps, lawyer and Chief of the Export Trade Division of the Federal Trade Commission, *ibid.,* p. 60.

[74] Among the new groups were the United Steelworkers of America, represented by their Research Director, Otis Brubaker, *ibid.,* p. 185, and the National Farmers Union represented by Angus McDonald, Assistant Legislative Secretary, *ibid.,* p. 136. The National Grange appeared through J. T. Sanders, *ibid.,* p. 243.

Chamber of Commerce,[75] the National Canners Association,[76] National Retail Lumber Dealers Association,[77] and local and state chambers and industrial associations.[78] Counsel for food and private truck owners' associations,[79] the American Bar Association,[80] and private witnesses [81] expressed the hope that Congress would do what was called for, although the witness for the truckers and the food dealers thought that Congress should be careful.[82] The chief witnesses, however, were the chairman of the Interstate Commerce Commission, who wanted references to his agency stricken from the proposed bill,[83] a group of witnesses from the Federal Trade Commission, and the research director for the United Steelworkers of America.

In the course of the questions put to the chairman of the Interstate Commerce Commission, it appeared that the questioners seemed less interested in the witness' problem than in trying to make it appear that the Interstate Commerce Commission promotes freight absorption [84] in order

---

[75] *Ibid.,* p. 168.   [76] *Ibid.,* p. 33.   [77] *Ibid.,* p. 55.

[78] *Ibid.,* pp. 118, 131, 111.   [79] *Ibid.,* p. 235.

[80] *Ibid.,* p. 49. See also American Bar Association resolution in support of congressional intervention, *ibid.,* p. 316.

[81] *Ibid.,* pp. 176, 163.   [82] *Ibid.,* p. 236.

[83] He was concerned lest one of the stated policies of the bill—"to foster competitive private enterprise by the treatment of transportation costs in interstate commerce so that access to distant markets may be available, when economically feasible, to any competing seller"— be construed to alter the jurisdiction of the Interstate Commerce Commission. He felt that it would be difficult for the Commission to determine economic feasibility and that it would lay a ground for attack upon its decisions by "disappointed litigants who might charge that they were denied access to distant markets by the Commission's action." He suggested that the reference to the Interstate Commerce Commission be deleted and indicated that he thought that the basic legislation under which the ICC operates adequately provided for consideration of the element of competition in rate making. *Ibid.,* pp. 7–9.

[84] *Ibid.,* pp. 14–15.

to encourage competition. The ICC on occasion permits blanket rates in order to allow sellers in two parts of the country to compete in the same market from which they are not equidistant. This produces a version of freight absorption inasmuch as the price to the consumer is not the sum of the cost of production and shipping. Commissioner Mahaffie refused to say that this practice was the same as the freight absorption with which the subcommittee was concerned, in spite of insistent prodding by Senator Capehart.[85] He did express his personal view that the "prohibition of any [i.e., all] absorption would be disturbing to business." [86] Capehart chose to regard this answer as an endorsement of his effort to prevent the Federal Trade Commission from requiring all sellers to adopt f.o.b. pricing, which was the theme of the Capehart hearings but was not the law as it existed nor the express policy of the Federal Trade Commission.

The witnesses from the Federal Trade Commission were Edwin L. Davis, Commissioner, and a group of Commission lawyers.[87] Missing from this group was Walter Wooden, Associate General Counsel of the Commission, who in the hearings on S. 241 had been subjected to a stiff cross-examination by Senator Capehart and by counsel for the Capehart Committee because he felt that f.o.b. pricing, although not the law, was desirable policy. The first presentation was made by Commissioner Davis; who took note of widespread misapprehensions that had followed the Cement Case in April 1948 but who thought that the misapprehension was abating.[88] He made the suggestion that

---

[85] *Ibid.*, pp. 15–18.   [86] *Ibid.*, p. 21.

[87] Allen Phelps, Assistant Chief Trial Counsel and Chief of the Export Trade Division of the Federal Trade Commission; Robert B. Dawkins, Special Legal Assistant to the Federal Trade Commission; and Joseph E. Sheehy, Associate Director of the Bureau of Legal Investigation of the Commission.

[88] *Ibid.*, p. 23.

Congress, by refusing to change the existing law, would do much itself to abate such confusion as might remain.[89]

Since the original drive to change the law was supposed to have been caused by the confusion among businessmen and their lawyers as to the meaning of the law and the intentions of the Federal Trade Commission, Commissioner Davis proceeded to show that the Commission had issued statements in explanation on two occasions and stood ready to issue further ones to clear up matters still obscure.[90] In its reply to questions put by the Chamber of Commerce of the State of New York, dated January 12, 1949, the Commission had refused to say that all basing-point systems were violations of the law or to predict all of the circumstances in which conspiracy might be proved. The Commission was specific in saying that it did not advocate required f.o.b. pricing.[91] In his testimony, Commissioner Davis was equally specific in saying that a seller could absorb freight or part of his manufacturing costs or any costs whatever in order, in good faith, to meet the equally low price of a competitor.[92] As to the proposed legislation, he was of the view that it was neither necessary nor desirable.[93] Commissioner Davis later gave to the subcommittee the views of a majority of the Commission on fifty-four questions deal-

---

[89] *Ibid.*

[90] FTC, *Notice to the Staff, In Re: Commission Policy toward Geographic Pricing Practices* (October 12, 1948); FTC Release, Letter from Commission to Secretary of Chamber of Commerce of State of New York, January 12, 1949.

[91] Commissioner Davis was emphatic in pointing out that "the Commission has not in a single case challenged the use of the basing point method of pricing per se, separate and apart from collusion. The Commission has not challenged freight absorption per se. The Commission has not required f.o.b. mill pricing. The Commission has not challenged the legality of the use of uniform delivered prices by an individual concern." *Senate Hearings on S. 236,* p. 24.

[92] *Ibid.,* p. 25.   [93] *Ibid.,* p. 26.

ing with Commission policy.[94] Apart from the propriety of using a public hearing to force from a quasi-judicial agency an assurance as to future policy, the Commission statement should have been sufficient clarification for all but the willfully self-confused.

Commissioner Davis commended to the attention of the subcommittee two FTC lawyers who had been requested to appear (Sheehy and Dawkins).[95] Both expressed objections to S. 236. Dawkins echoed the view of Commissioner Davis that the amount of uncertainty was subsiding under the influence of public discussion, and that S. 236 would not reduce uncertainty but would increase it by the use of new and ambiguous concepts and words that would require long litigation to clarify.[96] Another lawyer (Phelps), however, contradicted Commissioner Davis,[97] thought that there was a drive to impose f.o.b. pricing on all sellers,[98] and felt that Congress should act.[99] The chairman of the subcommittee thanked him for his "scholarly presentation." [100]

These differences of view expressed by witnesses from the Federal Trade Commission lent leverage to the subcommittee in its claim of excessive uncertainty and confusion arising out of the Cement Case. In the *Interim Report* to the Senate on S. 236, the contradictory statements of the FTC witnesses were laid end to end and pronounced "confusing." [101] They were made to appear more confusing than they actually would have been had the subcommittee heeded the explanation made by Commissioner Davis. He later pointed out that all the individuals had been invited in their personal capacities and that they had so testified; he then said:

---

[94] *Ibid.*, pp. 268–278. These replies constituted a clear answer to legitimate questions of doubt about the policies and expectations of the Commission.

[95] *Ibid.*, p. 27.   [96] *Ibid.*, p. 97.   [97] *Ibid.*, p. 65.

[98] *Ibid.*, p. 66.   [99] *Ibid.*, p. 67.   [100] *Ibid.*, p. 69.

[101] Sen. Doc. No. 27, p. 46 ff.

The Commission regards difference of opinion among staff members and even among Commissioners as a normal incident of the development of policy and of the interpretation of law; and believing that responsible interpretations of public questions contribute to the understanding thereof, the Commission is unwilling either to require all staff members to express only its official views or to muzzle all staff members who think for themselves.[102]

It may be said at this point that the subcommittee under both Capehart and Johnson seemed interested in obtaining assurances that the Commission would not press the enforcement of the law rigorously in the directions which the Supreme Court had indicated were open. Capehart had previously referred to a meeting with representatives of the Commission for the purpose of coming to some understanding.[103] At the time of the hearings of S. 236, however, the record did not show that such an understanding had been negotiated, and much, therefore, was being made of the contradictions. Subsequently the subcommittee took credit for producing mollifying disclaimers by the Commission and for the Commission's acceptance of the views of Commissioner Davis,[104] although it was still felt necessary to enact legislation to be sure that the Commission did not backslide.

One of the most thoroughly prepared presentations made to the Johnson Committee was that of Otis Brubaker, research director for the United Steelworkers of America.[105]

---

[102] *Senate Hearings on S. 236,* p. 275. The reference to disagreements among the members of the Commission is documented by the record of the hearings on S. 236. On February 18, 1949, Senator Johnson wrote to Commissioner Lowell Mason, who replied March 2, 1949, that he wished to express his disagreement with the majority of the Commission on matters before Congress. *Ibid.,* pp. 337–338.

[103] *Senate Hearings on S. Res. 241,* p. 1011.

[104] Sen. Doc. No. 27, p. 63.

[105] *Senate Hearings on S. 236,* p. 185 ff. The record of the study and

It offered evidence that the effects of the Cement Case allegedly feared were not taking place. Throughout the entire thirty districts of the USWA "we found not one single basic steel plant or one steel-fabricating plant which had been shut down because of the pricing change." [106] In the questioning of Brubaker after his direct statement, however, there was no effort to test the validity of his findings. Rather Capehart undertook to swoop him off into the empyrean of speculation—to a fictitious world where the only pricing alternative is required f.o.b., to a realm "where the big steel industries would welcome a law making it illegal to sell on any other than f.o.b. basis." [107] The conclusion is permissible that the subcommittee was more interested in proving its case than in hearing it refuted.

There was a hiatus between the third and the fourth of the four days of hearings on S. 236, a hiatus of about three weeks. In this period of time a change in strategy took place. Senators Johnson and Capehart was still pushing for permanent legislation, and Johnson instructed subcommittee counsel to revise the bill. Subcommittee counsel met with Commissioner Davis, who reportedly instructed the Federal Trade Commission staff to collaborate with subcommittee counsel in the preparation of a revised bill. Johnson approved the revision and told Commissioner Davis that he would accept the revision and try to get it through Congress "if the Commission formally approved the bill." [108] Commissioner Davis replied that the Commission opposed any legislation and that it would not approve the bill. An amended S. 236 was nevertheless prepared. It was said by the chairman of the subcommittee to have embodied the

---

the testimony of the representative of the United Steelworkers was of importance inasmuch as it supplied some of the basis for the attack upon the movement to obtain congressional relief which was made by Senator Wayne Morse. 95 *Cong. Rec.* 7025, 7027 (May 31, 1949).

[106] *Senate Hearings on S. 236,* p. 202.

[107] *Ibid.,* p. 224.   [108] Sen. Doc. No. 27, pp. 69–70.

advice of Assistant Attorney General Bergson at many points.[109]

In the amended bill, the references to the Interstate Commerce Commission which were not agreeable to the chairman of that body were eliminated. Provisions of the bill would have made it harder for the Federal Trade Commission to prove any violation of the antitrust laws in the absence of conspiracy, and even the value of some types of evidence that would tend to prove conspiracy was reduced. The original aim of the bill was intact and indeed strengthened, to wit, to enact a permanent amendment to the antitrust laws on the basis of the Capehart testimony, which was largely *ex parte,* and the three days of hearings under the nominal chairmanship of Senator Johnson.

The Myers Moratorium

Although S. 236 had been amended as a result of the hearings, the effort to get it adopted was abandoned [110] and support was given instead to a bill which Senator Myers of Pennsylvania had introduced before the hearings on S. 236 were finished: a bill to provide a legislative moratorium.[111]

---

[109] *Ibid.,* pp. 64–69, *passim.*

[110] Several factors led to this change in strategy. First, the subcommittee had failed to get Federal Trade Commission approval of the proposed legislation. This failure to approve could have lessened the chances of passage. Second, Assistant Attorney General Bergson, in a speech before the New York City bar on February 17, had said that he had opposed S. 236 because it provided permanent regulation of a subject then being adjudicated, but indicated that he would not be adverse to a moratorium that would permit Congress time to develop satisfactory permanent legislation, if any should be found to be needed. *Ibid.,* p. 71. Third, it appeared that considerable time might pass before Congress would adopt S. 236, if it ever did. The chances of getting a quick moratorium that would produce the same result for a shorter time then appeared to be quite attractive.

[111] Representative Walter of Pennsylvania introduced a similar bill in the House at the same time, H. R. 2222. In a speech to the Chicago Association of Commerce and Industry, Senator O'Mahoney said that

This bill, S. 1008, was referred to the Senate Committee on Interstate and Foreign Commerce, of which the Johnson-Capehart subcommittee was a part. Under the Legislative Reorganization Act of 1946, amendments to the Federal Trade Commission Act were put under the jurisdiction of the Committee on Interstate and Foreign Commerce, while amendments to the Clayton Act were placed under the jurisdiction of the Committee on the Judiciary. Ten days after the hearings on S. 236, Senator Johnson introduced a resolution to transfer jurisdiction of both S. 236 and S. 1008 from the Committee on Interstate and Foreign Commerce to the Committee on the Judiciary, and this was approved by the Senate.[112]

Before any hearings were held on the Myers Bill (S. 1008), the Committee on Interstate and Foreign Commerce made an interim report to the Senate on the original Capehart hearings, the hearings on S. 236 as amended, and on S. 1008.[113] The *Interim Report,* which more nearly resembled a thesis than a report, was an argumentative attack upon the Federal Trade Commission. Attention was given to the plight of those who, under required f.o.b. pricing, would not be able to relocate their plants or build a $300,000,000 steel mill.[114] Out of pages of testimony by the United Steelworkers' representative, the part which the authors of the *Interim Report* salvaged was a statement saying that a straight f.o.b. system was as undesirable as a straight basing-point system. The same witness also said that the law did

S. 236 was abandoned because the members of the committee were "so uncertain . . . of what the effect of that bill would be that they decided not to report it and instead to report a bill which was called the 'moratorium bill.'" 95 *Cong. Rec.* A4093, A4094 (June 28, 1949). The clarifiers, in short, were confused.

[112] S. Res. No. 76, 95 *Cong. Rec.* 1615 (February 28, 1949). According to Senator O'Conor of Maryland, the moving spirit in the transferring of jurisdiction was Senator McCarran of Nevada. 95 *Cong. Rec.* 7019 (May 31, 1949).

[113] Sen. Doc. No. 27.   [114] *Ibid.,* p. 21.

not require f.o.b. pricing and that no legislation, therefore, was needed to allow freight absorption. On the other hand, a considerable amount of space was given to the testimony of the small number of unions who were basing-point beneficiaries. There were tears for the proverbial victims of government regulation, "the small investor, widow, or orphan" who would "have unpleasant surprises with no fair warning." [115] The ambiguous surprises were evidently related to an asserted stock market decline in the securities of companies struck foully by the pricing policy which the Federal Trade Commission said it was not enforcing. Various statements of the staff of the Commission were examined for inconsistency with pedantic fidelity. Painstaking research was evident in the historical exposition of the Commission's well-known view that conspiracy is a bad thing and that basing-point systems lend themselves to violations of the antitrust laws. The good faith of the Commission was challenged in the statement that "the Commission's present disclaimer of any intention to require f.o.b. mill selling, and current confusion as to the legality of competitive freight absorption, may be examined in the light of this historical background." [116] Although no hearings had as yet been held on S. 1008, the hope was voiced that S. 1008 would be passed immediately by Congress [117] while further consideration was given to S. 236.

There were three days of hearings on S. 1008 at the end of March and the first of April, 1949. The bill itself was very simple.[118] It disclaimed the intent of Congress to deprive

---

[115] *Ibid.*, p. 27.　　[116] *Ibid.*, p. 45.　　[117] *Ibid.*, p. 72.

[118] See *Senate Hearings on S. 1008*, p. 1. Section 1 of the Myers Bill declared "that it has not been the intent of the Congress to deprive individual companies of the right to use delivered price systems or to absorb freight to meet competition in any or all markets, provided such activities are carried on independently and in good faith, and not through any combination or conspiracy in violation of the Sherman Act as amended." Section 2 provided as follows: "Until the expiration

individual companies of the right, independently, to use delivered price systems or to absorb freight to meet competition in any and all markets, provided good faith was present and conspiratorial design was absent. One part of the bill provided that for two years the Federal Trade Commission Act and the Clayton Act (both as amended) should not be construed as depriving individual companies of the right, independently, to use delivered price systems or to absorb freight to meet competition in any and all markets, so long as there was no conspiracy or combination to restrain trade. The scene of action was now the subcommittee of the Committee on the Judiciary, and the cast of characters had changed. The three members of the subcommittee were McCarran of Nevada, O'Conor of Maryland, and Wiley of Wisconsin.

The Senate Judiciary Committee hearings on S. 1008 were notable chiefly because the CIO as an organization appeared for the first time to object to the rate and the direction in which the move to write legislation was proceeding, the Federal Trade Commission took a clear position through one spokesman, and several members of Congress also testified. The spokesman for the CIO was the research director for the United Steelworkers of America, who had appeared in the hearings on S. 236.[119] He objected both to the idea of a moratorium and to the language of the proposed bill, feeling that the Supreme Court's expected decision in the Rigid Steel Case might dispose of many points

---

of two years after the enactment of this Act, the Federal Trade Commission Act, as amended, and the Clayton Act, as amended, shall not be construed as depriving individual companies, in the absence of conspiracy or combination or other agreement in restraint of trade, of the right to independently use delivered price systems or to absorb freight to meet competition in any and all markets." Section 3 provided, "Nothing herein contained shall affect any proceeding pending in any Federal court of the United States on February 1, 1949."

[119] Otis Brubaker, *Senate Hearings on S. 1008*, p. 19 ff.

said to be controversial, and that the Myers Bill was vague enough to permit the re-establishment, entire, of the steel industry's pricing practices before the Cement Case of 1948. He called attention to the study he had presented to the Johnson Committee,[120] felt that the Commission had settled the matters about which confusion was said to exist,[121] described how steel union locals were being solicited by steel companies to support S. 236 and S. 1008,[122] and pointed out that stockholders were being urged to write their Congressmen to the same effect.[123]

The Federal Trade Commission view was represented by the Associate General Counsel, who had testified before the Johnson Committee on S. 236.[124] The views he expressed were those of the Commission, with one dissent.[125] The dissent was included in the record in the form of a communication to Senator Johnson.[126] The Commission view in brief was that the adoption of the moratorium would increase any confusion that might exist as to the meaning and application of the Federal Trade Commission and Clayton Acts.[127] Although specific weaknesses of S. 1008 might be cured by amendment and revision, the Commission's objection went to the very idea of the moratorium itself, since any such moratorium would inevitably create a basis for further and additional uncertainties.[128] The Commission witness also felt that in the Rigid Steel Conduit Case then pending the Supreme Court might clear up many matters about which uncertainty had been expressed.

The members of Congress who testified were Senators Myers and Johnson and Representative Walter of Pennsylvania. Senator Myers of Pennsylvania, like the Commission

---

[120] *Ibid.*, p. 21.
[121] *Ibid.*, p. 25.
[122] *Ibid.*, p. 32.
[123] *Ibid.*, p. 34.
[124] Robert B. Dawkins, *ibid.*, pp. 69–82.

[125] *Ibid.*, p. 69.
[126] *Ibid.*, p. 82.
[127] *Ibid.*, p. 69.
[128] *Ibid.*, p. 71.

and CIO witnesses, indicated that he was looking forward to the Supreme Court's decision in the Rigid Steel Case before considering permanent legislation.[129] The Myers moratorium had been proposed, said the Senator, because the Johnson Bill (S. 236) dealt with a matter too complex for Congress to dispose of in speedy fashion.[130] Although the Myers Bill suggested a two-year moratorium, he was not insistent on this term.[131] Senator Johnson of Colorado took a short time to bring the record of alleged Commission inconsistencies up to date, including witnesses appearing as recently as the day before, in the mood and the manner of the *Interim Report* which bore his name.[132] His most original contribution was a classification which divided those who want to encourage competition and those who want no competition, with the Federal Trade Commission and the Supreme Court in the second category.[133] Representative Walter of Pennsylvania supported the proposed bill since he had introduced one like it in the House.[134] There were other witnesses, some of whom had appeared before the Capehart and Johnson Committees.[135] One of them, at least, seemed to have got into the wrong hearing because he wanted to talk about advertising allowances as they affected dress manufacturers and thought that, since moratoriums were in order, one might be fashioned for his problems. He indicated that he would settle for advisory opinions by the Federal Trade Commission "or somebody." [136]

---

[129] *Ibid.*, p. 5.   [130] *Ibid.*   [131] *Ibid.*, p. 7.

[132] *Ibid.*, pp. 85–89.   [133] *Ibid.*, p. 86.   [134] *Ibid.*, p. 8.

[135] See, for example, George Burger, National Federation of Small Business, *ibid.*, p. 45; Angus McDonald, National Farmers Union, *ibid.*, p. 59. See also American Steel Warehouse Association, *ibid.*, p. 95; Order of Railway Conductors, *ibid.*, p. 82; General Counsel Senate Subcommittee on Trade Policies, *ibid.*, p. 89.

[136] *Ibid.*, p. 14.

Chapter Four

The O'Mahoney Bill

The investigation of pricing practices made by the Senate committees from June 1948 to April 1949 covered a very wide range of alternative policies, without much specific attention to the particular phrases which might be used to carry these policies into law. The Capehart Committee produced no specific proposals for legislation. The Johnson Bill was abandoned. The Myers moratorium in effect would merely have deferred consideration of the words and phrases that would have stated a settled policy of national regulation of basing-point pricing systems. With the introduction of the Myers Bill in the Senate, however, there was set in train a series of events that involved the attention of the Senate and the House with the meanings of words for the rest of the First Session of the Eighty-first Congress.

"Geography Counts a Lot in Politics" [1]

On April 27 the Myers Bill was reported favorably to the Senate with an amendment.[2] The end of the moratorium was fixed by date (July 1, 1950), and there were changes in

---

[1] Senator Wiley, *Senate Hearings on S. 1008*, p. 79.
[2] 81st Cong., 1st Sess., Sen. Rep. No. 305 (1949), 95 *Cong. Rec.* 5092 (April 27, 1949). Even as amended, the bill was regarded by the Federal

wording designed to restrict the operation of the moratorium to the practice of freight absorption, without giving countenance to the systematic use of basing-point pricing. For example, the phrase "quote and sell at delivered prices" replaced "use delivered price systems." An appendix to the bill contained a brief citation of Supreme Court cases tending to uphold the constitutionality of legislative overriders of Supreme Court cases, and it was the judgment of the Committee on the Judiciary, speaking through Senator O'Conor, that enactment of S. 1008 was within the consitutional authority of Congress. There was, however, no statement as to the Supreme Court decisions which S. 1008 was setting aside. Senator Langer of North Dakota dissented from the Committee report and recommendation,[3] because the bill introduced at least four new terms and phrases in the antitrust laws without defining them.[4] It would, he said, have the practical effect of immunizing various monopolistic practices which the supporters of the bill would condemn; it would vitiate enforcement of the antitrust laws by substituting intent for practical effect as a test of violation; and it would legalize basing-point systems and phantom freight through the uses that can be made of freight absorption. Senator Langer concluded that Congress was invading the sphere of the judiciary and recommended that Congress either refuse to pass the bill or amend it further to protect the antitrust laws.[5] His dissent from the majority report of the Senate Committee on the Judiciary prepared the way for a strong attack upon the bill when it came up for debate.

Trade Commission as neither necessary nor desirable. See letter from the Commission to Congressman Patman of Texas. 95 *Cong. Rec.* A3361–A3363 (May 31, 1949).

[3] 81st Cong., 1st Sess., Sen. Rep. No. 305, pt. 2 (1949), p. 5.

[4] These were "engaging in competition;" "absorb freight;" "in any and all markets;" and "delivered prices."

[5] See note 3 above.

It came up on May 31, when Senator Myers moved its consideration.[6] Those who might have been opponents of the legislation, those who might have argued that Congress should let the Supreme Court work out the clarification of any possible confusion, were disarmed by the Court itself. One hour after the Senate Judiciary Committee had voted seven to two to report the Myers Bill favorably to the Senate, the Supreme Court handed down its decision in the Rigid Steel Case.[7] The Court had split four to four.[8] A half hour before the Myers Bill was to come up for debate, Senator O'Mahoney of Wyoming talked with Myers and others about a substitute bill that he wanted to introduce in place of the one that the Committee on the Judiciary had worked on.[9] An arrangement was made to permit O'Mahoney to discuss his proposed substitute before final vote on the Myers Bill. Senator O'Conor assumed charge of the Myers Bill, and the Senate proceeded to consider the measure, which was now moot because of the expected O'Mahoney substitution.

O'Conor's opening statement in explanation of the bill described the principal features of the measure. He was not accurate in implying that mere freight absorption as such was unlawful or that the only pricing alternative available to businessmen under the law was f.o.b. pricing.[10]

---

[6] 95 *Cong. Rec.* 7018 (May 31, 1949).

[7] *Ibid.*, p. 7159. *Triangle Conduit & Cable Co.* v. *Federal Trade Commission*, 168 F. 2nd 175 (C.C.A. 7th 1948), aff'd per curiam sub nom., *Clayton Mark & Co.* v. *Federal Trade Commission*, 336 U.S. 956 (1949).

[8] "Perhaps as a result of this split decision sentiment in the Senate in favor of permanent legislation in preference to a moratorium appears to have strengthened." Testimony of Herbert A. Bergson, Assistant Attorney General, in *H. R. Hearings on S. 1008*, p. 11.

[9] This was S. 1974, which was referred to the Committee on the Judiciary. 95 *Cong. Rec.* 7001 (May 31, 1949).

[10] See *ibid.*, p. 7020 (May 31, 1949), where Senator O'Conor used language that made it appear that the Federal Trade Commission felt

There was widespread confusion, he said; the expected "clarification" by the Supreme Court in the Rigid Steel Case had not materialized; and it was now more necessary than ever for Congress to intervene. The intervention prescribed by S. 1008 was a moratorium until July 1, 1950, on all proceedings against pricing practices except those where conspiracy or combination was involved. There was to be no permanent change in the law, and Congress was not committing itself to any particular course of action or policy after the expiration of the moratorium. He made a point of saying that the bill was not a "big business" bill but one that involved the entire economy.[11] After Myers' explanation, Senator Langer of North Dakota launched an attack on the bill, in the main following the points that he had raised in his dissent from the Senate Judiciary Committee Report on S. 1008 but adding new matter of a general nature, in a text full of personal reminiscences.[12]

The principal attack in this opening phase of the debate on S. 1008 was made by Senator Wayne Morse of Oregon.[13] He described the cross-pull and interplay of pressures working upon Congress, masterminded, he asserted, by the steel companies. The steel decision to go to f.o.b. pricing was not forced by the Cement Case because, as the Small Business Committee had reported in 1948 before the Cement Case, there had been a steady withdrawal of steel from those markets where freight was absorbed.[14] The Cement Case provided the steel companies with a pretext for getting rid of costly freight absorption in a sellers' market and for shifting the blame for the change to the Federal Trade Commission. Moreover, this maneuver transformed steel

that the Cement Case made freight absorption unlawful. He did not cite the express denial of this made by Commissioner Davis and referred to above.

[11] *Ibid.*, p. 7022.
[12] *Ibid.*, pp. 7023–7025.
[13] *Ibid.*, pp. 7025–7031.
[14] *Ibid.*, p. 7027.

buyers into an "army of zealous supporters of the modifica-
tion of the law which the steel industry desired." [15] He
charged deliberate misrepresentation of the Federal Trade
Commission's position on these matters and denied that the
record showed any ambition on the part of the Commission
to force enterprises to adopt f.o.b. pricing. He cited evidence to show that on June 2, 1948, at the outset of the
controversy, and in January, 1949, the position of the Federal Trade Commission had been clear that the Cement
Case did not outlaw all delivered prices or require only
f.o.b. prices.[16] He asserted that the propaganda line in favor
of revision of the laws was perfected in the summer of 1948.
The offensive phrase "basing point" was discarded and the
pricing practices of the steel industry were represented as
being no more than absorption of freight where necessary
in order to meet competition.[17] It was his conclusion, as it
had been that of Senator Langer, that the blanket authoriza-
tion in S. 1008 to absorb freight for the sake of quoting
identical prices would legalize the entire mechanism of the
basing-point system.[18] Langer had begun his speech on May
31. He yielded to Morse so that the latter could get his
speech in before he made a train. Langer resumed his remarks the next day, finishing his attack upon S. 1008 as
sponsored by Myers. But the attack on the Myers Bill was
flogging a dead horse, for it was now evident that agreement
was going to settle on the O'Mahoney substitute, and Langer accepted the substitute.[19]

---

[15] *Ibid.*   [16] See above, p. 114.

[17] 95 *Cong. Rec.* 7030 (May 31, 1949).

[18] Senator Myers showed himself to be concerned over some of
the implications of the Morse exposition of the activities of pressure
groups. At the end of the Morse speech, Senator Myers wanted his
"friend from Oregon" to understand that no steel companies or any
others came to Myers while the bill was being prepared. *Ibid.*, p. 7031
(May 31, 1949).

[19] *Ibid.*, p. 7050 (June 1, 1949).

The O'Mahoney Bill (S. 1974) had been referred to the Committee on the Judiciary when it was introduced on May 31. The next morning O'Mahoney met with members of the Committee on the Judiciary and discussed his bill with them, making some changes in it which he had not had time to incorporate in the text by the time he arose on June 1 to describe his bill. The clerk of the Senate made a notation of the changes as he described them. The bill was written in a hurry. It was proffered to the Senate without hearings. The Myers Bill provided for a short moratorium; O'Mahoney proposed moratorium forever. His substitute was a permanent revision of the antitrust laws so as "to declare that delivered prices and freight absorption are not unlawful per se." [20] The champion of the antitrust laws thus appeared as a champion of permanent amendment to the antitrust laws of a kind that even the sponsors of S. Res. 241 and S. 236 had not dared to propose.

There have been various explanations of O'Mahoney's maneuver. One of the favorable interpretations is the suggestion that O'Mahoney believed that Congress was in a mood to enact a serious renunciation of antitrust policy. In order to avoid a more serious rout, he "preferred a strategic retreat in the form of a compromise with the forces of monopoly." [21] Against this view, perhaps, is the fact that the authors of S. 236 did not think that they could get their bill through and that the Myers Bill, which the O'Mahoney Bill replaced, was more moderate than the O'Mahoney Bill, at least to the extent of being temporary and not permanent legislation. A sterner critic suggested that O'Mahoney had "become a convert to a different school

---

[20] *Ibid.*, p. 7064. The other of the two objectives of the bill was to "preserve the strength of the anti-trust laws."

[21] Letter to Congressman Wright Patman from Dr. Fritz Machlup, Johns Hopkins University, July 6, 1949, *Small Business Committee Hearings*, p. 212.

of economic thought" from that he had expressed as head of the Temporary National Economic Committee.[22] The most candid testimony as to what O'Mahoney had in mind is the testimony of Senator O'Mahoney. On the floor of the Senate O'Mahoney said: "I should like to say to the Senator [Kefauver] that one of the purposes which I entertained in offering this provision was to make sure that the system which has been used, without criticism, by the sugar beet industry, of selling at delivered prices by absorbing freight, should not now be disturbed." [23]

His faithfulness to his mission as a Senator with important state economic interests to promote is evident in his further statement: "I wanted to be sure that the great western industry was not being unduly affected by the decision." [24] In the course of testimony he gave to the House Judiciary Committee in support of his bill, Senator O'Mahoney also referred to the development of trona deposits in Wyoming by the Westvaco Company, whose representative he had accompanied to the Capehart hearings. O'Mahoney later said that he proposed his bill to clear up the law because he felt "it was essential that nothing be done to prevent the investment of private capital in new industry in the United States." [25] He had told the Westvaco Company representatives that he thought the law did not compel f.o.b. pricing and that (if conspiracy was absent) the company could sell its product in the market of any other company at a delivered price and absorb the freight. But no lawyer would advise the company so. O'Mahoney cited the four-to-four split of the Supreme Court in the Rigid Steel Case and

---

[22] Testimony of Walter Wooden, Associate General Counsel, Federal Trade Commission, *Small Business Committee Hearings*, p. 68. See Senator O'Mahoney's speech before the Chicago Association of Commerce and Industry, June 22, 1949, as an example of the asserted conversion. 95 *Cong. Rec.* A4093–A4094 (June 28, 1949).

[23] *Ibid.*, p. 7071 (June 1, 1949). [24] *Ibid.*

[25] *H. R. Hearings on S. 1008*, p. 4.

indicated that after that case it seemed clear to him "that we were erecting a barrier to the investment of private capital in the development of our natural resources and in the development of trade and commerce." [26] Beets and chemicals were clearly in the mind of the sponsor of the substitute for the Myers Bill, whatever other aims may have existed.

The Senate was patently confused, as the record shows. Some members, like Senator Tobey of New Hampshire, had come well prepared to fight against S. 1008 in the Myers version, on the ground that it would legalize or tend to legalize basing-point systems and make the problem of proof of violation of the statutes more difficult for the Federal Trade Commission, or that lawyers might so argue and thereby produce more eventual confusion than clarification. [27] Tobey felt that he was voting for something different in the O'Mahoney substitute for the Myers Bill. [28] But Senator O'Conor of Maryland, who was in charge of the Myers Bill, felt that there was no substantial difference between the two except that the O'Mahoney proposal would have made permanent what O'Conor and Myers had only dared to hope to make temporary. [29] Senator Myers thought that there was no difference either. As he said:

When I introduced Senate Bill 1008, in the nature of a

---

[26] *Ibid.*

[27] See the long statement inserted in the *Congressional Record* by Senator Tobey. 95 *Cong. Rec.* 7071–7091 (June 1, 1949).

[28] "Therefore I wish to go on record as saying that I am opposed to the bill (i.e., the Myers Bill) itself. I shall vote for the O'Mahoney amendment in the nature of a substitute." *Ibid.*, p. 7071 (June 1, 1949).

[29] "We feel that the amendment as proposed by the Senator from Wyoming accomplishes exactly what was intended to have been accomplished by the Committee on the Judiciary on a temporary basis, but now is accomplished on a permanent basis by the suggestion of the Senator from Wyoming, as amended in the several respects to which explanation has been given." *Ibid.*, p. 7091.

moratorium, in the nature of temporary legislation, I was hopeful that at least we might get that much action. However at that time I did not believe that it would be possible to get permanent legislation through the Senate. However with the assistance and guidance of the Senator from Wyoming, we are able to make permanent what we originally sought to make temporary. I congratulate him for his efforts.[30]

The Senate by a voice vote and with no real debate adopted the O'Mahoney Bill as a substitute for the Myers Bill and then passed it, not as S. 1974, but as S. 1008.[31] There

[30] *Ibid.*, p. 7092.

[31] As it passed the Senate, S. 1008 in Section 1 provided: "It shall not be an unfair method of competition or an unfair or deceptive act or practice for a seller, acting independently, to quote or sell at delivered prices or to absorb freight: Provided, That this shall not make lawful any combination, conspiracy, or collusive agreement; or any monopolistic, oppressive, deceptive, or fraudulent practice, carried out by or involving the use of delivered prices or freight absorption." *Ibid.* The Clayton Act as amended was further amended by adding that it "shall not be an unlawful discrimination in price for a seller, acting independently" to quote and sell at delivered prices, identical at different delivery points, "or if differences between such prices are not such that their effect upon competition may be that prohibited by this section." Similarly, it was not to be an unlawful discrimination in price for a seller, acting independently, "to absorb freight to meet the equally low price of a competitor in good faith (except where the effect of such absorption of freight will be to substantially lessen competition), and this may include the maintenance, above or below the price of such competitor, of a differential in price which such seller customarily maintains." The parenthetical phrase is the Kefauver amendment referred to below, note 34. Section 2(b) of the Clayton Act as amended was further amended to read: "Upon proof being made, at any hearing on a complaint under this section, that there has been discrimination in price the effect of which upon competition may be that prohibited by the preceding subsection, or discrimination in services or facilities furnished, the burden of showing justification shall be upon the person charged with a violation of this section, and unless justification shall be affirmatively shown, the Commission is authorized to issue an order terminating the discrimination: Provided further; That a seller may justify a discrimination (other than a discrimination which will substantially lessen competition) by showing that his lower price or the furnishing of services or facilities to any purchaser or

had been no hearings on it. Some of the Senators obviously did not understand what was happening. O'Mahoney gave only a very general kind of explanation. The bill seems not to have been in existence forty-eight hours before its passage.[32] It committed the Senate overnight to a policy that Capehart and Johnson had failed to establish after a struggle of almost a year. The reputation of the Senator from Wyoming as a champion of the antitrust laws seems to have been accepted as a guarantee of his proposal.[33] Only Senator Kefauver of Tennessee and Senator Long of Louisiana showed signs of doubt. Kefauver got O'Mahoney to accept an amendment that would have refused legal countenance

---

purchasers was made in good faith to meet an equally low price of a competitor, or the services or facilities furnished by a competitor." The parenthetical phrase is also a Kefauver amendment. Both amendments were designed to retain the rule of the Seventh Circuit Court of Appeals in *Standard Oil Co.* v. *Federal Trade Commission*, 173 F. 2nd 210 (1949), where the effect of price discrimination on competition was held to overcome the defense of good faith. 95 *Cong. Rec.* 7071 (June 1, 1949). At one place, Senator O'Mahoney told Kefauver that he did not think that his bill (before the Kefauver amendment) would "change the ruling under which the Federal Trade Commission now operates," but he later admitted that the effect of his language would be adverse to the rule in the Standard Oil Case (*Standard Oil Co.* v. *Federal Trade Commission*, 173 F. 2nd 210 [C.C.A. 7th 1949]). 95 *Cong. Rec.* 7066 (June 1, 1949). The fourth section of S. 1008 contained definitions, one of which was: "The term 'effect may be' shall mean that there is substantial and probative evidence of the specified effect." This would have reversed the rule of the *Federal Trade Commission* v. *Morton Salt Co.*, 334 U.S. 37 (1948), where it was held that a "reasonable possibility" of injury to competition could make a price discrimination unlawful. See also *Corn Products Co.* v. *Federal Trade Commission*, 324 U.S. 726, 742 (1945).

[32] Congressman Walter said that the bill as it passed the Senate had been drafted by Assistant Attorney General Bergson. 95 *Cong. Rec.* 8983 (July 6, 1949). At another time Senator Johnson of Colorado said that the Federal Trade Commission was the source of the bill. *Ibid.*, p. 11267 (August 11, 1949), and that Robert Dawkins was the author. *Ibid.*, p. 11268.

[33] See the comments of Senator Lucas of Illinois and Senator Myers of Pennsylvania to this effect. *Ibid.*, pp. 7092–7093 (June 1, 1949).

to freight absorption which "will substantially lessen competition." [34] The effect of this amendment was to weaken the defense of "good faith" and to restore the rule of the Robinson-Patman Act that discriminatory prices were unlawful (good faith or not) where they could not be justified by cost differentials and tended to lessen competition. After the vote Senator Long said that he was inclined to feel "that when everyone is as happy about a piece of legislation as Senators appear to be, someone is going to be fooled when he wakes up and sees what is in it." [35] A subsequent motion on June 6 to reconsider the bill was defeated,[36] and on that day the O'Mahoney version of S. 1008 was referred to the House Committee on the Judiciary.[37]

From House to House

The bill, which was given no hearings at all before it was proposed to and passed by the Senate, was given no hearings to speak of in the House. According to one witness, the Judiciary Committee announced a one-day hearing, which he heard about "by the grapevine." [38] One accomplishment of the one-day hearing was to prune the bill of the amendment that Senator Kefauver had had inserted. Although he accepted the amendment on the floor of the Senate,[39] Senator O'Mahoney appeared a week later at the House Judiciary Committee hearings to propose that it be taken out.[40]

---

[34] *Ibid.*, p. 7071. The verb "will" was to be important. See below, note 100, and pp. 151–157.

[35] 95 *Cong. Rec.* 7092 (June 1, 1949). Note that Senator Long was also in doubt and confusion as to what was taking place. He said that even though he was in favor of the O'Mahoney amendment, on the voice vote, he voted against the bill. He thought that the amendment improved the bill, a remark that is difficult to comprehend.

[36] *Ibid.*, p. 7248 (June 6, 1949).   [37] *Ibid.*, p. 7313.

[38] Angus McDonald, National Farmers Union, in *Small Business Committee Hearings*, p. 84.

[39] 95 *Cong. Rec.* 7071 (June 1, 1949).

[40] *H. R. Hearings on S. 1008*, p. 9. A later discussion showed that

Herbert Bergson, Assistant Attorney General for the Antitrust Division of the Department of Justice, also appeared and suggested that the Kefauver amendment be removed.[41] While O'Mahoney and Bergson were thus engaged in building up the defenses available to respondents charged with lessening competition, Congressman Walter announced that the Federal Trade Commission had authorized him to state that the Commission was not opposed to the bill,[42] although it had been opposed to the lesser regulation first proposed by Senator Myers. It is perhaps a tribute to the leadership of O'Mahoney that he had been able to get the Department of Justice, the Federal Trade Commission, Senators Myers, O'Conor, Capehart, Johnson, and McCarran, and Congressman Walter to unite in favor of his bill. Because of the weight of this influence and the speed with which the measure moved through legislative channels without adequate hearings, the critics of the O'Mahoney Bill could fight only a rearguard action.[43] This they did in brilliant fashion, first in the House and then in the Senate. They were caught unawares when O'Mahoney's substitute

---

the printed version of the Kefauver amendment was not in the form the author intended. It had passed in a form more restrictive of the Federal Trade Commission than he had at first thought. See 95 *Cong. Rec.* 11253 (August 11, 1949).

[41] *H. R. Hearings on S. 1008*, p. 12.

[42] *Ibid.*, p. 6, 28. In an ambiguous statement, the Commission seemed to imply that the Kefauver amendment needed to be eliminated or modified in order to make good-faith meeting of the lower prices of a competitor a complete defense to a charge of unlawful discrimination, although it did not make elimination of the Kefauver amendment a condition of approval. See reference to a caucus between Congressman Walter and Commission staff on June 7, 1949, in the letter of Commissioner Davis to Congressman Walter, dated June 9, 1949. *H. R. Hearings on S. 1008*, pp. 60–62.

[43] The *Journal of Commerce,* in an editoral of June 8, 1949, was suspicious of the approval extended to S. 1008 by the Federal Trade Commission and of Senator O'Mahoney's sponsorship of the permanent legislation. See *H. R. Hearings on S. 1008,* p. 68.

passed the Senate, but they fought literally from house to house and won a temporary stalemate when the Senate failed to act on the conference version of the O'Mahoney Bill at the end of the First Session of the Eighty-first Congress.

The first attack took place in the House Judiciary Committee. Although it was evidently intended originally that the subcommittee would hold hearings of only one day to hear O'Mahoney and Bergson, opportunity was provided for Congressman Wright Patman to make a statement.[44] The occasion was the meeting of the full Committee on the Judiciary under the chairmanship of Congressman Celler of New York to decide what action it would take on S. 1008. Before it went into executive session on June 14 to decide to report the bill favorably, Patman and three other Congressmen were heard. Patman urged the Committee to hold a complete and full hearing because the bill, in his opinion, would "put a loophole in the anti-trust laws that a B-36 could fly through." [45] There was no other argument he could make since the subcommittee had already reported to the full Committee, and the discussion of the merits was presumably foreclosed, although there had never been any public discussion anywhere on the merits. Congressman Jennings of Tennessee tried to get Patman shut off [46] but without success.[47] Much of the questioning of Congressman Patman was heckling and argumentative. Congressman Robert J. Corbett of Pennsylvania, representing the Pittsburgh area, said that he supported the bill because "business does ask for an immediate decision on this problem," [48] and a Congressman from Peoria, "where a number of large, bulky industries are operating," agreed with Corbett.[49] With these statements, which took an hour and a quarter,

---

[44] H. R. Hearings on S. 1008, p. 17 ff.   [45] Ibid.   [46] Ibid., p. 23.
[47] Ibid., p. 24.   [48] Ibid., p. 31.   [49] Ibid., p. 35.

the Committee went into executive session and decided to report the bill favorably.

The bill was reported to the House, June 21, 1949.[50] The Committee report recommended the deletion of the Kefauver amendment [51] and spoke of clarification when it should have spoken of reversal of the courts. The Cement Case, the Rigid Steel Conduit Case, and the rule in the Standard Oil Company case—all were now involved, since the bill would have given new defenses to those practicing freight absorption, making prices identical with those of competitors, and injuring competition, so long as "good faith" was present. The Kefauver amendment at least would have sustained the rule of the Standard Oil Case.[52] The O'Mahoney version reversed it. As to Rigid Steel, Representative Walter said that the Federal Trade Commission was embarrassed to admit that it had made a mistake in pressing for favorable judgment on Count II in the Rigid Steel Case.[53] The O'Mahoney Bill would probably have inhibited the Commission from proceeding against firms consciously paralleling prices, regardless of the effect on competition, where deliberate conspiracy was absent.

On June 30, 1949, the Rules Committee of the House granted an open rule providing for three hours of general debate on S. 1008.[54] Representatives Celler and Walter of the Committee on the Judiciary urged the granting of the rule, and Patman opposed it unsuccessfully. The best he could do was make a speech warning the members of the House that S. 1008 was on its way.[55] He was active in another direction, however. As chairman of the House Select

---

[50] 95 *Cong. Rec.* 8083 (June 21, 1949).
[51] 81st Cong., 1st Sess., H. R. Rep. No. 869, to accompany S. 1008, 1 (1949).
[52] See above note 31.   [53] *H. R. Hearings on S. 1008,* p. 27.
[54] 95 *Cong. Rec.* D448 (June 30, 1949).
[55] 95 *Cong. Rec.* 8768 ff. (June 30, 1949).

Committee on Small Business, he undertook to hold hearings on S. 1008 which he said had been denied to him and to small business groups.[56] And for five days witnesses made appearances before the Small Business Committee or sent statements attacking S. 1008. Professional economists,[57] representatives of small business organizations,[58] wholesale and retail distributors,[59] the National Farmers Union,[60] the American Trucking Association, Inc.,[61] and the staff of the Federal Trade Commission [62] made a record of protest of three hundred pages, the theme of which was that S. 1008 would weaken the antitrust laws, cancel recent gains in the clarification of the laws, create more confusion and litigation, and make it easier for violators to justify infractions and harder for the Federal Trade Commission to halt such infractions. Walter Wooden, Associate General Counsel of the Commission, thought that S. 1008 would set back the Commission twenty-four years to the time of the old Cement Case.[63]

Having failed to prevent the granting of a rule to S. 1008, Patman then sought to delay the schedule of the Rules Committee in setting the time for the debate on S. 1008, but failed in this also.[64] In the course of discussing the schedule, however, Patman was able to forewarn the House of the

---

[56] Celler of New York found this maneuver "unseemly" because the Patman Committee was not a legislative committee, had no direct power to recommend legislation, and had no jurisdiction over S. 1008. Jurisdiction was in the Committee on the Judiciary, of which Celler was chairman. *Ibid.*, p. 8989 (July 6, 1949).

[57] *Small Business Committee Hearings*, pp. 135, 212, 215.

[58] *Ibid.*, p. 225.   [59] *Ibid.*, pp. 3, 4, 9, 21.

[60] *Ibid.*, p. 75.   [61] *Ibid.*, p. 102.

[62] *Ibid.*, pp. 30, 141, 202.

[63] *Ibid.*, p. 36. *Cement Manufacturers Protective Association* v. *United States*, 268 U.S. 588 (1925).

[64] 95 *Cong. Rec.* 8856 (July 5, 1949). Majority Leader McCormack hinted that Patman's request was tardy and that the bill might have been scheduled to Patman's satisfaction had he been more prompt in his request.

principal objections that his select committee had developed.[65] He also kept the Appendix of the *Congressional Record* filled with editorials and extended remarks showing the impact of basing-point systems on various geographical areas in the country.[66] The rule was called up as scheduled, and the House debate on S. 1008 began on July 6, 1949.[67]

The ignorance and confusion of the Congressmen in discussing the measure were depressing.[68] Brown of Ohio asserted that there had been "rather extensive hearings" on the bill before the subcommittee and then the full Committee on the Judiciary,[69] which was not so. The attitude of the Department of Justice was variously expressed, Sutton of Tennessee saying that he had talked with the person in charge of the Antitrust Division of the Department of Justice by telephone the day before and had been told that the legislation was not necessary at all,[70] and Walter of Pennsylvania asserting that Bergson (head of the Antitrust Division) had said that "it was absolutely necessary" that the bill be enacted.[71] This dispute was settled only when Majority Leader McCormack declared that the bill had the

---

[65] *Ibid.*, p. 8859 ff.

[66] *Ibid.*, pp. A4553, A4254, A4279. See also *ibid.*, pp. A3353, A3377, A3393 (May 31, 1949). Congressman Walter inserted a speech he made before the Pennsylvania Bar Association in which the decisions of the Federal Trade Commission on pricing were found to resemble the philosophy of a former Soviet Commissar of Justice. Special reference was made to Count II in the Rigid Steel Case. S. 1008 was designed to combat the "Krylenko philosophy" represented by the Federal Trade Commission. 95 *Cong. Rec.* A4256 (July 5, 1949).

[67] *Ibid.*, pp. 8982–8996 (July 6, 1949).

[68] Congressman Lyle of Texas made an accurate observation when he remarked that, "generally, legislation coming to the floor under a rule is better understood than this particular bill." *Ibid.*, p. 8982.

[69] *Ibid.*   [70] *Ibid.*, p. 8983.

[71] The record of the hearings before the House Committee on the Judiciary does not disclose such a statement by Bergson. It does quote him as saying, "Insofar as the Department of Justice is concerned, we have never urged the necessity or desirability of legislation with re-

approval of the Commission, the Department of Justice, the Bureau of the Budget, and the White House.[72] Patman said that O'Mahoney had "agreed to this substitute" (for the Myers moratorium) "only when the Kefauver amendment was added to it." [73] The record of course shows that he personally appeared before the House Judiciary Committee to get the Kefauver amendment stricken.

The chief accomplishment of the House was to write in another version of the Kefauver amendment after Patman failed to prevent the debate on the bill scheduled by the Rules Committee.[74] Willis of Louisiana led the first attack to restore the Kefauver amendment or another version of the amendment,[75] but this was defeated.[76] The second (and successful) effort to undo the work of the Committee on the Judiciary in striking out the Kefauver amendment was led by Carroll of Colorado.[77] The object of the Carroll amendment, as of the Kefauver and Willis amendments, was to deprive respondents under the Robinson-Patman Act of the defense of good faith where differential prices to meet those of a competitor (without differentials of cost) substantially lessened competition. Like the Kefauver and

spect to the pricing practices to which the present bill is directed." *H. R. Hearings on S. 1008,* p. 11.

[72] 95 *Cong. Rec.* 8989 (July 6, 1949). Patman was of the opinion that the Department of Justice was willing to restrict the operations of the Federal Trade Commission out of a sense of rivalry. *Ibid.,* p. 9039 (July 7, 1949). He could not understand why the Federal Trade Commission had changed its position. *Ibid.,* pp. 9039, 9040.

[73] *Ibid.,* p. 8984 (July 6, 1949).

[74] The vote on the rule was easily carried (*ibid.,* p. 8992), and the House proceeded to consider the measure on its merits, with time divided equally between opponents and proponents for three hours. *Ibid.,* p. 8993.

[75] *Ibid.,* p. 9052 (July 7, 1949).

[76] *Ibid.,* p. 9064. It is of interest that 143 Congressmen out of the total membership of 435 voted down the Willis amendment by a vote (on division) of 80 to 63.

[77] *Ibid.*

Willis amendments, its effect was to retain the rule of the Standard Oil Case as decided by the Seventh Circuit Court of Appeals.[78] The Carroll amendment was adopted by the Committee of the Whole House [79] after a wearying debate in which few were on the floor and the speakers complained about the noise.[80] Since the House passed S. 1008 in a different form from the Senate, the measure was almost certainly headed for a conference committee unless the Senate accepted the House version.[81] This would have been true also if the Judiciary Committee version of the measure had been adopted intact by the House, since that version had eliminated the Kefauver amendment.

With the action of the House on the Carroll amendment, a sharp and fairly definite issue was joined for the first time. There was now a line, on one side of which the spokesmen for the Robinson-Patman Act could stand, and on the other, the spokesmen for legislative intervention on behalf of the steel, oil, cement, and building materials industrial groups, all affected by recent decisions. The question was not now the abstract one of basing-point systems and required f.o.b.

---

[78] *Ibid.*, p. 8995 (July 6, 1949).

[79] *Ibid.*, p. 9074 (July 7, 1949). The vote was 117 to 81. Where the Kefauver amendment had used the words "except where the effect of such absorption of freight will be to substantially lessen competition," the Carroll amendment said, "except where such absorption of freight would be such that its effect upon competition may be that prohibited by this section." Where the Kefauver amendment used the words "other than a discrimination which will substantially lessen competition," the Carroll amendment said, "if the discrimination is not such that its effect upon competition may be that prohibited by this section." Compare the Carroll amendments with S. 1008 as it passed the Senate, above, note 31. As S. 1008 passed the House, the phrase "substantial and probative evidence" in the definition of "the effect may be" had been changed to "reasonable possibility," thus restoring the rule of the Morton Salt Case. See above note 31.

[80] See remarks of Christopher of Missouri, 95 *Cong. Rec.* 9070, 9071 (July 7, 1949), and White of Idaho, *ibid.*, p. 9073.

[81] The House passed the bill by voice vote after a motion to recommit to the Committee on the Judiciary was defeated. *Ibid.*, p. 9075.

pricing, nor freight absorption as such, nor moratoriums. After the action of the House, Senator Long of Louisiana warned the Senate that he recognized the existence of a drive to end the Robinson-Patman Act and referred to a statement in the *Journal of Commerce* which spoke of Celler of New York as the sponsor of such a drive.[82] A statement attributed to Celler suggested that the conference committee might not have to take either the Kefauver or the Carroll amendments.[83] Long put the Senate on notice that he regarded the issue as a serious one and was prepared to make a fight on it.

On July 26 the Vice President laid before the Senate the amendments made by the House to S. 1008, and McCarran of Nevada moved that the Senate disagree with the House and go to conference.[84] This was quickly agreed to by the Senate, and McCarran, O'Conor, and Wiley were appointed Senate conferees. Long and Kefauver immediately protested the action, charging McCarran with violation of an understanding to give notice to Kefauver when the conference vote would arise in order to permit them instead to move to concur in the House amendments.[85] The McCarran motion to send the bill to conference, *sotto voce,* almost succeeded in preventing the Senate from debating S. 1008 at all. Senate protocol, had McCarran consented, would have nullified the vote to send the bill to conference. He, however, would agree only to a debate on Long's motion to reconsider, which is not a debate on the merits.[86] The debate was held on August 10, 11, and 12, and it failed to persuade the Senate to recall its decision to send S. 1008 to conference.[87] Before the matter was sent on its way to the House

---

[82] *Ibid.*, p. 9125 (July 8, 1949).   [83] *Ibid.*

[84] *Ibid.*, p. 10150 (July 26, 1949).   [85] *Ibid.*, pp. 10150–10151.

[86] See discussion of this point by Senator Morse, *ibid.*, pp. 11272–11273 (August 11, 1949).

[87] The motion to reconsider was rejected August 12, 1949. *Ibid.*, pp. 11325–11360 (August 12, 1949).

again with a request to appoint conferees, Senator Lucas of Illinois said that had he known the bill was going to cause so much trouble and take up so much time, it never would have got off the calendar. He had been persuaded to take it off the calendar by Senator Myers of Pennsylvania, who had assured him "that it was a moratorium bill, which would probably require a couple of hours." [88] The weapon that McCarran had against the Long-Kefauver group throughout the three-day debate was the rule of the Senate that a motion to table the motion to reconsider would have the effect of shutting off debate immediately.[89] This advantage was not pressed, however.

The familiar ground was traversed once again, the chief difference being the new alertness of senators who had had the time and the inclination to inform themselves about matters upon which they had voted unknowingly when the O'Mahoney substitution for the Myers moratorium was made. O'Mahoney expressed again his interest in the development of trona deposits in Wyoming and his desire to make sure that Wyoming concerns would be permitted to absorb freight and quote delivered prices.[90] He also said that he thought his sponsorship of S. 1008 was consistent with his views when he was head of the TNEC. He said that he had been glad to accept the Kefauver amendment when it was introduced originally and hoped that it, or language like it, would come out of the conference committee intact.[91] He did not say that he had gone to the House Judiciary Committee to urge its removal.[92] Senator Myers said

---

[88] *Ibid.*, p. 11153 (August 10, 1949). Senator Lucas on two occasions tried and failed to get the debate limited by unanimous consent. He succeeded on the third attempt, but only after the supporters of the motion to reconsider had developed their attack at length. *Ibid.*, pp. 11176, 11247, 11286 (August 11, 1949).

[89] *Ibid.*, p. 11153 (August 10, 1949).   [90] *Ibid.*, p. 11170.

[91] *Ibid.*, p. 11172.

[92] At still another place in the debate, on Aug 11, Senator O'Ma-

that he had no objection to either the Kefauver or the Carroll amendments but thought that the bill should go to conference because there were such deep cleavages on both sides.[93]

The principal speeches in favor of the motion to reconsider the vote to send the bill to conference were made by Senators Douglas, Long, Kefauver, Hill, and Morse. Senator Douglas presented the most coherent and logical exposition to be made on either side of the controversy.[94] He took the bold view that the bill, even with the Carroll amendment, would legalize basing-point systems and that, although the Carroll amendments improved the measure originally introduced, it would still be better to have no bill at all.[95] The principal instrument for the suppression

---

honey again said that he had accepted the Kefauver amendments in the Senate because he "believed they were totally in harmony with the purposes of the author of the substitute." *Ibid.*, p. 11265 (August 11, 1949). He failed to state at this time also that he had gone to the House Judiciary Committee to have the amendments stricken.

[93] *Ibid.*, p. 11175 (August 10, 1949).

[94] Senator Capehart was the originator of several short, sharp exchanges with Senator Douglas. The first exchange ended with the following colloquy: Mr. Capehart: "If the Senator wants an argument and a fight I will be very happy to give it to him. The Senator seems to be inviting it." Mr. Douglas: "I fight only in a good cause. If the Senator wants to take me on while I am defending a good cause, I am willing." *Ibid.*, p. 11177 (August 10, 1949).

[95] *Ibid.* He mentioned trade-marked consumer goods like chocolate bars and other candies, chewing gums, cigars, soap, cosmetics, drugs, shirts, soft drinks, and the like which sell all over the country at the same price (indicating freight absorption) and are protected by trade-mark. As to these the Federal Trade Commission had not proceeded against the uniform prices of trade-marked commodities and there was no prospect that it would. These are different from the standardized commodities in which there is little difference of quality, and price competition is the only kind that counts. Among the latter are steel, cement, lead, steel pipe and conduits, corn syrup, beet sugar, some forms of lumber, and brass. He said that the makers of the latter had been fighting behind the skirts of the first to legitimatize their own monopolistic practices.

of price competition is the basing-point system, and this the O'Mahoney Bill, even with the House amendment, would sanctify.[96] The alleged confusion following the Rigid Steel Case existed only in the minds of those sponsoring the O'Mahoney measure and not in the minds of the courts or the Federal Trade Commission. The fact that the Court split four to four in the Rigid Steel Case need not have made legislation any more necessary than the four-to-four split in the Oregon minimum wage case in 1917.[97] Any further amplifications or refinements of statements about the law and its application should be undertaken by the administrative and the judicial processes. The present laws are adequate to deal with the situation and new legislation is unnecessary.[98]

Kefauver of Tennessee repeated many of the points that had been mentioned and developed some further.[99] The O'Mahoney Bill he thought was unnecessary. It added to and did not lessen confusion. But if it should be enacted, it

---

[96] Douglas cited a letter written to him at his request by the Chairman of the Department of Mathematics at Haverford in which it was estimated that the probability of eight identical bids in 102 counties was one in eight followed by 214 zeroes. The Illinois Department of Highways in 1947 had received bids from eight cement companies which were identical within each of the 102 counties in the state. *Ibid.,* p. 11180.

[97] *Stettler* v. *O'Hara,* 243 U.S. 629 (1917).

[98] 95 *Cong. Rec.* 11181 (August 10, 1949). The Kefauver and Carroll amendments would only have "limited the bare-faced use of the basing point system," not made it obviously unlawful. *Ibid.,* p. 11185. Capehart said that Douglas was confusing the right of individual sellers acting independently to absorb freight with the basing-point system. There is perhaps less confusion than overlapping between the two. Not all freight absorption is basing point in structure, but typical basing-point systems involve freight absorption. A bill making all non-conspiratorial freight absorption lawful regardless of effect on competition could be understood to legalize basing-point systems, as Douglas asserted.

[99] Kefauver's principal presentation is to be found in 95 *Cong. Rec.* 11252 ff. (August 11, 1949).

should contain the Carroll amendments. The junior Senator from Tennessee in fact thought that the Carroll amendments were broader and provided more protection to small business than his own.[100] Kefauver reviewed the cases which the O'Mahoney Bill would affect (indeed, set aside): Corn Products, Staley, Cement, Rigid Steel, and Standard Oil— in short, all the cases in which the profile of the law was becoming more and not less clear and certain.[101] Like Douglas, Kefauver hoped that the bill would be defeated. The minimum condition of acceptance, he felt, should be the adoption of the Carroll amendments.[102] There was a strong implication that the Senators sponsoring the bill did not know what they were doing when Kefauver said that the purpose of the measure was to emasculate the antitrust laws, a purpose that the sponsoring Senators did not embrace, but which was the design of "the great lobby that is behind the bill." [103]

Hill of Alabama and Morse of Oregon made the last two speeches of importance in favor of the motion to reconsider. Hill drew freely upon the views of witnesses before the Patman Small Business Committee,[104] and the reported views of the Federal Trade Commission,[105] the Department of Justice,[106] and the press.[107] Morse of Oregon,

---

[100] *Ibid.*, p. 11253. When he first proposed his amendment, Kefauver proposed to insert the words "except where the effect of such absorption of freight will be to substantially lessen competition." He then thought that the word "will" was incorrect since the word "may" customarily appears in antitrust legislation, and substituted the word "may" for the word "will" in the printed copy of his bill. It was adopted by the Senate with the word "will," however, raising a matter of some concern to the conference committee when it looked for a version of the Kefauver-Carroll amendments that would be satisfactory to both the House and the Senate.

[101] *Ibid.*, p. 11252.
[102] *Ibid.*, p. 11261.
[103] *Ibid.*
[104] *Ibid.*, pp. 11266, 11271.

[105] *Ibid.*, p. 11268.
[106] *Ibid.*, p. 11267.
[107] *Ibid.*, p. 11271.

although feeling that the bill would eventually pass into law,[108] nevertheless conducted a vigorous attack upon it. He deplored what seemed to him to be a breach of the usual senatorial practice when sentiment exists to reconsider a vote by which bills are sent to conference. The customary practice he had found was to permit reconsideration by unanimous consent, without debating the motion.[109] This courtesy had been withheld by the chairman of the Senate Judiciary Committee, who had originally called for a vote on sending the bill to conference when Kefauver, with whom he had had an agreement to give prior notice, was not in his seat.[110] Morse wanted the record to show that the proponents of the bill wanted to take refuge in the protection of a technicality in the rule.[111]

Morse preferred the Carroll amendment to the Kefauver amendment because the latter contained the inadvertent word "will" and he applauded Kefauver's forthrightness in accepting the Carroll amendment in place of his own.[112] He made an exposition of the actual operation of basing-point systems,[113] thereby carrying forward the excellent lecture given to the Senate by Douglas and others on economics. He twitted O'Mahoney with a news release issued by the Senator from Wyoming, dated July 11, 1948, in which the basing-point system was condemned, the reader

---

[108] In a colloquy with Senator Douglas, Senator Morse said: "But I am sure the Senator from Illinois will agree with me that the probabilities are that Senate Bill 1008 will be finally passed by the Senate." *Ibid.*, p. 11274. And again, "But I recognize that a bill is going to be passed, and therefore I am going to do the very best I can to patch it up." *Ibid.*, p. 11280.

[109] *Ibid.*, p. 11272.   [110] *Ibid.*, p. 11273.

[111] Long of Louisiana was also absent, being "on my way to the Senate Chamber at the time the motion was made." *Ibid.*, p. 10150 (July 26, 1949). The agreement was made between McCarran and Kefauver. Russell of Georgia had also asked McCarran to be notified. Long spoke of the "low tone of voice" in which McCarran had put the motion to send the bill to conference. *Ibid.*, p. 10151.

[112] *Ibid.*, p. 11274 (August 11, 1949).   [113] *Ibid.*, pp. 11274–11284.

was warned that the steel industry would try to lay the basis for a demand that Congress change the antitrust law, and a case was made for a good faith abandonment of the basing-point system in favor of f.o.b. pricing.[114] He thought that the news release left some in doubt as to how the Senator from Wyoming could justify his position on S. 1008.

On the last day of the three-day debate on the motion to reconsider, the time was divided equally (under a unanimous consent agreement) between the supporters and opponents of the motion. Wherry of Nebraska led off against the motion to reconsider by asserting that the bill (S. 1008) had been used as a medium for airing wholesale violations of the antitrust laws. He thought that S. 1008 was designed to restore the competitive conditions "which were revolutionized by the Supreme Court opinion in the Cement case." [115] The issue was a simple one, and he proceeded to explain it in terms of horse trading on the farm. Douglas made a summary of his previous speech.[116] O'Conor of Maryland concentrated upon the Carroll amendments, which he thought meant to "amend the Robinson-Patman Act except in any respect in which it is in force." [117] Among the authorities invoked in favor of S. 1008 was John D. Clark of the Council of Economic Advisers, described by Johnson of Colorado as a great liberal who, although his father left him a fortune, "did not become a playboy at all." [118]

The suggestion made the day before by Morse, that Sena-

---

[114] *Ibid.*, pp. 11284–11285.   [115] *Ibid.*, p. 11326 (August 12, 1949).
[116] *Ibid.*, pp. 11329–11331.   [117] *Ibid.*, p. 11335.
[118] *Ibid.*, p. 11268 (August 11, 1949). See testimony of Clark cited by O'Conor, *ibid.*, p. 1135 (August 12, 1949). Long of Louisiana suggested that Clark was one of the "great Standard Oil executives" who had been "one of the foremost advocates of the legalization of the basing-point system itself" and that if the bill met with Mr. Clark's approval that fact might "indicate that the bill might actually legalize the basing-point system." *Ibid.*, p. 11268 (August 11, 1949).

tor O'Mahoney was professing a view inconsistent with one he held on July 11, 1948, was further developed by Long.[119] O'Mahoney maintained his position that S. 1008 contained nothing which affected the basing-point system or the multiple basing-point system.[120] He argued that if S. 1008 was defeated, steel could go back to f.o.b. mill prices and then prevent any other state from developing a steel industry.[121] It was put to him that he had once said that it was desirable public policy for the steel companies to go on an f.o.b. pricing basis. O'Mahoney's answer was that the TNEC report had indicated that a change in f.o.b. pricing must allow industry time for adjustment. He saw around him now opportunities for new competitive enterprises to enter industry and believed that they could not do it without being permitted to absorb freight.[122]

Sparkman of Alabama reviewed the history of the pressure that had been organized to produce changes in the antitrust laws by Congress.[123] He paid special attention to the effect of the abolition of the basing-point system on the sugar beet industry of Colorado, Wyoming, and other mountain states and concluded that the result would not be harmful to that industry in those states.[124] This seems to have been an appeal to the chief proponents of the legislation from important sugar beet states, Johnson of Colorado and O'Mahoney of Wyoming. Pepper of Florida developed the case against the basing-point system with special reference to Florida.[125] With some further remarks by Long and Kefauver, the struggle to get the Senate to reconsider the

---

[119] *Ibid.*, p. 11343 (August 12, 1949).   [120] *Ibid.*, p. 11344.
[121] *Ibid.*   [122] *Ibid.*, p. 11345.
[123] He also utilized the material reported by James W. Daniel, Washington correspondent of the *Rocky Mountain News*, December 17 and 22, 1948, describing the activities of an organization which set out to produce a "grass roots demand" for change in the law. 95 *Cong. Rec.* 11347 (August 12, 1949).
[124] *Ibid.*, pp. 11347–11350.   [125] *Ibid.*, pp. 11350–11354.

motion to send the bill to conference ended. It was a struggle that had been waged in the main by Senators from southern and midwestern states against Senators from the steel
and beet sugar states.

Before the vote was taken on the motion to reconsider,
McCarran undertook to defend O'Mahoney, as Johnson
had previously done.[126] The McCarran statement was notable chiefly for the suggestion that the O'Mahoney Bill was
more antimonopolistic than "any bill which was likely to
come out of the Committee on the Judiciary after the year
of study which was contemplated during the period of
moratorium" which the Myers Bill provided.[127] The motion to reconsider the vote to send S. 1008 to conference was
lost twenty-eight to forty-nine,[128] and McCarran was stopped
by Langer of North Dakota in a maneuver to have O'Mahoney and Jenner of Indiana added to the conference committee.[129]

The First Conference Report

The final passage at arms in the First Session of the
Eighty-first Congress took place over the conference committee report, which was submitted in the closing days of
the session.[130] As reported by the conference committee,
the compromise bill was unacceptable to Celler, chairman

---

[126] Johnson had said, "The chemical industries of the West wanted
to go ahead without further delay. They had to have matters clarified
so they could develop the industries they had in mind. Industries
wanted to get under way in Wyoming. They were demanding that the
matter be settled. They persuaded the Senator [i.e., O'Mahoney] they
needed action at once and the present bill is the result." *Ibid.*, p. 11345.

[127] *Ibid.*, p. 11354.   [128] *Ibid.*, p. 11360.

[129] McCarran asked for unanimous consent to augment the number
of Senate conferees and to add Jenner and O'Mahoney, but Langer
objected and unanimous consent was therefore not secured. *Ibid.*

[130] After the Senate action sending the measure to conference, the
House insisted on its amendments, agreed to the conference (*ibid.*, p.

of the House Judiciary Committee, and Willis of Louisiana.[131] It was acceptable to the three Republican conferees and one Democrat, Representative Walter of Pennsylvania, who was on the high seas but had cabled his proxy, not to a member of his party, but to a member of the minority party.[132]

S. 1008, as finally proposed in the conference report, amended the Federal Trade Commission Act to provide that it should not be regarded as an unfair trade practice for sellers acting independently to absorb freight and quote delivered prices.[133] The benefits of the act were withheld from any combination, conspiracy, or collusive agreement, and from any monopolistic, oppressive, deceptive, or fraudulent practice carried out by the use of freight absorption or delivered prices. This provision had been included in both House and Senate versions of S. 1008. Neither the Carroll nor the Kefauver amendment, as such, was accepted by the conference committee, but language from both was borrowed. The Robinson-Patman Act was amended to make it lawful for sellers independently to absorb freight or quote delivered prices unless the effect of these practices "upon competition will be to substantially lessen competition." This was language from the Kefauver amendment that Kefauver had repudiated. Even where the forbidden effect was shown, however, the conference report provided that a meeting in good faith of the lower prices of

11583, August 16, 1949) and appointed conferees August 16, 1949. The conference report, H. Rep. No. 1422, was submitted to the House on October 14, 1949, and debated. *Ibid.*, p. 14605 ff. (October 14, 1949).

[131] *Ibid.*, p. 14605 (October 14, 1949).

[132] Michener of Michigan. Walter's views about the legislation were closer to those of Michener than to either of the other two conferees of his own party. See Michener's statement, *ibid.*, p. 14613.

[133] *Ibid.*, pp. 14613–14615.

a competitor should be a complete defense to a charge of unlawful discrimination, regardless of its effect upon competition. It would therefore be possible for the Federal Trade Commission to prove a prohibited discrimination to which good faith would be a complete defense.

The press reported (as the conference report indicated) that S. 1008 would overrule the Seventh Circuit Court decision in the Standard Oil Case, where a prohibited effect upon competition vitiated the defense of good faith in a charge of unlawful price discrimination.[134] Moreover, the language of the proposed bill required the Commission to demonstrate illegal effects of price discrimination with "reliable, probative and substantial evidence." This threw out the rule of the Morton Salt Case, where the Commission had been required to prove only a "reasonable possibility" that the effect of a price discrimination would injure competition unlawfully.[135] The general exemption extended to nonconspiratorial freight absorption would have nullified the holding on Count II in the Rigid Steel Conduit Case and would have weakened the theoretical basis of the Cement Case, and the Glucose cases which preceded it.

Carroll of Colorado supported Celler's objection to the conference report and explained the circumstances under which the word "will" had come into the Kefauver amendment instead of "may." He proposed that the report be recommitted or that no legislation on the subject at all should be sought.[136] Others felt as Carroll did.[137] Strong statements in support of the conference report were made by Halleck of Indiana [138] and Michener of Michigan.[139] The proceedings were short, and, after a motion to recom-

---

[134] *Wall Street Journal,* October 13, 1949, p. 8, col. 2.

[135] *Federal Trade Commission* v. *Morton Salt Company,* 334, U.S. 37, 68 S.Ct. 822 (1948), p. 830.

[136] 95 *Cong. Rec.* 14607 (October 14, 1949).

[137] For example, Boggs of Louisiana, *ibid.,* p. 14608.

[138] *Ibid.,* pp. 14608–14609.   [139] *Ibid.,* pp. 14613–14615.

mit was lost,[140] the conference report was adopted by the House by a vote of 200 to 104.[141]

With the submission of the conference report to the Senate,[142] the opponents of S. 1008 had picked up another ally—time.[143] The Senate was in the last days of the First Session of the Eighty-first Congress, and Congressmen wanted to expedite their business in order to get home. O'Conor was reported to be confident that he had enough votes to push the bill through.[144] The pressure was so great that the sponsors of the conference report actually managed to slip it through the Senate in a Saturday night session with what Douglas described as "supersonic speed." [145] The action was recalled by the timely attentiveness of Douglas and Long. The Senator from Illinois said that he and Long were standing close to the Chair, but even then they could not hear the question which was stated, "and we were startled by the almost instantaneous announcement that the report had been agreed to." This tactic was reminiscent of the manner in which the motion to send the bill to conference had been put over. If Douglas and Long had not been watching for the Saturday night motion, the Senate would have enacted a fundamental reform of the antitrust laws that had never·had hearings in either the House or the Senate, that few legislators understood, and that had been put on the books by inadvertence.

---

[140] *Ibid.*, p. 14616. The vote was 138 to 178, with 116 not voting.

[141] *Ibid.*, pp. 14616–14617. There were 128 not voting.

[142] *Ibid.*, p. 14702 (October 15, 1949).

[143] See *ibid.*, pp. 14720–14721 (October 17, 1949), where Lucas of Illinois arranged the schedule of the Senate, including the conference report debate.

[144] The *Journal of Commerce*, October 18, 1949, p. 2, cols. 6–8. Senator Long told reporters that Douglas would not filibuster, but that he had no objection to doing so. See also *Journal of Commerce*, October 19, 1949, p. 1, col. 8, where mention is made of a sizable stack of books brought to the Senate by Long.

[145] 95 *Cong. Rec.* 14781 (October 17, 1949).

The last debate on S. 1008 began when Douglas objected
to the conference report in its entirety.[146] He expressed the
opinion that S. 1008 legalized the basing-point system and
the postage stamp and zone systems of pricing, and would
produce a reversal of the entire policy of the government
in the pricing field.[147] In addition, he felt that the bill really
repealed the Robinson-Patman Act.[148] Hill of Alabama contributed a recollection of William Jennings Bryan, who
once in a debate against a tariff bill referred to the banyan
tree which entices the unwary native to seek its fruit only
to be crushed by the powerful limbs of the tree.[149] Capehart wanted to talk about the Miller-Tydings Act, which
Douglas said was as relevant to S. 1008 as canasta.[150] As he
had warned in an early phase of his speech, Douglas at its
conclusion moved that further consideration of the conference report on S. 1008 be postponed until January 20,
1950.[151] O'Conor immediately moved to table the motion,
and on the yeas and nays the motion was lost, twenty-nine to
twenty-nine, the Chair indicating that its vote would be in
the negative.[152]

The denouement was supplied by O'Mahoney, who
turned against the bill he had sponsored and gave his support to Douglas. He expressed his pleasure that the Douglas
motion was not laid upon the table,[153] and he urged that
it be adopted. His principal point was that the conference

---

[146] Douglas got unanimous consent to hold the floor on October 17
and to permit him to resume the debate the next morning, October
18. *Ibid.*, p. 14784.

[147] *Ibid.*, p. 14834 (October 18, 1949).   [148] *Ibid.*, p. 14835.

[149] *Ibid.*, p. 14836. Douglas thought that this illustration was more
graphic than the spider and fly analogy.

[150] *Ibid.*, p. 14836.

[151] Douglas' first motion was to recommit the report to the conference committee with the request that it report on January 20, 1950.
This was ruled out of order since the House had already acted. *Ibid.*,
p. 14841.

[152] *Ibid.*, p. 14842.   [153] *Ibid.*

committee version of S. 1008 permitted the Federal Trade
Commission to proceed against prohibited forms of freight
absorption only where the effect of the absorption *will* be
to lessen competition substantially, not where there might
be a reasonable probability of this result.[154] The committee
had retained language from the original or inadvertent
version of the Kefauver amendment; O'Mahoney thought
that the Carroll version was preferable. O'Mahoney warned
that if consideration was not postponed, he would have to
vote against the bill that he had introduced.[155] The conference bill not only did not clear away misunderstandings
but created fresh ones. O'Mahoney said that he had always
understood independent freight absorption to be legal and
was glad to have the recent opinion of the Fourth Circuit
Court of Appeals in the case of *Bond Crown and Cork Company* v. *Federal Trade Commission* confirm this belief.[156]
He concluded by explaining why he had got into the controversy in the first place—to help Wyoming beets and
chemicals [157]—but he now felt that the conference report
version of his bill would work to the disadvantage of these
industries by "locking up the natural resources of the West
in the hands of the monopolists." This statement (perhaps
it might be called a "recantation") was documented by a
letter from O'Mahoney to Mr. Robert D. Pike, in which the
latter was assured that the courts, the Commission, and the
Department of Justice would continue to support the legality of independent freight absorption.[158]

With the conclusion of O'Mahoney's speech, the opposition to Douglas' motion collapsed. The Senate quickly
agreed by voice vote to postpone consideration of the conference report to January 20, 1950.[159]

---

[154] *Ibid.,* pp. 14842–14845.   [155] *Ibid.,* p. 14845.
[156] 176 F. 2nd 974 (C.C.A. 4th 1949). 95 *Cong. Rec.* 14844 (October
18, 1949).
[157] 95 *Cong. Rec.* 14845 (October 18, 1949).
[158] *Ibid.,* pp. 14847–14848.   [159] *Ibid.,* p. 14848.

A Temporary Balance

The drive to amend the antitrust laws and overrule major decisions of the federal courts had begun in the summer of 1948, when steel customers, and others, stimulated by the new pricing policy of the steel industry, appeared on the stage of the Capehart Committee and asked that Congress "clarify" the law on pricing. The trouble was not that the law was unclear but that it was becoming clearer as the Federal Trade Commission and the courts applied the Federal Trade Commission and Clayton Acts (as amended) to new situations. The principal effect of the two measures to enact permanent amendment to these statutes—S. 236 and O'Mahoney's S. 1008—would have been to set aside the new decisions. A trend was to be stopped and perhaps reversed, not made more viable in the directions freshly opened.

After the somewhat elaborate propaganda prepared by the Capehart hearings for a Congress that the voters did not elect, the effort to write a permanent statutory amendment of the antitrust laws proceeded briefly, but was soon abandoned because of the complexity of the problem and the desire of the proponents of change for quick results. The Myers moratorium was to serve this desire. At the critical point, however, the proponents of legislative intervention against the Commission and the courts found themselves being led, to their joyful surprise, by Senator O'Mahoney, who seems to have been influential in bringing along the Commission and the Department of Justice also. If Kefauver had not amended S. 1008, however inadvertently, as it whisked through the Senate, one of the fastest-breaking squeeze plays in recent legislative history would have reversed developments in the law of pricing that had taken years to mature. The Kefauver amendment slowed up proceedings in the House, made a conference necessary, and thereby gave time for an opposition to crystallize and organize. Even with this small gain, two stratagems threatened to deprive the new opposition of full opportunity to state and discuss its objections. These were the maneuvers that almost sent S. 1008 to conference on tiptoe and then almost whirled the conference report through the Senate with "supersonic speed."

Few Congressmen seemed to know quite what they were doing, and on S. 1008, at least, there was almost no way for them to find out, since the O'Mahoney Bill was given no hearings in the Senate and no public hearings in the House Judiciary Committee. The only public hearings it received were held by a committee that had no jurisdiction over the measure. The Capehart hearings were useless as a basis for legislation. The residuum which the Capehart hearings left was that the witnesses, understandably, would feel uncomfortable in the dream world of required f.o.b. pricing that was imagined for them. The hearings on S. 236 were perfunctory at best, and full investigation of alternatives was missing.

The Federal Trade Commission looked no more sure of itself at points than some of the Congressmen. Under pressure, the Commission seemed to abandon at least one position that it had assumed before the courts and permitted itself to be reported as not objecting to the O'Mahoney Bill, although it had declined to support either S. 236 or the Myers moratorium. Moreover, direct statements were made in Congress to the effect that the Commission staff was responsible for language in the O'Mahoney Bill.

It need not be supposed that those who supported the O'Mahoney Bill were willful wreckers of the antitrust laws, for the choices were not simple and clear-cut. Few argued that required f.o.b. pricing was desirable. Most accepted the view that independent freight absorption made in good faith with no adverse effect upon competition was desirable. But neither Johnson, Myers, nor O'Mahoney had succeeded in producing a bill to protect this kind of freight absorption without at the same time lending countenance to practices that would be restrictive of competition, be hard to detect, and be harder to prove. It is not difficult to understand that the harassed Congressman, importuned by restless constituents, preferred to risk abuse of the law if he could protect the concerns of those innocent in intention. Indeed, O'Mahoney himself seemed to have made somewhat this kind of choice. The alternatives, however, become a little clearer if it is established that the fears are unfounded. One does not then have to assume the risk.

The struggle was not over, however. The most that had been accomplished was a precarious balance of power which the advocates of revision were not quite able to tip decisively in their favor. The opponents of revision, on the other hand, were incapable of doing more than hold; in this their effort was helped by the desire of the revisionists to close business for the First Session. The showdown was to come in the Second Session.

Chapter Five

The President

Defeats Congress

Throughout the controversy over S. 1008 in both sessions of the Eighty-first Congress, the Federal Trade Commission continued to assert that it did not regard independent freight absorption as a violation of the Clayton and Robinson-Patman Acts.[1] And there is reason to believe that many of the cement companies continued to practice independent freight absorption after the Cement Case. For example, the Commission, at the request of Senator Douglas of Illinois, made known the results of a questionnaire sent to cement producers which asked whether they proposed to practice such independent freight absorption after the Cement Case, and a majority of those responding said that they did.[2] There was also some evidence in the Capehart

---

[1] See statement of Commissioner Edwin L. Davis, *Senate Hearings on S. 236*, referred to and discussed above, pp. 113–115.

[2] 96 *Cong. Rec.* 7866–7869 (May 31, 1950). Douglas in a letter to the Chairman of the Federal Trade Commission dated March 16, 1950, asked for information about the pricing practices of cement companies. The information supplied by the Commission was a résumé of the reports of compliance which were filed pursuant to the cease and desist order in the Cement Case in September of 1948. The information related to the practices obtaining in September, 1949, five months after the Supreme Court decision, or to the practices that the respondents at that time intended to employ in the future. There

hearings that at least one cement company did not think that it was inhibited from absorbing freight so long as it was not in conspiracy or collusion.[3] And, of course, Senator O'Mahoney at the end of the First Session of the Eighty-first Congress had said that he was satisfied that the law did not prevent independent freight absorption.

These persistent disclaimers, however, did not quiet anxiety, some real and some assumed, about the meaning of the law and the status of freight absorption in the courts

---

were fifty-five respondent cement producers, operating some 152 plants. Of this number, only five companies operating fifteen plants said definitely that they would not absorb freight, and of these only three companies operating three plants said that they would not absorb freight because of the Cement Case. Of this report, Senator Douglas said, "One hundred and thirteen plants out of 152 have in effect stated that they would absorb freight. They know that it is not illegal unless it is used as an unfair method of competition. The claim that this bill is needed in order to permit freight absorption is thus disproved by the actual practices of the cement industry, including the Universal Atlas Co., under existing law." *Ibid.*, p. 7869 (May 31, 1950). The Universal Atlas Cement Company is a subsidiary of the United States Steel Corporation, which helped to generate pressure for a revision of the antitrust laws by changing its pricing practice to f.o.b. mill in July, 1948. See above. Senator Douglas also asked the Federal Trade Commission to supply information about intercorporate relationships among companies which reported that they did not intend to absorb freight in any manner, but the Acting Chairman of the Commission did not have such information. *Ibid.*, p. 7866 (May 31, 1950).

[3] See testimony of Edward A. Zimmerman, in *Senate Hearings on S. 236,* p. 247. One evidence of change in the pricing practices of cement companies was supplied by Senator Douglas in a series of tables he introduced in the Senate on May 31, 1950, identified as "Summary of Identical Bids on Cement to State and Federal Government Agencies by Cement Companies before and after the Supreme Court Decision of April 26, 1948, in the Cement Institute Case," 96 *Cong. Rec.* 7858 (May 31, 1950). The tables showed identity of bids before the Cement Case and diversity after it. Of this evidence, Douglas said, "It proves conclusively that the basing point system was responsible for the absence of price competition and the almost absolute identity of prices which had prevailed for over 40 years in the cement industry." 96 *Cong. Rec.* 7858 (May 31, 1950).

and the Federal Trade Commission. The movement to revise the antitrust laws which was temporarily halted in October 1949 was resumed in January 1950, and it eventually succeeded, in Congress. The revisionists (the O'Mahoney group) found it considerably less difficult to get their measure through the Second Session than they had in the first. They suffered eventual defeat however in the White House when the President joined the antirevisionists and vetoed the bill, after having permitted the Bureau of the Budget to state earlier that S. 1008 was in accord with the program of the President.[4]

There was at least one point of difference between the First and Second Sessions in the consideration of S. 1008. In the Second Session the members of Congress, with some exceptions, seemed to know what the stakes were in the controversy. Although the dispute over technical details was tortuous and complex, Congressmen were able eventually to make up their minds on the controversial measure, thanks to the determined persistence of the antirevisionists in holding, on the floor of the Senate, the hearing which S. 1008 had not been accorded in committee.[5] In the Second

---

[4] Much was made by Senator O'Conor of Maryland and others of the endorsement given to S. 1008 by the Bureau of the Budget. See for example the statement by Johnson of Colorado that "on June 28, 1949, the Bureau of the Budget wrote the chairman of the Rules Committee that this bill, then in stronger form than at present, was in accord with the program of the President." *Ibid.*, p. 7940 (June 2, 1950). To those who are familiar with the proposed legislation and the program of the President, it will be evident that such accordance sometimes means only that the President has no policy to state which is, at the time, different from the policies of the official groups in the executive establishment who have some interest in the subject matter.

[5] Despite the irrefutable record, O'Conor of Maryland in the final stages of the debate on S. 1008 sought to establish the proposition that the hearings accorded were not only ample but extensive. *Ibid.*, pp. 7731–7732 (May 25, 1950). In reaching this result he counted as "hearings" the sessions of the Senate Committee on Interstate and Foreign Commerce on Sen. Res. 241, S. 236, and S. 1008 in the Myers version,

Session, the measure was referred to as a "basing-point bill" even by its supporters, although the nomenclature was not universal, and some preferred to consider it as a "freight absorption bill." [6]

The Autumn Maneuvers

When Congress convened for the Second Session, it was evident that a considerable amount of maneuvering had

---

none of which dealt with the bill before the Senate. Johnson of Colorado was even more specific if just as inaccurate in his conclusion. He counted thirty days of hearings, twenty-two in the Senate and eight in the House. Of the eight in the House, five were held by the House Small Business Committee, which had no legislative jurisdiction of S. 1008, one was held by the Rules Committee, which dealt with the scheduling of the bill in the House, and one was held by the House Judiciary Committee, which opened its door to Congressman Patman briefly before deciding formally to report the bill favorably to the House. Of the twenty-two days of supposed hearings in the Senate, all took place before O'Mahoney introduced his substitute for the Myers moratorium, upon which the Senate held no hearings of any kind. The only effective hearings, indeed the only hearings in the Senate on the O'Mahoney version of S. 1008, were the eight days of debate on conference reports (not on the bill itself) which the anti-revisionists forced through the original Kefauver amendment. See 96 *Cong. Rec.* 7942 (June 2, 1950) for Johnson's summary of the legislative history.

[6] When the O'Mahoney version of S. 1008 was introduced in the Senate, and in much of the early discussion of the measure, brief as it was, the proposal was represented as one to permit independent freight absorption, and it was argued that it was not designed to legalize basing-point pricing practices. In the Second Session of the 81st Congress, however, the bill was freely referred to as a basing-point bill. See 96 *Cong. Rec.* 4450 (March 31, 1950) where in a colloquy between Ferguson of Michigan and McCarran of Nevada the bill is called a basing-point bill without any effort to employ the earlier periphrasis. Some members of the House of Representatives, however, thought that it was of some value to make the proper distinctions. Walter of Pennsylvania felt that S. 1008 should not be called a basing-point bill because it merely legalized independent freight absorption. *Ibid.,* p. 2504 (February 28, 1950). Kilburn of New York said, "It is no more a basing-point bill than the FEPC bill, and any charge made that it would reestablish the basing-point system is without foundation." *Ibid.,* p. 2506 (February 28, 1950).

taken place among the parties-in-interest since the October decision to defer further action until January 20, 1950. The Patman-Douglas-Long group had organized increased pressure upon Congressmen through groups speaking for small businessmen, and the O'Mahoney group had drafted the support of the Department of Justice in the drive against the Federal Trade Commission and its policies. Thus these two combinations of groups struggled with each other to write the rules on basing points, with most of the leverage in Congress working for O'Mahoney's advantage. Behind him were the most powerful of the unofficial groups—the industrial forces—and an array of official agencies like the Department of Justice and the Bureau of the Budget, strong in prestige and influence.

One of the many paradoxes of the struggle over the basing-point legislation was the insistence of all the revisionists (the O'Mahoney combination) that they were helping small business and protecting its interests by supporting S. 1008, although the standard organizations of small businessmen had been lined up by Patman in opposition to O'Mahoney's designs.[7] The Capehart Committee had

---

[7] Few of the Congressmen showed their awareness of the many paradoxes but among them was Senator Langer of North Dakota. He referred to the two revisionist arguments that canceled each other: (1) that failure to enact S. 1008 would make ghost towns of the steel- and cement-producing centers; and that (2) failure to enact S. 1008 would create local monopolies in the steel- and cement-producing centers. Said Langer, if these predictions were to come true simultaneously, "we should find all the steel fabricators converging on Pittsburgh, and find there nothing but a ghost town, because the steel industry would have moved to where the fabricators came from and would there have established themselves little local monopolies." *Ibid.*, p. 4598 (April 3, 1950). Wherry of Nebraska referred to the bill as one "in the interest of all industry, and especially of the small businessmen of the country." *Ibid.*, p. 700 (January 20, 1950). Later he said, "The junior Senator from Nebraska yields to no Member of the Senate or to anyone else as a defender of small business." *Ibid.*, p. 7956 (June 2, 1950). But he showed annoyance at the organizations of druggists

previously piped the "small business" pitch to which the revisionist tune was later played. But the organized small businessmen groups had had small say in the Capehart proceedings and no visible influence there. They became more insistent (although still small of voice) during the hearings on S. 236 and on the Myers version of S. 1008, and were in full cry in the Patman Committee on Small Business. During the autumn months of 1949, all members of Congress (especially Senators) were subjected to forceful and frequent pressure by small business organizations whose spokesmen pounded out the theme that S. 1008 was offensive to small business.[8] Most of those who acknowledged this

---

and gasoline dealers. See *ibid.*, p. 7957 (June 2, 1950) where he reports the judgment of the Wisconsin Supreme Court affirming the conviction of some gasoline dealers of conspiracy to fix prices.

[8] According to the National Farmers Union, as reported in its weekly news letter of April 21, 1950, a coalition of small business groups and their farm and labor allies and supporters was organized by Congressman Patman of Texas as an antimonopoly committee, the purpose of which was to resist the enactment of S. 1008. The organizations so combined were the American Farm Bureau Federation, The American Federation of Labor, American Retail Federation, Congress of Industrial Organizations, Cooperative League of the United States, Credit Union National Association, Inc., International Association of Machinists, National Association of Independent Tire Dealers, National Association of Retail Druggists, National Candy Wholesalers Association, National Congress of Petroleum Retailers, Inc., National Council of Farmer Cooperatives, National Federation of Independent Business, Inc., National Food Brokers Association, National Grange, National Rural Electric Cooperative Association, Railway Labor Executives Association, and United States Wholesale Grocers Association. See 96 *Cong. Rec.* 7795–7796 (May 26, 1950), for letters and lists of groups joined in the struggle to defeat S. 1008. Many of the Congressmen who were pressured by these organized groups reacted with uneasiness and resentment. Bricker of Ohio, for example, said that "those who support the Federal Trade Commission's policies of soft competition have conducted a thorough, and somewhat unsuccessful, campaign to enlist the aid of small business." *Ibid.*, p. 7898 (June 1, 1950). Johnson of Colorado spoke in similar vein, "Opposition to the bill has come mainly from the retail druggists who have attacked it as a peril to their businesses. It is my considered opinion that these in-

pressure publicly said that they would still support S. 1008, that is, that they would go ahead to help "small business" whether the spokesmen for small business wanted them to or not, but some were made unsure by the pressure applied against them.[9] This pressure continued up to the final action on the bill. On the day of the Senate vote which finally passed the bill, every member of the Senate received a telegram against the measure, signed by spokesmen for the

---

spired attacks by some retail druggists are based wholly on false and misleading information which has been given to them. It is my further belief that this misinformation was willfully given to the retail druggists by those who would use these retailers as tools to accomplish a purpose which is not in the interests of those druggists." *Ibid.*, p. 7940 (June 2, 1950). O'Mahoney of Wyoming was more specific: "We are seeking to maintain a competitive system, but the great campaign alleging that we are upsetting the Robinson-Patman Act has emanated chiefly from the Retail Druggists Association, which was the sponsor of the Miller-Tydings law, the sole purpose of which was to eliminate competition." *Ibid.*, p. 7913 (June 1, 1950).

[9] Thye of Minnesota showed constant concern. He mentioned the large number of telegrams and letters "both from druggists within my State and from the National Druggists Association, as well as from those engaged in the grocery business," all of them asking him to vote against S. 1008. *Ibid.*, pp. 680–681 (January 20, 1950). He said that he had "been besieged with telegrams and telephone calls from druggists who ask that I block this proposed legislation." *Ibid.*, p. 703 (January 20, 1950). Later he said, "I have heard from the meat dealers in my State. I have had numerous letters from the Drug Association; in fact some of them most caustic in their criticism of me because I had not definitely stated that I would oppose this conference report. In fact, some of the letters, as I stated, have almost been bordering on insult because I had not committed myself positively to vote against this report." *Ibid.*, p. 7734 (May 25, 1950). A "large number of students at the University" also took a hand when they sent Senator Thye a petition deploring the effect of S. 1008 on the Clayton and Robinson-Patman Acts. *Ibid.* Robertson of Virginia seemed somewhat more resolute and although he said that "all of us have been flooded with letters" and pointed a finger of suspicion at "the patron of the Patman-Robinson Act," his chief concern at an early stage of the proceedings in the Second Session was apprehension lest the House conferees tie up S. 1008 if recommitted to them, "so that the Senate could not get the measure back before it again." *Ibid.*, p. 680 (January 20, 1950).

United States Wholesale Grocers Association, Inc., the National Federation of Independent Business, the National Congress of Petroleum Retailers, the National Association of Retail Druggists, the National Association of Independent Tire Dealers, the International Association of Machinists, the National Farmers Union, and the Cooperative League of the United States, but it failed to prevent the enactment of legislation which Senators said was for the benefit of the groups which rejected it.[10] The refusal to conform to the views of the established organizations interested in small business may seem somewhat perverse when one considers O'Mahoney's statement that it was "representatives of some of the large concentrated industries" that had "delude[d] independent competitors into the belief that now, if they individually adopted delivered prices, or if they individually absorbed freight, they would be violating the law." [11]

Although the main effort of the O'Mahoney group in the interval between the two sessions of Congress was bent toward enlisting the support of the Department of Justice in a minimum revision of the conference report, there were various supporting actions. For example, the combination of groups that had participated in the Capehart hearings was re-formed on a reduced scale under the title, The Coun-

---

[10] Statement of Fulbright of Arkansas, in which he chided Wherry of Nebraska for his attitude toward the organized small business groups, recalling that Wherry in the past had "seemed to have some regard for the established organizations which are interested in small business." *Ibid.*, p. 7958 (June 2, 1950).

[11] Statement made in colloquy with Douglas of Illinois. *Ibid.*, p. 7817 (May 26, 1950). At a later point, O'Mahoney, in support of the measure that would have made it more difficult for the Federal Trade Commission to control price combines, aspersed the organized druggists with the remark, "If the National Retail Druggists had their way, price competition would be unlawful." *Ibid.*, p. 7971 (June 2, 1950).

cil for the Clarification of Pricing Practices. A group of thirteen members, it was made up (in the main) of members of the Capehart Advisory Committee, a former member of the Capehart Committee, and witnesses who had appeared before that committee to testify for legislation. Legal and public relations services were provided by the former counsel of the Capehart Committee, who was said by Senator Langer of North Dakota to have received a retainer of $1,500 a month.[12] The Senator from North Dakota could have been wrong about the fee, however, for the report of counsel under the Regulation of Lobbying Act for the fall quarter of 1949 lists reimbursable expenditures in approximately this amount.[13]

It was a principal stratagem of the O'Mahoney revisionists in the interval between the two sessions of the Eighty-first Congress to exploit the rivalry and conflict of interest between two official groups, the Department of Justice and the Federal Trade Commission.[14] Although O'Mahoney in October 1949 had indicated that he believed that independent freight absorption was legal and that new assurance of this was provided by the decision of the Fourth Circuit Court of Appeals in the Bond Crown and Cork Company Case,[15] he nevertheless went ahead to push S. 1008 to enactment. To meet some of the objections of the Patman-Douglas-Long combination to the conference report,

---

[12] *Ibid.*, p. 4598 (April 3, 1950).

[13] *Ibid.*, p. 1243 (January 31, 1950). In the group comprising the Council for the Clarification of Pricing Practices, Senator Langer noted that two were college professors, and he wondered aloud whether academic salaries had advanced enough to permit the payment of any considerable part of the expenses of the Council. *Ibid.*, p. 4598 (April 3, 1950).

[14] See above, p. 33 ff., for a discussion of the concept of officiality and the role of official agencies in the struggle of groups for advantage and security.

[15] 95 *Cong. Rec.* 14844–14845 (October 18, 1949).

O'Mahoney arranged for its revision with the assistance of the Department of Justice. At O'Mahoney's suggestion [16] the Senate managers worked with staff members of the Department to rewrite phrases of S. 1008 that dealt with the degree of proof required to establish the existence of certain unlawful pricing practices.

The critical language was contained in Section 4D of the bill. Section 4 set out definitions of the words and phrases used in S. 1008, and Section 4D defined the phrase "effect may be" to mean that "there is reliable, probative, and substantial evidence of the specified effect." The phrase "effect may be" is to be found in Section 2a of the Robinson-Patman Act, which declares that certain price discriminations are illegal, among them being those where the "effect . . . may be to substantially lessen competition." Section 4D as the conferees had phrased it would have made the proof of illegal price discrimination by the Federal Trade Commission more difficult. The Morton Salt Case had said that the Commission could inhibit price discriminations where there was a "reasonable possibility" that competition would be substantially lessened. Under 4D, the Commission would have had to establish the *injury*, not the *possibility*, by reliable, probative, and substantial evidence. The conferees said that they had simply borrowed the language of the Administrative Procedure Act of 1946, but the effect of this language was to work a considerable weakening of the Robinson-Patman Act.[17] There had been strong

---

[16] O'Conor of Maryland asserted this, 96 *Cong. Rec.* 678 (January 20, 1950).

[17] The conference report asserted that 4D applied only to S. 1008 and did not apply to other parts of the Robinson-Patman Act. But S. 1008 amended the Robinson-Patman Act, and it is not to be supposed that the courts would have defined "effect may be" in contradictory ways in the same statute. *Ibid.*, p. 679 (January 20, 1950). The Department of Justice did not agree with the conclusion of the conference report that limited the effect of 4D to S. 1008 but assumed that 4D applied throughout the Robinson-Patman Act wherever the critical

criticism of Section 4D, as there had been of other sections of S. 1008, by the antirevisionists when the conference recommendations and report were filed in the Senate, and the criticism did not abate after the Senate decided to postpone its deliberations from October to January.

In order to forestall a repetition of this criticism O'Mahoney called upon the Department of Justice to lend a hand. He arranged a conference which was attended by J. Howard McGrath, Attorney General of the United States, Peyton Ford, Assistant to the Attorney General, Herbert Bergson, head of the Antitrust division of the Department of Justice; McCarran of Nevada, chairman of the Senate Judiciary Committee; Johnson of Colorado, chairman of the Senate Committee on Interstate and Foreign Commerce; and Senator Myers of Pennsylvania, the author of the original version of S. 1008 which had been abandoned in favor of O'Mahoney's.[18] The Attorney General was invited to submit a formal opinion analyzing each section of the conference report and expressing his view as to whether new language should be adopted. He was also asked to suggest the wording that might be used. The Justice Department did submit such a formal analysis, with recommendations for changes in wording. The first three sections of S. 1008 were passed over without objection, but it was recommended that Section 4D be rewritten. The Justice Department, in a letter over the signature of Peyton Ford, recommended that the bill be amended to read as follows: "D. The term 'the effect may be' shall mean that there is reasonable probability of the specified effect."[19] The recommendation of the Department of Justice restored to

phrase appeared. The Federal Trade Commission also believed that 4D applied generally to the Robinson-Patman Act. *Ibid.,* pp. 608–609 (January 19, 1950).

[18] *Ibid.,* p. 678 (January 20, 1950).

[19] For the full text of the Ford letter see *ibid.,* p. 4492 (March 31, 1950).

the bill the version of 4D that the House had originally written, the effect of which was to retain the rule of the Supreme Court in the Morton Salt Case.[20]

Although the Senate managers for S. 1008 did not feel that any revision of 4D was really necessary, they nevertheless agreed to work for the change recommended by the Department of Justice, even though it meant accepting the House version of 4D that they had once rejected. The Senate managers could not make this change unilaterally, however, nor could any informal arrangement or understanding between the Senate and the House managers effect the legal position of S. 1008, which stood as a measure reported out of conference, to be accepted or rejected as such by the Senate. The conference report had already been adopted by the House [21] in its entirety; the Senate could no longer amend it. The only question before the Senate in January 1950 was the adoption or rejection of the conference report in toto. It was decided by the Senate managers under the leadership of O'Mahoney, therefore, to ask the Senate to reject the conference report and to send it back to the conferees for revision of 4D in accordance with the recommendations of the Department of Justice. This then was the strategy of the revisionists, perfected the week before the date scheduled for further discussion of the conference report.[22]

Although in an earlier stage of O'Mahoney's fight to get Congress to enact S. 1008 (specifically, in the First Session of the Eighty-first Congress) the Department of Justice and the Federal Trade Commission were both recorded as not objecting, the apparent harmony of view was both deceptive

---

[20] Compare the Department of Justice version of 4D with that of the House described above, p. 141 n. 79.

[21] 95 *Cong. Rec.* 14616–14617 (October 14, 1949).

[22] Peyton Ford's letter, addressed to Senator O'Conor was dated January 13, 1950. 96 *Cong. Rec.* 4492 (March 31, 1950). The scheduled date to discuss S. 1008 was January 20, 1950.

and brief. For the interests of the Department of Justice and the Federal Trade Commission were not the same, although they both dealt with aspects of the antitrust laws. The Department concerned itself with prosecutions for violation of the Sherman Act and the Commission dealt with violations of the Clayton and the Robinson-Patman Acts, being involved with the Sherman Act only when the violation of that act was also an unfair trade practice under the Clayton and Robinson-Patman Acts. The Department of Justice was not particularly friendly to the Robinson-Patman Act, and, indeed, the Assistant Attorney General in charge of the antitrust Division had appeared in opposition to that act when it was being considered by Congress.[23] Being, by nature of their responsibilities, involved in the prosecution of criminal actions under the Sherman Act, lawyers in the Department of Justice are constantly under pressure to supply a degree of proof of fact which civil actions and the litigation of cease and desist orders do not require. The nature of their court room responsibilities may generate a somewhat different outlook in the Justice lawyers, although this possibility will not bear too much emphasis. Bricker of Ohio put the conflict of interest with downright, if erroneous, simplicity when he said that he intended to vote for the conference report favoring S. 1008 because that report supported "the Justice Department's policies of free competition and reject[ed] the Federal Trade Commission policy of restricting competition."[24]

It will be recalled that while the pressure was on it during the First Session of the Eighty-first Congress, the Federal Trade Commission had had some difficulty in presenting a united front on the issues raised by S. 1008. The Commissioners were split and the staff of the Commission was also

---

[23] This point was made by Kefauver of Tennessee in debate with O'Mahoney of Wyoming, *Ibid.*, p. 7737 (May 25, 1950).

[24] *Ibid.*, p. 7898 (June 1, 1950).

split. But the Commission eventually made up its mind that S. 1008 was an unnecessary statute, that it weakened the antitrust laws, and that it should be thoroughly and completely opposed. By the beginning of the Second Session, the Commission definitely opposed the measure and thus was brought into clear conflict with the Department of Justice, which did not oppose the bill at all [25] but co-operated with O'Mahoney in revising it to facilitate its enactment.

Since the strategy of the revisionists brought them into collaboration with the Department of Justice, the opposing strategy of the antirevisionists moved them to enlist the aid of the Federal Trade Commission. On January 19, 1950, the day before the Senate was scheduled formally to open consideration of the conference report on S. 1008, Kefauver of Tennessee placed in the *Congressional Record* two letters from the Federal Trade Commission in answer to his request for a statement of Commission views about S. 1008.[26] The first letter represented the majority view in the Commission and the second was the separate and dissenting view of the Acting Chairman of the Commission, Lowell Mason. These communications were accompanied by a Commission analysis of the conference committee version of S. 1008, an analysis which Kefauver had requested. The Commission was unequivocally of the opinion that the

[25] In the same month, January 1950, the conflict of view between the Department of Justice and the Federal Trade Commission was illustrated in another official forum. The Department of Justice normally argues cases on behalf of the Federal Trade Commission in the Supreme Court but did not do so in the Standard Oil Case, reputedly because the Department did not agree with the Commission's position in that case, that good faith was not a complete defense in complaints of price discrimination under the Robinson-Patman Act. See article by Joseph R. Slevin, *Journal of Commerce,* January 19, 1950, and discussion of the Department of Justice's failure to appear for the Commission in 96 *Cong. Rec.* 701–702 (January 20, 1950).

[26] 96 *Cong. Rec.* 608–609 (January 19, 1950). Kefauver made his request for a statement of Commission views on January 11, 1950.

bill as reported by the conference committee would seriously weaken the Clayton Act. Its comment particularly criticized Section 4D and the conflict between Sections 2B and 3.[27] In criticizing 4D, the Commission expressed the same attitude as did the Department of Justice, but in pointing out the conflict betwen 2B and 3, it was opposed where the Department of Justice was indifferent.[28] The analysis

---

[27] Section 2B made it lawful for sellers independently to absorb freight or to quote delivered prices unless the effect of these practices "upon competition will be to substantially lessen competition." But Section 3 provided that a good faith meeting of the lower prices of a competitor should be a complete defense to a charge of unlawful discrimination, regardless of its effect upon competition. See above, pp. 151–152, on this point.

[28] Of the relation between 2B and 3, the Ford letter to O'Conor had said that although 2B, "rejecting the defense of good faith competition where its effect will be to substantially lessen competition, appears both undesirable and somewhat inconsistent with section 3, permitting this defense without a similar qualification, the matter is one of legislative policy for the Congress to determine." 96 *Cong. Rec.* 4492 (March 31, 1950). Senator Kefauver of Tennessee on April 6, 1950 wrote to the Department of Justice to ask whether the Department had any objection to the contradiction between 2B and 3 apart from legislative policy as to the merits of the bill. In a letter to Kefauver, dated April 13, 1950, The Assistant to the Attorney General, Peyton Ford, replied that the Department did not think that the two sections contradicted each other but that they were somewhat inconsistent. The removal of the defense of good faith in 2B was limited to price discriminations rooted in the practice of freight absorption. The absolute defense of good faith in section 3 extended to all other discriminations. Price discriminations based upon freight absorption were not under the protection of the absolute defense of good faith available to other forms of price discrimination. Hence the two provisions were inconsistent but not contradictory. The Department of Justice had no objection to the enactment of 2B and 3 in their inconsistency, if not their contradiction. 96 *Cong. Rec.* 7737 (May 25, 1950).

However, the two provisions were not merely inconsistent because one made good faith a limited defense where price discrimination was grounded in freight absorption and the other made good faith an absolute defense where the price discrimination was not based in freight absorption. From this point of view they were perfectly consistent because they applied a different kind of defense for a different

of S. 1008 which the staff of the Commission prepared for Kefauver concluded with a strong and somewhat provocative statement that the "elementary injustice to small business which S. 1008 proposes should be obvious to all Members of Congress, whether or not the portent to our political system is so." [29] Members of Congress were reminded by the Commission of their national party platform pledges on monopoly and small business, which were quoted in full. These statements exuded good feeling for "small business, the bulwark of American enterprise," and promised an "aggressive antimonopoly action" designed to produce a "strengthening of existing anti-trust laws." [30]

Lowell Mason, Acting Chairman of the Federal Trade Commission, who had not seen eye to eye with the Patman-Douglas-Long combination in Congress nor with his fellow members in the Commission, disassociated himself from the majority of his colleagues and supported the conference report on S. 1008 with the exception of 4D, in place of which he favored the House version, which the Department of Justice supported.[31] Later the antirevisionist combination made use of an analysis of S. 1008, unfavorable to the bill, which had been prepared by a former chairman of the Federal Trade Commission, thereby making more marked the

---

kind of discrimination. Section 3 of the conference committee report actually produced a contradiction, for the defense that was denied to some in 2B was available to all in section 3, without exception. Discriminators by freight absorption practices could get under section 3 what they were specifically denied under 2B. The contradiction was created by the action of the conferees in rejecting both the Kefauver and Carroll amendments to section 3, for the proviso in either of those amendments would have made 2B and 3 consistent. The Federal Trade Commission thought that the inconsistency amounted to a contradiction. See the analysis of S. 1008 made by the Commission staff at the request of Kefauver. 96 *Cong. Rec.* 613–614 (January 19, 1950).

[29] *Ibid.*, p. 615 (January 19, 1950).
[30] *Ibid.*   [31] *Ibid.*, p. 609 (January 19, 1950).

eccentricity of the acting chairman's position in relation to that of his colleagues,[32] present and former.

Back to Conference

The execution of the revisionist (O'Mahoney) strategy to send the conference report back to the conferees, to enable them to rewrite Section 4D, proceeded as planned. On January 20 the Senate resumed consideration of the conference report. The question before the chamber was on the motion to agree to the conference report. O'Conor of Maryland, as one of the managers for the Senate, told the Senate that the managers would be willing "to see the conference report rejected" and "seek a new conference with a view to amending Section 4D along the lines of the Justice Department's recommendation." [33] He explained that the Justice Department felt that 4D should be rewritten to conform to the House version, said that the Senate managers did not really think that such a step was necessary, supplied a statement of the views of the managers contrary to that of the Justice Department on the point, but indicated that the managers were willing to have the question opened again.[34] Robertson of Virginia supported the conference report without change and wanted O'Conor's assurance that if S. 1008 went back to conference, the bill would be returned to the Senate again.[35] He was afraid that the House conferees might somehow contrive to tie up the measure, and he wanted to be sure that the referral of the bill back to conference was not a maneuver to put it to sleep.

The antirevisionists were not reluctant to have the bill

---

[32] The analysis, dated March 8, 1950, was made for Rankin P. Peck, President of the National Congress of Petroleum Retailers, by Robert E. Freer, and was placed in the *Record* by Long of Louisiana. 96 *Cong. Rec.* 4493–4495 (March 31, 1950).

[33] *Ibid.*, p. 679 (January 20, 1950).

[34] *Ibid.*, pp. 677–679 (January 20, 1950).

[35] *Ibid.*, pp. 679–680 (January 20, 1950).

sent back to conference, although Douglas thought that the conference committee would be limited to the few matters in disagreement between the two houses. Because of this limitation, the second conference could only patch and plaster infirmities of phrase and thought that were serious enough to require surgery. The vice of the bill, he thought, was not the weakness of a few words; the vice of the bill was that it legalized the basing-point system beyond the power of the conferees to change.[36] Douglas regretted that the Justice Department had not seen fit to disagree with Sections 1, 2, and 3, which would fasten the basing-point system into the law by the consent, indeed by the contrivance, of Congress.[37]

An effort was made by Long to have Kefauver added to the list of Senate managers, on the ground that he was a new member of the Senate Judiciary Committee. O'Conor said that he had no power to appoint the conferees, but that if the "present conferees happen to be members of the conference committee appointed by the Presiding Officer

---

[36] *Ibid.*, p. 683. Sections 1 and 2B of S. 1008 according to Douglas would legalize three essential features of the basing-point system: a delivered price; identity of price at any given location; and absorption of freight. The proper title of the bill, he suggested, should have been "An act to nullify the Sherman Anti-trust Act and an Act to repeal the Clayton Act." 96 *Cong. Rec.* 683–684 (January 20, 1950). Tobey of New Hampshire, who had first opposed S. 1008 in the Myers version and then supported the O'Mahoney version because he thought it was different (95 *Cong. Rec.* 7211, June 1, 1949), seemed to agree with Douglas and said that the bill ought to be amended with language to make it clear that the antitrust laws were being repealed. Said Tobey, "Hang a sign up in the sky which he who runs may read, so that when anyone votes for that amendment or against it we can know whether he is in favor of or in opposition to the anti-trust laws of the country." 96 *Cong. Rec.* 684 (January 20, 1950). Tobey, however, was evidently not captive to his own cliché for he finally voted in favor of S. 1008, presumably identifying himself as one of those ready to repeal "the principles and tenets and ideals of the Sherman Anti-trust Law and the Clayton Act."

[37] *Ibid.*, p. 685 (January 20, 1950).

of the Senate," they would welcome any suggestions Kefauver might have.[38] Long persisted in seeking a definite statement from O'Conor, who said that he would have no objection to Kefauver as a conferee, although, "of course, I should assume the chairman of the Judiciary Committee, the senior Senator from Nevada, would of course be the first to be consulted on the question." Kefauver was not appointed.[39] The attempt by Long to have Kefauver appointed as a conferee was the only notable effort on the part of the antirevisionists to modify and divert the direction of the revisionist maneuver, which had been carefully prepared and which unfolded in a smooth and easy operation. Some time was spent by Thye of Minnesota, who urged hasty passage of the measure because it was strongly desired by Minnesota canners, lumbermen, and cement, coal, and lumber dealers, who were said to be confused by the existing law; [40] by Martin of Pennsylvania, who also wanted quick action, many of the small businesses in Pennsylvania having been put in great confusion by the Supreme Court decision in the basing-point case; [41] by Johnson of Colorado, who congratulated O'Conor for his good faith, intelligence, and good judgment, asserting that he thought that "we have the votes in the Senate today to adopt the report without any change"; [42] and by Capehart, who wanted to fence with Long on the policy of compulsory f.o.b. pricing, which no one was advocating.[43]

Further time was consumed by Douglas, Long, and Kefauver in talking over a variety of matters connected (in some instances, remotely) with the basing-point problem.

---

[38] *Ibid.*, p. 680 (January 20, 1950).

[39] *Ibid.*, p. 703 (January 20, 1950). The conferees were McCarran, O'Conor, and Wiley, the same three who had brought in the first conference report.

[40] *Ibid.*, p. 681 (January 20, 1950).

[41] *Ibid.*   [42] *Ibid.*

[43] *Ibid.*, pp. 682–683 (January 20, 1950).

One matter of interest was the new relation assumed by Congress toward the Supreme Court in the last few years. Douglas thought there was "too much of a tendency . . . on the part of the legislators to protect monopoly when the courts are trying to protect competition." Said Douglas:

That movement began a few years ago when the Supreme Court in the Southeastern Underwriters case declared fire insurance companies to be engaged in interstate commerce. What happened then, Mr. President? Congress then passed a law taking the fire insurance companies out of interstate commerce, and putting them back under State regulation, which, because of the 48 conflicting jurisdictions, would largely be ineffective.

Then Governor Arnall started suit against the railways for their combinations fixing freight rates which had the effect of imposing excessive freight rates on the South and on the West. . . . I am sorry to say that Governor Arnall was not properly supported by the South and the West in regard to the decisions which he succeeded in having made.

Then what happened? The Reed-Bulwinkle bill was passed which permitted the railroads to get together and make combinations and to fix freight rates. Thank heavens, the President vetoed that bill; but Congress passed it over his veto.[44]

These were illustrations of recent tendency. Long of Louisiana summarized the trend in these words: "Although many of us had the idea that the United States Supreme Court was the court of last resort, yet it seems that, so far as the major industries of the country are concerned, the Congress of the United States is the court of last resort." [45] Kefauver joined the discussion by quoting the platform pledges of the Republican and Democratic parties in 1948, and the three Senators maintained an amiable conversation among themselves with the help of leading questions which implied the expected answers. Sports-minded listeners might have been reminded of the way in which basketball players pass the

[44] *Ibid.*, p. 685 (January 20, 1950).   [45] *Ibid.*

ball back and forth to each other as they stall for time. The difference was that the Douglas antirevisionist team had no lead to protect. At best, the score was momentarily tied. Langer of North Dakota got into the play long enough to remind the Senate of his dissent from the Senate Judiciary Committee's favorable recommendation of the Myers version of S. 1008, and Long and Douglas commended him for it, the latter remarking that it had been like a "fire bell clanging in the night," demonstrating thereby that the clichés were not all on the Republican side of the aisle.[46]

Before the vote on the motion of O'Conor to recommit the bill to conference, the antirevisionist group found itself briefly at cross purposes. Kefauver told the Senate that he was considering making a motion to instruct the conferees not to report until June 30, in order to await an expected decision from the Supreme Court in a case involving the Standard Oil Company of Indiana. He felt that nothing greatly untoward had happened to industry as a result of the Cement Case and believed that a further wait before making a final decision on S. 1008 would do no harm.[47] Long, however, asked Kefauver if he wouldn't be willing to withhold his motion to postpone consideration in order that S. 1008 might be expedited and the time of the Senate saved. He said:

Some of us feel that the conference may be able to arrive at some agreement whereby the amendment offered by the Senator or the amendment offered by Representative Carroll of Colorado, might be preserved. I am certainly hopeful of that. I wonder if the Senator would be willing to withhold his motion and wait to see what the effect of the conference report actually will be.[48]

---

[46] *Ibid.*, p. 687 (January 20, 1950).

[47] *Ibid.*, p. 688 (January 20, 1950).

[48] *Ibid.*, p. 688 (January 20, 1950). There seems to have been little reason for Long to think that the conference committee would change the bill in the respects he wished. Douglas had pointed out earlier in

Kefauver's answer to Long's suggestion that he withhold his motion to postpone the report of the conference committee was somewhat stiff. He said that he had not been made privy to any agreement about what was going to happen in the conference. Long then told Kefauver that he had been talking to O'Conor and to McCarran of Nevada about the possibility of Kefauver's being appointed to the conference committee, and Kefauver said that perhaps he and Long might get together later on the matter.

The conference report was rejected by voice vote and the original Senate managers were named by the President *pro tempore* of the Senate as the managers for the second conference with the House members.[49] The House took corresponding action and S. 1008 was back in the conference committee.[50]

_____

the debate that the competence of the conference committee was limited to matters of disagreement between the House and the Senate. Since the conference had rejected the Carroll and the Kefauver amendments once, it was unlikely that they would accept either. They would have no jurisdiction to make any extensive changes. Without an instruction to the conferees there was little reason to believe that they would voluntarily assume to do what they had previously refused to do, and Long made no mention of any instruction to the conferees in this regard. He had, of course, suggested to O'Conor that Kefauver might be added to the conferees, but O'Conor was evasive, and in fact Kefauver was not appointed to the conference committee. If Long had been relying upon Kefauver to persuade the conferees to make the desired changes, he evidently had not made Kefauver privy to his plan. He could not have been relying upon the House managers because after the adoption of the conference report in the House, the House managers were discharged and in January there were no House managers. See *ibid.*, p. 680 (January 20, 1950), where O'Conor tells Johnston of South Carolina that the House managers are not a party to the plans of the Senate managers for Section 4D because there were no House managers.

[49] *Ibid.*, p. 703 (January 20, 1950).

[50] On February 28, Congressman Celler of New York, chairman of the House Judiciary Committee, moved that the House insist upon its amendment to S. 1008 and agree to the further conference which had been requested by the Senate. This motion carried by vote of 240 to

The Second Conference Report

Late in the discussion of the revised conference report, Senator Lucas, the majority floor leader, said, "I have been a Member of the Senate twelve years, and there has been only one instance in which any Senator admitted that I

---

144. See 96 *Cong. Rec.* 2501 (February 28, 1950) for Celler's motion, and *ibid.*, p. 2515 (February 28, 1950) for the vote. Celler had refused to sign the first conference report. 95 *Cong. Rec.* 14605 (October 14, 1949). Borrowing from Winston Churchill, Celler referred to the first conference report as a "riddle inside an enigma wrapped in mystery." 96 *Cong. Rec.* 2502 (February 28, 1950). But the fact that he had not signed the conference report did not mean that "we should not have a second try at it." Out of the hour allotted to the discussion of the proposal to comply with the Senate request for a further conference, Patman of Texas got nine minutes to argue against the motion. His principal point was that the conferees would not be able to make a good bill out of a bad one, because the range within which they could recommend changes was too narrow, being limited to the precise matters in disagreement between the Senate and the House. Of S. 1008, he said that he had "never known a proposal before a legislative body to be less understood generally than this bill." *Ibid.*, p. 2503 (February 28, 1950). Walter of Pennsylvania said that he expected the Supreme Court to reverse the Seventh Circuit Court decision in the Standard Oil Case and predicted that those who opposed S. 1008 would want to enact it and would then be "most vociferous in demand for its passage." *Ibid.*, p. 2504 (February 28, 1950). Just why the antirevisionists would want to support a bill to overrule the Seventh Circuit Court after the Supreme Court had overruled the Seventh Circuit Court was not made clear by Walter. Evins of Tennessee referred to a resolution adopted by a majority of the members of the Select Committee on Small Business of the House of Representatives, to oppose sending the bill back to conference and said that the resolution had been urged by small business and other groups. *Ibid.*, p. 2506 (February 28, 1950). Graham of Pennsylvania on the other hand said, "Oddly enough the great big manufacturers in my district are not the ones who are urging that this measure be sent back to conference. It is the small manufacturers in my district who have made this request." *Ibid.*, p. 2507 (February 28, 1950). Crawford of Michigan and Graham together developed the theme that to fail to enact S. 1008 would help big business, and that to put S. 1008 on the books would help small business. *Ibid.* Davenport of Pennsylvania in a richly mixed metaphor said, "Is the basing point cry a smoke screen behind which selfish interests

changed his mind as a result of a speech I made." [51] There
is no evidence that any Senator's mind was changed as a
result of the debates that took place on the second conference report, and it could well have been, as Johnson of
Colorado indicated on January 20, that the revisionists had
the vote at that time, and could have passed the bill forth-
with, without sending it back to conference.[52] There was
plenty of evidence, however, that it was unnecessary to
understand the bill in order to know how to vote. The conference committee wasted little time in doing its work, and
its second report was back in the House three days after the
House had agreed to the conference asked by the Senate.[53]
Two weeks after the conference had been appointed, the
second conference report had passed the House.

The second conference report differed from the first.
Section 4D had been revised in line with the recommendation of the Department of Justice and the desire of the

---

from outlying regions of the country are attempting to rape the great
steel centers of America?" *Ibid.,* p. 2507 (February 28, 1950). That it
was not necessary to understand S. 1008 in order to vote for it is evident in Davenport's further statement, "We are for the wise adjustments worked out by the Federal Trade Commission in the pricing of
steel." *Ibid.* He voted against a motion to kill the bill by recommitting
it to committee. *Ibid.,* p. 3332 (March 14, 1950). Although the antirevisionist case was clearly stated on the floor by Boggs of Louisiana
(*ibid.,* pp. 2510–2514, February 28, 1950), the motion to instruct the
House conferees to insist on the House amendments (i.e., the Carroll
amendment among others) was lost, 210 to 161. *Ibid.,* pp. 2515–2516
(February 28, 1950). Celler, Walter, Michener, Willis, and Case of
New Jersey were the House managers. Of these only Willis was identified as a supporter of the antirevisionists. There were none among
the Senate managers. Willis was the only conferee to refuse to sign the
second conference report. *Ibid.,* p. 4452 (March 31, 1950).

[51] *Ibid.,* p. 7835 (May 31, 1950).

[52] *Ibid.,* p. 681 (January 20, 1950).

[53] Michener of Michigan submitted the second conference report to
the House on behalf of Celler of New York on March 3, 1950 (96 *Cong.
Rec.* 2782, March 3, 1950), and it was ordered to be printed (*ibid.,*
p. 2789, March 3, 1950).

Senate managers and O'Mahoney. The hope that Long had expressed that a more thoroughgoing revision might be made was disappointed. The suggestion of some that the conference might reconsider basic decisions was not fulfilled. The revisionists had made a small gesture of appeasement and now, armed with the necessary votes, were determined to temporize no longer. In the House, some members on the antirevisionist side struggled to develop narrow and fortuitous tactical advantages, but their efforts were doomed.[54] Their words reached a majority that had already closed its mind.

The debate on the second conference report in the House was inconsequential. Patman urged that the bill be recommitted to the conference committee and Carroll made a motion to that effect at the end of the allotted hour, but the motion was lost.[55] The most complete exposition of views was made by Jackson of Washington, who introduced evidence that the effect of the basing-point system was adverse to the Pacific Northwest. Mitchell of Washington made the same point.[56] Boggs of Louisiana introduced evidence tend-

---

[54] At the start of the House debate of one hour on the second conference report, for example, Boggs of Louisiana asked unanimous consent to extend the debate by thirty minutes, but the minority floor leader, Halleck of Indiana, objected and the extension was lost. Halleck's point was that the House was busy and that there had already been enough debate on the matter. *Ibid.*, p. 3321 (March 14, 1950). Some use was made of the Appendix to the *Congressional Record* to publicize the antirevisionist side. Page A1960 (unbound) (March 13, 1950), for example, was a reprint of the Freer analysis of S. 1008 prepared for Peck of the National Congress of Petroleum Retailers. Pages A1242–1245 (unbound) were a printed statement and tables by the head of the Economics Department at Vanderbilt University, George Stocking, tending to show that although the Birmingham steel mills probably enjoyed the lowest cost in the country, they have secured a relatively small share of the home market.

[55] 96 *Cong. Rec.* 3332 (March 14, 1950).

[56] *Ibid.*, pp. 3324–3326 (March 14, 1950), for Jackson's presentation and pp. 3331–3332 for Mitchell's.

ing to show that the effect of the basing-point system in steel was harmful to the South.[57] One of the Pennsylvania representatives said that he supported S. 1008 because it was "good for the United States of America—not for any particular people, not for any particular section, but for the whole country." He then spoiled the effect of this high-minded homily by saying that "as steel goes, so goes the Nation." [58] A point of order was made three times in the course of the hour that a quorum was not present, and on two of these occasions a quorum was not in fact present. When the vote was taken, however, the revisionists had won.[59]

Having been steam-rollered in the House, the antirevisionists prepared for their last congressional stand in the Senate, where McCarran, on March 31, submitted the second conference report [60] and then moved that the Senate agree to it. The Senate did not agree at the time because it was involved with a displaced persons bill and a rivers and harbors bill, and partisans of both did not want to be diverted from them, but Long of Louisiana later made an extensive speech which covered familiar ground and filled

---

[57] *Ibid.*, pp. 3328–3329 (March 14, 1950).

[58] This was Kearns, *ibid.*, p. 3331 (March 14, 1950). Another Pennsylvanian, Davenport, used his speech of February 28 almost verbatim, including in both places the metaphorical question concerning cries, smoke screens, and rape. *Ibid.*, p. 3330 (March 14, 1950). He was more candid than his colleague, Kearns, about the relation of the steel industry to S. 1008 and its interest in it. Davenport said that if "the steel industry is forced to an f.o.b. mill pricing system as a permanent way of doing business chaos will arise with a return of a buyers' market in steel." Of the pricing to be legalized by S. 1008, "How much fairer to the people of the Pittsburgh area whose livelihoods are tied directly and indirectly to the steel industry." *Ibid.*, p. 3330 (March 14, 1950).

[59] The second conference report was adopted by voice vote after Carroll's motion to recommit was lost by 175 to 204. *Ibid.*, p. 3332 (March 14, 1950).

[60] *Ibid.*, p. 4452 (March 31, 1950).

the record with a variety of insertions, printed statements, chapters from books, and other evidences to support his view that S. 1008 was a weakening of the antitrust laws, and especially of the Robinson-Patman Act, into the history of which he went in detail.[61] The principal new matter introduced was a letter opposing S. 1008 which was signed by seventy-six economists, most of them connected with colleges and universities.[62] The showdown on S. 1008 took place during the last week of May and the first of June, and the only stir between Long's speech and the climax of the controversy was a speech by Langer on April 3, 1950, when he put together forty-five minutes granted him by McCarran of Nevada and fifteen minutes contributed by Kilgore of West Virginia out of time allotted to a discussion of the displaced persons bill.[63]

On May 25, 1950, O'Conor moved that the Senate proceed to the consideration of S. 1008. Lucas immediately tried to get an accurate estimate of the length of the discussion, urging dispatch, and asserting: "I think every Senator knows at this moment exactly how he intends to vote on the conference report. I do not think any arguments are going to change the result." [64] O'Conor assured him that the supporters of the second conference report would not need more than two or three hours, and Long said that the opponents would need two or three days. There was no unanimous consent agreement to organize and limit the debate and to fix a time for voting, and Lucas, as majority floor leader, found it difficult to schedule the legislative traffic

---

[61] *Ibid.*, pp. 4468–4510 (March 31, 1950).

[62] *Ibid.*, pp. 4495–4496 (March 31, 1950).

[63] *Ibid.*, pp. 4597–4602 (April 3, 1950). Much of the speech of Langer was an account of the State Cement Commission of South Dakota established in 1919 to construct and operate a cement plant in the state, and the experience it had with the cement industry.

[64] *Ibid.*, p. 7730 (May 25, 1950).

so as to permit Congress to finish up its business quickly and thus avoid a sultry summer in Washington. He had no way, of course, of prophesying that Congress was going to be preoccupied with the Korean War, and that it would be unable to get away for the fall campaigns before September. Long, who had thought that the conference committee would produce a better second report than he was justified in hoping for, on this occasion thought that perhaps even one day's full debate, with all Senators present, would suffice the antirevisionists. Lucas replied to this optimism:

Of course, I should like to have a full attendance of Senators in all debates, but if the future can be judged by what has occurred in the past, I fear there will not be many Senators listening to the debate. During the past two months many important measures have been debated when, as the Senator from Louisiana knows, very frequently there were only three or four Senators listening.[65]

In the proceedings that followed, the O'Mahoney group emphasized the extent to which the measure had been heard, considered, and argued, which the members said was considerable.[66] O'Conor reviewed the legislative history of S. 1008, ascribing its origin to the alleged confusion resulting from the Supreme Court decisions in the Cement and Rigid Steel cases. Much of the opposition to the bill, he said, arose from a misconception and misinterpretation of what it actually did. In illustration of his point about the misconception of the opposition, O'Conor referred to

---

[65] *Ibid.*

[66] *Ibid.*, p. 7731. Kefauver, at the end of the debate on June 2, made a point of order designed to delay proceedings further, as discussed below, but he wanted to make it at the start. While O'Conor had the floor on May 25, and after he had moved consideration of S. 1008, Kefauver asked him to yield for the purpose of making the point of order which he said might make the subsequent debate unnecessary, if upheld. O'Conor, however, refused to yield for this purpose and the debate went on.

Sections 2B and 3.[67] Section 2B was the work of the second conference committee and represented another stage in the battle over the Carroll and Kefauver amendments. At the end of the First Session of the Eighty-first Congress, it will be recalled that O'Mahoney had said that the conference committee had used the language of the Kefauver amendment in its report. O'Mahoney then indicated that he would be willing to accept the Carroll amendment. The second meeting of the conference committee not only patched up Section 4D in accordance with the advice of the Department of Justice, but tinkered with the language which had been borrowed from the Kefauver amendment in setting out the conditions under which good faith would be a defense in an action for unlawful price discrimination. But instead of taking either the Carroll amendment or the Kefauver version, the second conference committee invented and substituted still another form of words, of which the most critical were "except that this shall not make lawful any combination, conspiracy, or collusive agreement; or any monopolistic, oppressive, deceptive, or fraudulent practice." This language was not at all equal to the Carroll

---

[67] The exact text of Section 2B was as follows: "Upon proof being made, at any hearing upon a complaint under this section, that there has been discrimination in price the effect of which upon competition may be that prohibited by the preceding subsection, or discrimination in services or facilities furnished, the burden of showing justification shall be upon the person charged with a violation of this section, and unless justification shall be affirmatively shown, the Commission is authorized to issue an order terminating the discrimination: *Provided further,* that a seller may justify a discrimination by showing that his lower price or the furnishing of services or facilities to any purchaser or purchasers was made in good faith to meet an equally low price of a competitor, or the services or facilities furnished by a competitor, and this may include the maintenance, above or below the price of such competitor, of a differential in price which such seller customarily maintains, except that this shall not make lawful any combination, conspiracy, or collusive agreement; or any monopolistic, oppressive, deceptive, or fraudulent practice." *Ibid.,* p. 7732 (May 25, 1950).

amendment as a limitation on the good faith defense. Under the Carroll amendment good faith would not have been a defense where the effect of price discrimination upon competition might be adverse. The substitute language in effect left good faith an absolute defense. But O'Conor said in answer to a query put by Long of Louisiana that the conferees had consulted the congressional parliamentarian on their authority to write new language different from that of the Kefauver and Carroll amendments, and that they had then devised the form of words adopted, a form of words which "in the opinion of the conferees serves to take their place quite adequately." [68]

There was weakness in the argument made by O'Conor and O'Mahoney—that the guarantees to small business were strong because good faith would not be available as a defense if there was collusion or combination—and this weakness was hit hard by Long. The antitrust laws since 1890, he said, had made collusion and combination in restraint of trade a violation of the laws. To say that good faith was a good defense unless collusion or unlawful combination was present was simply to say that defendants would not be permitted to argue that their motives were pure when they committed an unlawful act. On the other hand, where proof of collusion or unlawful combination depended upon the existence of an unlawful intent, the absence of such an intent was always open to demonstration. Good faith in such circumstances, therefore, was always a defense. According to Long the language adopted by the conferees could not have been more than surplusage.[69]

---

[68] *Ibid.*, p. 7733.

[69] Long adverted to some of these considerations in a colloquy with O'Conor and Thye. *Ibid.*, p. 7734. O'Mahoney was pursued by Long to answer whether it was necessary to make illegal what was already illegal, and he replied after evading a direct response, "Does the Senator [Long] want to take the position that the conferees should have rejected this prohibition? I am willing to repeat the prohibition

Under pressure O'Mahoney then contradicted an important position that he had adopted in the First Session. When he had joined the effort of Douglas to postpone action on S. 1008 until the Second Session, he had done so presumably because the conferees had brought in the Kefauver amendment and not the Carroll amendment. The first conference committee action, said O'Mahoney, had so perverted his intention for S. 1008 that it would be necessary to reject the conference report entirely unless the offending language was removed and the Carroll amendment substituted for it. But when the conferees rejected both the Kefauver and the Carroll amendments and brought in a form of words that contained neither, and Long wanted to restore the Carroll amendment, O'Mahoney refused to support the Carroll amendment which, short months before, was so critical to him that he had had to repudiate the bill which failed to contain it. Of the Carroll amendment, in May 1950, O'Mahoney said that it was necessary for him to object to it because "it broadens the law and makes the law incapable of understanding." [70] Moreover, he then unmistakably implied that he would have preferred the Kefauver amendment and that the House had made the Senate version of S. 1008 unacceptable by substituting the Carroll amendment.[71]

---

of the antitrust law every day of the year, every hour of the day, every minute of the hour, and, if I could, every second." Mr. Long: "If we were to follow the argument from the Senator from Wyoming, we would be great statesmen if we took the whole United States Code and reenacted it every day." *Ibid.*, p. 7736.

[70] *Ibid.*, p. 7739.

[71] "I accepted the amendment offered by the Senator from Tennessee. . . . But when the bill went to the House, the Representative from Colorado caused the word 'may' to be inserted. Of course, the word 'may' is as broad as a barn door." *Ibid.*, p. 7739. This was grossly misleading because the Colorado representative did not cause a substitution of "may" for "will" as this statement of O'Mahoney's implies. It was O'Mahoney who had had the Kefauver amendment stricken from the bill in the executive session of the House Judiciary Com-

Consistency, as political speakers are often happy to point out, is the hobgoblin of small minds, but O'Mahoney must have set new marks for greatness if the contrary of this proposition is true. He had accepted the Kefauver amendment when it was first proposed in 1949. He then had it removed in the House Judiciary Committee. When it appeared in the conference report he said he would have to reject the conference report because it contained the language of the Kefauver amendment. At this time he indicated that he preferred the Carroll amendment. When the second conference report rejected both the Kefauver and the Carroll amendments, O'Mahoney said that the Carroll amendment was objectionable and strongly implied that he preferred the Kefauver amendment but that, since it was not possible to have the Kefauver amendment, he would take the language of the second conference report in preference to the Carroll amendment. From this tergiversation, it is permitted to conclude that O'Mahoney was less concerned with making and sticking to a single comprehensible position on the legislation which he had fathered than he was in getting it passed. He agreed with both advocates of strict adherence to the antitrust laws and with those who would have radically revised them. He carried water upon both shoulders and, if he did not get himself wetted thereby, it was only because the issues were so complicated, the stakes were so obscure to all but a few, and the trouble to understand the disputation was so tedious.

Perhaps the appeal to argument and debate was as futile as Lucas of Illinois had said that it would be. But the Sisyphean task went forward. Hubert Humphrey of Minnesota,

mittee, so that that Committee reported the bill to the House without it. It was only when the bill appeared in the House without the Kefauver amendment that Carroll of Colorado proposed alternative language. It was this alternative language that O'Mahoney had said was so crucial to S. 1008 that he would have to reject the conference report which omitted it.

co-operating with the Long-Kefauver-Douglas group, made a speech on the general effect of the antimonopoly laws on the economy and the menace of the growing concentration of economic power.[72] In this he was aided by Douglas, who interrupted at appropriate times to help emphasize some points in the argument that bigness, although not "bad" in and of itself, might produce lamentable consequences which legislation should seek to cure and regulate. O'Mahoney bespoke assurance from Humphrey that the latter did not suggest that S. 1008 had been introduced by O'Mahoney "at the behest of or in cooperation in any way directly or indirectly with the great concentrations of economic power which he has mentioned." [73] Humphrey made the civil gesture, but Douglas would not permit courtesies to conceal O'Mahoney's amazing sponsorship of a "big business" bill. He pointed out that although he would not impute to O'Mahoney the influence of steel, oil, or cement interests in the formulation of the bill, these groups, he said, had an important stake in S. 1008. The drive to change the law started after the Cement Case of 1948; the leader of the steel industry, Mr. Benjamin Fairless, "then came out and said that there must be a change in the law." Following the decision of the Seventh Circuit Court of Appeals in the Standard Oil Case, the oil industry had joined the drive, said Douglas. O'Mahoney, the professional foe of big business, was (willing or not) the front for an industrial drive to reverse the Federal Trade Commission and the Supreme Court. Douglas and O'Mahoney wrangled about the obligation of Congress to rewrite court decisions for the benefit of businessmen until Humphrey had to ask them to continue their debate on their own time.[74]

---

[72] Ibid., pp. 7781–7812 (May 26, 1950).   [73] Ibid., p. 7789.
[74] The colloquy went as follows: Mr. O'Mahoney. "The bill does not reestablish the basing point system as an instrument of monopoly."

O'Mahoney and Douglas on separate days made formal presentations of their respective views, and then Majority Floor Leader Scott Lucas of Illinois insisted upon bringing the matter to a close under threat of keeping the Senators in unwelcome night sessions until the basing-point bill was disposed of.[75] Even with this official pressure from the party

Mr. Douglas. "We shall argue that at Thermopylae." Mr. O'Mahoney. "Let us argue it here. Let us not postpone it. Why should we have to go to Greece for it?" Mr. Douglas. "We will have Thermopylae here." *Ibid.*, p. 7790.

[75] See *ibid.*, pp. 7813–7820, for O'Mahoney's presentation and pp. 7851–7869 (May 31, 1950) for the presentation of Douglas. In the course of O'Mahoney's presentation, Douglas got the Senator from Wyoming to agree that dicta in the Cement Case had been misinterpreted by spokesmen for the steel and the cement industries to make small businessmen believe that independent freight absorption was illegal. *Ibid.*, p. 7817 (May 26, 1950). Douglas then asked whether it was necessary to enact new legislation to clear up a misapprehension that may have been deliberately planted. O'Mahoney said that he believed that it was necessary in fairness to those who desired to enter into competition with big business. At one point Douglas referred to S. 1008 as a bill fathered by O'Mahoney "in a moment of inadvertence," but O'Mahoney objected to this. Douglas replied, "I will strike out 'inadvertence' and say 'which, unfortunately the Senator from Wyoming fathered.'" *Ibid.*, p. 7818. McMahon of Connecticut showed more sympathy for the manufacturers of Connecticut than for the druggists of Connecticut, the letters from whom he said had been "written here in Washington" and "shipped out to the states." *Ibid.*, p. 7819.

In Douglas' formal presentation of the basing-point problem, he lectured the Senate like a university professor. The basing-point system of quoting delivered prices was traced to Carnegie, who used it in pricing steel beams in 1880 following, said Douglas, the model of the German cartels which Carnegie had visited the year before. The system was extended throughout the steel industry gradually to the point where, with a standardization of steel production, it became possible to destroy price competition without resort to open cabals or the somewhat more devious device of the famous "Gary dinner." *Ibid.*, pp. 7851–7852 (May 29, 1950). S. 1008 legalized the basing-point system by protecting three of four ingredients essential to its operation: delivered prices, identical prices, and freight absorption. The fourth ingredient—standardization of product—was of course already legal. Section 1 of S. 1008 in specific words legalized freight absorption and

leader, the antirevisionists, fighting a rear-guard action, managed to squeeze out two final days of debate on the subject. Some of this new time was taken, however, by conservative spokesmen from Pennsylvania and Ohio who had not participated in any of the previous debate on S. 1008 and who wanted to get themselves recorded on the issue. According to Bricker of Ohio, the controversy over basing-point practices was "forced" on Congress by a Supreme Court that had made judicial legislation. The Federal Trade Commission was viewed with disfavor for trying, since the early 1920's, to foist compulsory f.o.b. pricing upon American industry. The Department of Justice was viewed with high favor by contrast with the Commission, which "seems to be dedicated to a policy of protecting competitors from the natural consequences of hard-hitting competition." [76] As one who wanted to expose competitors to the "natural consequences of hard-hitting competition," Bricker hoped that small business would support S. 1008 in preference to the restrictive devices with which the Federal Trade Commission would shackle competition. Much of Bricker's talk assumed, as had Capehart in the hearings of 1948, that the issue was really whether business should be required to adopt a compulsory f.o.b. system of quoting prices. Bricker was candid in stating that one of the effects of S. 1008 would be the reversal of the decisions in the Standard Oil and Morton Salt cases. Martin of Pennsylvania, like Bricker, expressed concern lest the f.o.b. system

---

delivered prices, and Section 2(b) legalized identical prices by allowing sellers to absorb freight to meet the equally low prices of competitors in good faith. *Ibid.*, p. 7863. In the opinion of Douglas, the effect of the Cement Case decision was clear to the steel industry, which, he asserted, adopted f.o.b. pricing for a double reason—to get a price increase and to blame it upon the decision, and to get people to put pressure upon Congress to legalize the basing-point system of quoting delivered prices. Similarly, the Cement Case decision was clear to most of the cement companies, he said.

[76] *Ibid.*, p. 7898 (June 1, 1950).

of quoting prices create local monopolies. The bill was vital to Pennsylvania workers, presumably because it would protect the position of Pennsylvania industry in the national market.[77] Why Pennsylvania interests should be protected from the competition of new rivals in other states while small businessmen were being counseled by Bricker to put away crass thoughts of protection was not made clear. The revisionists in effect rested their case with these statements by the Senators from Pennsylvania and Ohio.

In an appeal to the basic groupings affected by the outcome of the struggle over S. 1008, the opponents of the measure made earnest arguments in an attempt to convince them that the bill was disadvantageous to their interests. For example, Kefauver sought to persuade the representatives of states in the West, the South, and New England [78] that the basing-point system permitted "predatory dumping" by large concerns which would drive little concerns out of business and retard the economic expansion of undeveloped areas. Douglas joined the appeal to basic group interests, arguing that the basing-point system enabled mills in the basing-point areas to penetrate the West and the South far more than the southern and western mills could penetrate the basing-point areas. Kefauver drove his arguments with especial force against the polite indifference of the Senators from the "traditional steel producing centers of Pennsylvania, Ohio, Illinois, and Maryland," who had long made up their minds as to how they would finally vote. Certainly there had been ample signs of this. In the House vote on the conference report, only two members from the Pennsylvania delegation had voted against the measure. Of the Chicago delegation, only one had voted against the bill. None of the Maryland delegation had voted against

[77] *Ibid.*, p. 7917.　　　　[78] *Ibid.*, p. 7903.

the bill.[79] But Kefauver patiently persisted. He particularly asked the legislators from steel-producing states to heed the fact that the prosperity of their states depended upon the prosperity of the country at large, but the final voting did not disclose that this appeal to a conception of the public interest beyond the boundaries of the constituencies represented by the legislators had much effect.

It was with some sacrifice that the vote on S. 1008 was scheduled, by unanimous consent, for Friday afternoon, June 4, 1950, at two o'clock. The sacrifice was borne by Long of Louisiana who was ill, but who consented to fly to Washington for the Friday vote after strong efforts had been made by the antirevisionists to postpone a vote until the following Monday.[80] Because of a speaking engagement at the University of Tennessee, Kefauver arranged for the two o'clock vote instead of one at four, which had been proposed, and the floor leaders agreed to call the Senate in session at eleven in the morning instead of at noon, its customary time, so as to permit the expression of last minute sentiments. The time of two hours, fixed by the unanimous consent agreement, was divided equally between the supporters and opponents of S. 1008, with O'Conor of Maryland in charge for the supporters and Long of Louisiana in charge for the opponents. As is usual, the time allotted

---

[79] *Ibid.*, p. 7910. See below, p. 210 ff., for an analysis of all of the votes on S. 1008 in all of its stages.

[80] 96 *Cong. Rec.* 7915 (June 1, 1950). Douglas made a point of saying, "I believe that for the sake of the *Record* it should be indicated that the Senator from Louisiana had not in any way tried to hold up the proceedings of the Senate, or to filibuster, nor is he interfering with the ordinary procedure of business. He is getting up from a sick bed and coming here when he is in no condition to come. He is doing so in an endeavor to facilitate and not to delay the business of the Senate." This disclaimer may have been given point by the fact that Long was fully prepared to filibuster the first conference report. See above p. 153 n. 144.

was divided up into bits and pieces of a few minutes each.

During the last two hours of debate, the ground covered had been well traveled many times before, but there were a few expressions and short statements of interest. Johnson of Colorado, favoring S. 1008, for example, said that congressional support for the bill was "wholly nonpolitical," a statement that the subsequent vote did not entirely justify.[81] The Senator from Colorado, like others among the supporters of S. 1008, acknowledged the pressure that had been exerted against the bill by the organized druggists. The hand of Congressman Patman of Texas was seen behind much of the pressure, and Johnson made particular note that, of an estimated more than two hundred insertions in the *Congressional Record* on the subject of basing points, Patman had been responsible for approximately one hundred.[82] Johnson produced a printed formal reply to the extensive analysis of S. 1008 and the basing-point system which Douglas had delivered a few days before. This step was taken for the sake of "lawyers, business men and even students of history who read the *Congressional Record*."

Hill of Alabama spoke against S. 1008, saying that the basing-point system, far from being a natural development to be protected from artificial interferences, was an "unnatural" development having its early origins in pools and gentlemen's agreements.[83] Wherry of Nebraska struck a somewhat defeatist note when he remarked that if the elimination of freight absorption (which was not in issue) created new industry in one section of the country, it must do so at the expense of other sections of the country.[84] This was similar to the view expressed by Martin of Pennsylvania and some members of the Pennsylvania delegation in the House that the effect of failing to enact S. 1008 would be

[81] 96 *Cong. Rec.* 7976 (June 2, 1950). See below, pp. 198, 209 ff.
[82] 96 *Cong. Rec.* 7942 (June 2, 1950).   [83] *Ibid.,* p. 7948.
[84] *Ibid.,* p. 7955.

unemployment in Pennsylvania. This kind of appeal could be based only upon the assumption that existing economic advantages should be frozen, which was inconsistent with the creed of a Bricker that competitors should not be protected from the natural consequences of hard competition. The Wherry argument also assumed that prosperity was a scarce commodity which had to be rationed and that some sections of a tightly knit and interdependent economy could prosper at the expense of others. Some credence to the second of these assumptions was given by spokesmen from the "colonial" sections of the country—those from the South and the West which suffered in competition with the East by a combination of railroad rate and basing-point price practices—who argued that the industrial East profited from the disadvantages that their sections were forced to endure. Fulbright admitted that any dislocation in existing price structures could result in temporary harm to existing business but that the same was true of technological advance. Said the Senator from Arkansas, "It is human nature that the few who are hurt are likely to complain while those who have some good fortune do not seem to bother about mentioning it." [85]

With the time for voting at hand, a last stratagem was attempted by Kefauver, who tried to dispose of S. 1008 on a point of order, which failed to secure the necessary votes. The point of order was that the conferees had exceeded their instructions when they brought in the second conference report. Kefauver argued that Senate Rule XXVII limits conferees to the forms of phrase and expression contained in the respective Senate and House versions of legislation. The conferees, as O'Conor had previously explained, had taken neither the Kefauver nor the Carroll amendments but had devised new language with the aid of the parliamentarian, which they thought conveyed the sense of

[85] *Ibid.*, p. 7960.

the two versions of S. 1008, even though the exact language was not used. The ruling on the point of order was adverse to Kefauver. Senate Rule XXVII does not require that the exact forms of phrase and expression used in conflicting versions of the same bill be utilized by the conferees. Their duty under the rule is discharged if they heed the prohibition not to eliminate matter that has been agreed upon. There was no agreement on either the Kefauver or the Carroll amendments. By declining to accept either, the conferees had not eliminated any matter agreed upon.[86]

When the point of order was overruled, the time appointed for voting under the unanimous consent rule arrived and the conference report was adopted by a vote of forty-three to twenty-seven, with twenty-six not voting. Thirty Republicans and thirteen Democrats made the majority. Twenty-five Democrats and two Republicans made the minority. Of those not voting, sixteen were Democrats and ten were Republicans. Of the twenty-six not voting, the Douglas-Long-Kefauver combination would have picked up eight nay votes from the Democrats and five from the Republicans for a total of thirteen. These added to the twenty-seven votes cast against S. 1008 would have produced a total of forty votes at the most. The two Republicans who voted against the conference report were Senators McCarthy and Wiley of Wisconsin.[87]

---

[86] *Ibid.*, p. 7976.

[87] Wiley at least voted against the tenor of his indicated opinion. When he sat as a member of the Senate Committee on the Judiciary in the sketchy hearings on S. 1008 (the Myers version) in March and April 1949, he expressed concern for the economic situation of the many industries in his state: pea canners, evaporated milk canners, meat packers, box makers, cheese processors, and so on. As he confessed, "I would not want to look after my own to the detriment of someone else, but I would not want to disintegrate a great wealth in my State." *Senate Hearings on S. 1008*, pp. 78–79. McCarthy took no obvious part in the deliberations, debate, discussion, or negotiations which brought the bill to a final vote.

Veto Politics

With the passage of the basing-point bill, the last phase of the struggle began. The constitutional period of ten days within which the President must sign, not sign, or veto a bill was a period of concentrated pressure upon the White House by the antirevisionist legislators and the established organizations which speak for small business, farm, and labor constituencies. The issue on the complicated and controversial problem of delivered pricing practices was finally resolved into a simple question of "yes" or "no." The President had been represented previously by O'Mahoney to be in favor. But the President vetoed the measure after his Democratic National Committee Chairman had polled the constituencies which constituted the bulk of the Truman administration's political strength.

A word must be said about the procedure by which measures enacted in Congress are signed or vetoed. The Bureau of the Budget receives enrolled bills from Congress and makes as recommendation to the White House whether to approve or veto. If the recommendation is to veto, the Bureau of the Budget prepares a draft veto message which may either be accepted by the President as his own or be used as a working paper for the preparation of the message which actually accompanies the bill when it is returned to Congress without the President's approval. The Bureau of the Budget is organized by divisions, and it is the Division of Legislative Reference which performs the principal staff work on recommendations pertaining to enrolled bills. Its normal procedure is to consult the staff members in the Bureau of the Budget who habitually deal with the subject matters contained in the measure. Other agencies of the federal government which have a subject matter jurisdiction are also consulted, and numerous conferences of all the parties are not unusual. The role of the Bureau of the Budget is like that of a congressional committee in some respects: it too holds "hearings," attempts to obtain a consensus of the parties-in-interest and to produce a single recommendation which represents an accommodation of most of the views which bear on the issue. It sometimes happens, however, that political considerations are important to a decision on enrolled bills. The Bureau of the Budget does not ordinarily concern itself with considerations of this kind. If such considerations are present in force, the task of deciding the policy will be taken by the President directly or—which is the same thing—by his aides in and out of the White House. Officials of the Bureau of the Budget in such circumstances will supply technical advice and staff services, but the center of decision is not in the Bureau but in the White House.

When O'Mahoney in 1949 reported the Bureau of the Budget's pronouncement that S. 1008 was in accord with the program of the President, it amounted to no more than the assertion that the President had no objection—at the time. It did not mean that the President had a specific and detailed policy on industrial pricing practices, with which S. 1008 was in accord. The consensus of official agencies in support of S. 1008 which O'Mahoney secured in 1949—from the Bureau of the Budget, the Federal Trade Commission, the Department of Justice—was a tribute more to the reputation and personal influence of the Senator from Wyoming than a clear and certain solidarity of the official family behind his proposals. The opposition headed by Patman in the House and by Douglas, Long, and Kefauver in the Senate had not really brought its guns to bear. The influence of these two factions was not strong enough to prevent enactment in the two houses of Congress, but the combined influence of these two factions brought to bear upon the smaller target of the White House family was superior to that which O'Mahoney had been able to organize.

The President was pulled this way and that in the fateful ten days. The day after passage of the bill the *New York Times* reported that there were no indications as to whether the President would approve or disapprove. S. 1008 was described as one of the most controversial business measures in the then current session of the Eighty-first Congress. Although the steel industry desired legislation legalizing freight absorption and a delivered price system, industry sources were said to be reluctant to express opinions on the measure. The confidence that some industry sources had in the outcome, however, is expressed in the statement attributed to United States Steel that it was "carefully reviewing the bill and will make a statement when the bill becomes law." [88] The *Wall Street Journal* was cautious. It said that Truman had never told anyone how he would act on the measure but pointed out that John D. Clark of the Council of Economic Advisers (and therefore presumably close to the President) was in favor of it. In view of the asserted desire of the revisionists to clarify the law, the conclusion of the *Wall Street Journal* was ironic. "Because of the wide disagreement over what the new bill actually means," it reported, "business probably cannot be completely certain what pricing practices are legal—even if the bill becomes law—until it has finally been interpreted by the Supreme Court." [89]

The names of the many callers upon the President and his political aides were familiar to those who were acquainted with the controversy. Congressman Wright Patman of Texas led the way when he visited the President soon after the passage of S. 1008 to urge him to veto the legislation. [90]

---

[88] *New York Times*, June 3, 1950, p. 19, col. 1.

[89] *Wall Street Journal*, June 3, 1950, p. 3.

[90] *New York Times*, June 7, 1950, p. 42, col. 3.

The principal congressional delegation, composed of six Senators and five Representatives, met with Truman a week later and also urged him to veto the bill. These were Hill of Alabama, Lehman of New York, Kefauver of Tennessee, Sparkman of Alabama, Douglas of Illinois, and Humphrey of Minnesota, all from the Senate; and Patman of Texas, Evins of Tennessee, Karst of Missouri, Boggs of Louisiana, and Mitchell of Washington, from the House of Representatives.[91] All were Democrats and most had played an active part in the congressional struggle. Spokesmen for organized groups opposed to the bill met with Chairman Boyle of the Democratic National Committee: the National Federation of Independent Business, the United Automobile Workers of America, the Cooperative League, the National Association of Retail Druggists, the U.S. Wholesale Grocers, and the National Association of Independent Tire Dealers. According to one account they argued that a sure way to guarantee a Republican Congress in the 1950 congressional elections would be to permit Truman to sign S. 1008. If the bill became law, it was said, the President's small business program would be worthless, and the burden of asserted freight rate increases would fall upon farmers and consumers. Perhaps most important was the suggestion that the President's attitude on S. 1008 would be an important test of his good faith in championing the interests of small business groups and farmers. O'Mahoney of Wyoming, Myers of Pennsylvania, and Mayor David Lawrence of Pittsburgh also saw President Truman and asked him to sign. Karst of Missouri saw the President in St. Louis as well as in the White House as a member of the delegation of Democratic Congressmen and repeated his advice to veto. A radio news commentator for the American Federation of Labor urged his listeners to send telegrams to the White House urging a veto of S. 1008.

---

[91] *Ibid.*, June 14, 1950, p. 47, col. 1.

On June 16, 1950, the President sent a veto message to the Congress.[92] It was a very calm, short, and temperate document. The veto was put on the ground, among others, that the bill, intended to clarify the law, would obscure it, with the result that businessmen, administrative agencies, and the courts would find it more difficult, not less, to apply the legal safeguards against monopoly and unfair competition. Indeed the bill, "as it has finally emerged from the legislative process," was so far from clear that each of its major provisions was capable of widely conflicting interpretations. "There is every reason to believe," the veto message said, "that if S. 1008 were to become law there would be as much uncertainty about its meaning in the business community and the administrative agencies of the Government as there has been in the Congress."

The sources of new confusion in S. 1008 were particularized. Section 1, which would declare it lawful for businessmen acting independently to absorb freight and quote delivered prices, also lent itself to interpretations that would permit the resumption of basing-point practices recently found to be illegal. Supporters of S. 1008 had interpreted Sections 2 and 3 as a guarantee to sellers of freedom to meet a competitor's price in good faith, regardless of the effect of such action on competition, but the opponents of the bill believed that the provisions of S. 1008 would nullify the Robinson-Patman Act with its protections against ruthless price discrimination. In the light of these conflicting interpretations, said the veto message, many years of complex litigation would be required to give the provisions of S. 1008 clear and specific content, certainly a slow and difficult process.

More important than this, however, was the risk that the bill would eventually be interpreted to reduce the protection afforded the public by the antitrust laws. The meaning

---

[92] 96 *Cong. Rec.* 8721–8722 (June 16, 1950).

of S. 1008 was so uncertain that no one could tell how its enactment would change the content of those laws. In particular, the Federal Trade Commission might be handicapped in proving the existence of conspiracies and in stopping unfair price discriminations. Thus the maintenance of the antitrust laws, intact and without weakening revisions, was at the center of the veto, and the Federal Trade Commission view of these laws and their enactment prevailed over that of the Department of Justice.

The message admitted that the apprehensions described were not certainties, but they were unacceptable risks. There would be justification for taking extreme risk if the present state of the law were in fact "so confused as to appreciably hamper business operations and there were no alternative methods for resolving these difficulties. At the present time, this is clearly not the case." Admitting some earlier uncertainty, the message declared that now "it is quite clear that there is no bar to freight absorption or delivered prices as such." Thus the President gave businessmen the assurance that the Federal Trade Commission had supplied, that the Fourth Circuit Court had stated in the Bond Crown and Cork Company Case, and that Senator O'Mahoney said that he believed all along, despite his efforts to get his bill through Congress.

The *New Republic* thought that the veto was a "wise veto," but the *Wall Street Journal* said that businessmen had got a "sympathetic but not very helpful rebuff" from President Truman.[93] The *Christian Science Monitor* thought that the veto was probably one of the gentlest and kindest in many a year, especially in view of the fact that S. 1008 was legislation supported by the Chamber of Commerce and the National Association of Manufacturers.

---

[93] *New Republic,* July 3, 1950, p. 7. *Wall Street Journal,* June 17, 1950, p. 2.

Joseph Harsch's explanation of the veto in the *Monitor* was that although Truman was under great pressure from within his official family to sign the bill, and although he would have felt happy to be able to do so, yet he feared to risk the loss of old friends when Douglas took the lead against the bill.[94]

What the decision in fact represented was a choice between the right and the left wings of the Democratic Party. In critical issues before the controversy on the basing-point bill, President Truman had more than once aligned himself with the liberal wing of the party against the conservative wing. Indeed, he alienated much of his Southern support in the 1948 election when he indicated that he took seriously the pledges in the party platform in the matter of the civil rights of Negroes. The President undoubtedly would have welcomed the opportunity to make new friends for himself by endorsing the basing-point bill (if he would have made new friends, which is doubtful), but not at the risk of destroying the base of his political power, which was composed of labor, farmer, and small business elements.

Other reactions were mixed. Congressman Walter of Pennsylvania talked about overriding the veto, but most of his colleagues believed that the chance of an overrider was slim. Hill of Alabama and Patman of Texas were, of course, enthusiastic. McCarran was sorry. O'Mahoney continued to make himself pleasant to both sides. In an echo of his statement in the Senate the year before, when action on the first conference report was postponed to January 1950, O'Mahoney said that businessmen could take a great deal of encouragement from the President's veto message. "It says," declared O'Mahoney, " 'fear not when acting individually, you can sell at delivered prices and you may absorb

---

[94] *Christian Science Monitor*, June 17, 1950, p. 1.

freight.' " This cheery advice was not encouraging to the general counsel for the United States Chamber of Commerce, who said that the veto was a "terrific slap at business." [95] Governor Duff of Pennsylvania said at the Governors' Conference in June that he believed that the veto of the basing-point bill would be a major issue in Pennsylvania in the fall. He thought that the veto would discourage that diffusion of industry that was so essential in an atomic age. The Pennsylvania delegation in Congress, however, had argued that the steel industry would be scattered all over the United States to the disadvantage of Pittsburgh, and many of the revisionists said that failure to enact S. 1008 would establish regional "monopolies," that is, decentralized industry. Governor Duff also said that a ban on the basing-point system would lead eventually to government subsidies for new steel plants and then to the nationalization of the steel industry. [96]

The steel industry continued its policy of f.o.b. pricing, although there were reports that it had been prepared to adopt a limited amount of freight absorption had S. 1008 become law. [97] That the continued use of f.o.b. pricing was not mandatory but was a matter of choice is evident in the reported opinion that the Truman veto did not "positively preclude such pricing practices" (that is, freight absorption), but that the resumption of freight absorption would require "a conclusive declaration of permission from the Federal Trade Commission or a sharp downturn in demand for steel." [98]

Perhaps the most interesting of the developments following the presidential veto of S. 1008 was the action taken

---

[95] *New York Times,* June 17, 1950, p. 18, col. 1, continued at p. 22, col. 5.

[96] *New York Times,* June 19, 1950, p. 15, col. 3.

[97] *Ibid.,* June 25, 1950, Section III, p. 1, col. 7.   [98] *Ibid.*

by the Senate Committee on Interstate and Foreign Commerce, whose chairman in the Eighty-first Congress was Johnson of Colorado. Directly after the veto the Committee posted a five-man "watchdog" subcommittee to exercise surveillance over the manner in which the Federal Trade Commission handled cases involving freight absorption and delivered prices. The reason, according to Chairman Johnson, was a belief that "frequent shifts" in the positions of the Federal Trade Commission on pricing questions "had destroyed public confidence and required close day by day watchfulness over its activities in this field." [99] Johnson named himself to the subcommittee and Senators Myers of Pennsylvania, O'Conor of Maryland, Capehart of Indiana, and Bricker of Ohio. Of the principal steel-producing states, only Illinois was unrepresented, but neither Lucas nor Douglas was a member of the Committee on Interstate and Foreign Commerce. Two other members of the Committee might have been eligible, however, Magnuson of Washington and Johnson of Texas, both Senators from states in a "colonial" status to the industrial East. These two were the only members of the Senate Committee on Interstate and Foreign Commerce to vote against S. 1008. All the others voted for the measure, including, of course, the members appointed to the subcommittee. The "watchdog" subcommittee was therefore composed of critics of the Federal Trade Commission and friends of the business groups that were defeated in the White House. Having failed to secure the enactment of legislation to moderate the full enforcement of the antitrust laws, the membership of the "watchdog" subcommittee stood ready to pressure the Commission without the authority of enacted legislation. There is a sense in which the action appropriated to the subcom-

---

[99] *Ibid.*, June 23, 1950, p. 36, col. 4.

mittee some measure of the full power to carry out the anti-trust laws which Congress had vested in the Commission.[100]

---

[100] In two articles which were reprinted in the *Congressional Record* by Wherry of Nebraska and Thye of Minnesota, David Lawrence expressed himself in somewhat extravagant language. Governor Duff of Pennsylvania had merely thought that the veto paved the way for the nationalization of the steel industry. Lawrence felt that the veto had made a government of laws and not of men obsolete, because businessmen were not governed by the laws of Congress any more but by the whims of fallible bureaucrats. 96 *Cong. Rec.* A4902 [unbound] (June 23, 1950), 96 *Cong. Rec.* A4788 [unbound] (June 20, 1950). He also said that the veto represented undemocratic influence by pressure groups, by which he presumably meant the pressure groups who won, not the pressure groups who lost. Of particular interest was his observation that Truman could not really say what the Federal Trade Commission might do in bringing or not bringing suits, because the Commission is "an independent agency—indeed . . . a quasi-judicial commission." The implication is that it would be unseemly for the President to direct the activities of such an agency. The Johnson subcommittee of the Senate Committee on Interstate and Foreign Commerce did not show such scruple. Basing his authority to exercise surveillance over the Federal Trade Commission on Section 136 of the Legislative Reorganization Act, Johnson said that he proposed to ask the Commission to submit to the subcommittee copies of all "orders, decisions, briefs, pleadings, and other papers" which may be publicly filed in any of the pending cases referred to in the President's veto message. He also planned to submit to the Chairman of the Commission questions designed to elicit answers that will "give businessmen further assurances of the legality of their competitive pricing practices." After receipt of the answers to these questions, the Senator said that he proposed to hold public hearings in which the Chairman of the Federal Trade Commission would be the first witness. Johnson said that the subcommittee would report to the 82nd Congress the "progress or lack of progress" in clearing away confusion and uncertainty. This planned campaign to pressure the Federal Trade Commission into enforcing the statute which Congress did not pass over the veto is without precedent. *Ibid.*, p. A4861 [unbound] (June 22, 1950).

Chapter Six

Politics as Process

More than one of the speakers in the debate on S. 1008 said that the issues it raised were above politics. This was not true in either of the two senses in which the word "politics" may be properly understood—as the struggle of groups to write in their favor the rules by which the community is governed or in the more customary and popular sense as partisan party division. In its first and broader sense, politics was amply demonstrated in every aspect of the tortuous struggle over basing-point policy, from the beginning to the end. In its popular sense, politics was present in the pattern of voting in the House and the Senate and in the maneuvers that led to the veto of S. 1008 by the President.

One of the many curiosities and anomalies of the history of S. 1008 is the fact that it was adopted by a Democratic Congress in which a preponderance of Republicans were for the measure and a preponderance of Democrats were against it, under circumstances which made it appear as though it were a Democratic proposal. The Senate leaders for the bill were O'Mahoney, Myers, O'Conor, Johnson of Colorado, and McCarran of Nevada, all Democrats. The House leader was Celler of New York, also a Democrat. O'Mahoney was armed with official endorsements in 1949, which included the White House (ambiguously identified), the Bureau of the Budget, the Federal Trade Commission, and the Department of Justice. It might have been assumed that the Democrats in the House and the Senate, being in the majority in both, would have led the way toward the enactment of S. 1008.[1] But a majority of the Democrats in both houses were in fact opposed to the measure, although a majority of the Republicans were overwhelmingly in favor. Thus an important measure seemingly sponsored by Democratic officialdom was opposed by a majority of the Democrats in Congress and finally vetoed by a Democratic president. The other side of the paradox is the fact that the minority party commanded a majority of the votes under the auspices of majority party leadership. This paradox was made possible by the fact that enough Democrats joined the Republicans to make a legislative, if not a party majority, for the bill.

The Voting Pattern

There were five critical roll calls in the House and three in the Senate in the course of the enactment of S. 1008. All other votes were voice votes and it is therefore impossible to know how individuals voted.

The first roll call vote in the House took place on October 14, 1949, when Patman moved to recommit the first conference report on S. 1008 and to instruct the House managers to insist upon the House amendments. This was a delaying tactic to prevent a final vote on S. 1008 in the First

---

[1] The Senate party ratio remained fixed throughout both sessions of the 81st Congress (53 Democrats and 42 Republicans), but the numbers changed in the House. There were 261 Democrats in January 1949, 262 in January 1950 (this includes the Democrat-Liberal, Roosevelt), and 258 in November 1950. There were 171 Republicans in January 1949, and 169 throughout 1950. The only minor party member was Marcantonio, the American Labor Party Congressman from New York, defeated for re-election in 1950.

Session of the Eighty-first Congress. A vote in favor of the motion was a vote against S. 1008. The motion was lost 138 to 178. One hundred and twenty-nine Democrats (including Roosevelt, the Democratic-Liberal Representative, who will be counted as a Democrat hereafter) and 9 Republicans voted for the motion while 62 Democrats and 116 Republicans voted against it.[2] The second roll call in the House

TABLE I. The Five Roll Calls in the House on S. 1008.

	Democratic yeas	Republican yeas	Democratic nays	Republican nays	Total yeas	Total nays
1	129	9	62	116	138	178
2	86	114	98	6	200	104
3	95	145	131	13	240	144
4	76	134	142	19	210	161
5	154	20	72	132	175 *	204

* This total includes the vote of Marcantonio of the American Labor Party.

(also on October 14, 1949) was on the motion to agree to the conference report and therefore pass it on to the Senate. A vote in favor of the motion was a vote in favor of S. 1008. The vote was 200 to 104 in favor. Eighty-six Democrats and 114 Republicans voted for the motion, while 98 Democrats and 6 Republicans voted against it.[3]

The third, fourth, and fifth roll calls in the House took place in 1950, during the Second Session of the Eighty-first Congress. The first vote took place on February 28, 1950, on the motion to send S. 1008 to further conference, in line with the understanding engineered by O'Mahoney between the First and Second Sessions to modify some of the language of the bill to conform with the recommendations of

[2] If the paired votes are counted, 10 Republicans voted in favor of the motion and 135 against; 149 Democrats voted in favor and 65 against.

[3] If the paired votes are counted, 130 Republicans voted in favor of the motion and 7 against; 91 Democrats voted in favor and 117 against.

the Department of Justice. A vote in favor of the motion was a vote in favor of S. 1008. It was passed by a vote of 240 to 144. Ninety-five Democrats and 145 Republicans voted for the motion, while 131 Democrats and 13 Republicans voted against it.[4] The second roll call came on the same day when Carroll moved that the House instruct the House conferees to insist upon the House amendments. This motion was adverse to S. 1008. Before the House could vote on this motion, Congressman Walter of Pennsylvania moved to table the motion to instruct. A vote in favor of the motion to table was a vote in favor of S. 1008. The motion to table carried by a vote of 210 to 161. Seventy-six Democrats and 134 Republicans voted for the motion, while 142 Democrats and 19 Republicans voted against it.[5] The third House vote took place on March 14, 1950, when a motion to recommit S. 1008 to committee was rejected. A vote in favor would have been a vote against S. 1008. The vote to recommit was 175 for and 204 against. One hundred and fifty-four Democrats, 20 Republicans and Marcantonio of the American Labor Party voted for the motion, while 72 Democrats and 132 Republicans voted against it.[6]

In the Senate there were three roll call votes, two in 1949 and one in 1950. The first was Douglas' motion on August 12, 1949, to reconsider sending S. 1008 to conference. A vote in favor of the motion was a vote against S. 1008. The motion to reconsider was rejected by 49 to 28. Twenty-four Democrats and 4 Republicans voted for the motion while

---

[4] If the paired votes are counted, 152 Republicans voted in favor of the motion and 13 against; 100 Democrats voted in favor and 142 against.

[5] If the paired votes are counted, 141 Republicans voted in favor of the motion and 19 against; 83 Democrats voted in favor and 155 against.

[6] If the paired votes are counted, 20 Republicans voted in favor of the motion and 141 against; 170 Democrats voted in favor and 79 against.

20 Democrats and 29 Republicans voted against it.[7] In October, 1949, Douglas moved that consideration of S.

TABLE II. The Three Roll Calls in the Senate on S. 1008.

	Democratic yeas	Republican yeas	Democratic nays	Republican nays	Total yeas	Total nays
1	24	4	20	29	28	49
2	8	21	23	6	29	29
3	13	30	25	2	43	27

1008 be postponed until 1950, and O'Conor immediately moved to table Douglas' motion. The motion to table failed to carry in a tie vote, 29 to 29. A vote for the motion was a vote for S. 1008. Eight Democrats and 21 Republicans voted for the motion, while 23 Democrats and 6 Republicans voted against it.[8] The last vote was the showdown, the vote which enacted the basing-point bill and sent it on its way to the White House. This vote, on June 2, 1950, was on the acceptance of the conference report, which passed 43 to 27. Thirteen Democrats and 30 Republicans voted for the motion, while 25 Democrats and 2 Republicans voted against it.[9]

The principal cleavage throughout was party-wise, as the record shows. The Democrats tended to vote against S. 1008 at all stages, and the Republicans tended to vote for it. In this sense it may be said that S. 1008 was a Republican measure and that the Republican Party line in Congress was to support the bill, while the Democratic Party line was to oppose the bill despite its official endorsements. There

---

[7] If the paired votes and announcements of preference are counted, 7 Republicans voted in favor of the motion and 35 against; 26 Democrats voted in favor and 21 against.

[8] If the paired votes and announcements of preference are counted, 28 Republicans favored the motion and 8 opposed it; 8 Democrats favored and 27 opposed it.

[9] If the paired votes and announcements of preference are counted, 34 Republicans favored the motion and 6 opposed it; 18 Democrats favored and 30 opposed it.

TABLE III. Voting Patterns in Selected States.

States	Democratic pattern Republicans voting	Democrats voting Democratic pattern	Republican pattern Democrats voting	Republicans voting Republican pattern	Not voting, or no clear pattern	Total number of Representatives
STEEL STATES						
Illinois	6	3	0	13	4	26
Maryland	3	1	0	2	0	6
Ohio	2	10	0	11	0	23
Pennsylvania	12	2	0	18	1	33
NEW ENGLAND						
Connecticut	2	1	0	3	0	6
Maine	0	0	0	3	0	3
Massachusetts	4	2	1	7	0	14
New Hampshire	0	0	0	2	0	2
Rhode Island	0	2	0	0	0	2
Vermont	0	0	0	1	0	1
SOUTH						
Alabama	3	5	0	0	1	9
Arkansas	3	4	0	0	0	7
Florida	4	1	0	0	1	6
Georgia	2	6	0	0	2	10
Kentucky	3	4	0	0	2	9
Louisiana	0	7	0	0	1	8
Mississippi	4	3	0	0	0	7
North Carolina	3	5	0	0	4	12
South Carolina	2	3	0	0	1	6
Tennessee	2	5	1	1	1	10
Virginia	7	0	0	0	2	9
MIDWEST						
Illinois	6	3	0	13	4	26
Indiana	0	7	0	4	0	11
Iowa	0	0	1	7	0	8
Kansas	0	0	0	6	0	6

TABLE III. Voting Patterns in Selected States (*continued*).

States	Democrats voting Republican pattern	Democrats voting Democratic pattern	Republicans voting Democratic pattern	Republicans voting Republican pattern	Not voting, or no clear pattern	Total number of Representatives
Michigan	0	4	1	11	1	17
Minnesota	0	4	1	4	0	9
Missouri	1	11	0	1	0	13
Nebraska	0	1	0	3	0	4
North Dakota	0	0	2	0	0	2
South Dakota	0	0	0	2	0	2
Wisconsin	0	2	3	4	1	10
WEST						
Arizona	0	2	0	0	0	2
California	1	9	0	11	2	23
Colorado	0	3	0	1	0	4
Idaho	0	1	0	1	0	2
Montana	0	1	0	1	0	2
Nevada	0	1	0	0	0	1
New Mexico	2	0	0	0	0	2
Oklahoma	3	5	0	0	0	8
Oregon	0	0	0	4	0	4
Texas	11	7	0	0	3	21
Utah	0	2	0	0	0	2
Washington	0	2	2	2	0	6
Wyoming	0	0	0	1	0	1

was cross voting, of course, but more Democrats voted the Republican side than Republicans voted the Democratic side. There were 36 Democrats who followed the Republican pattern on all five votes in the House, and 5 Republicans who followed the Democratic pattern.[10]

[10] The "pattern" as it is here used is a concept of behavior based upon the performance of the legislators in the entire voting history

Many of the Republican-voting Democrats were from the states of Illinois, Maryland, Ohio, and Pennsylvania, to whom a special appeal had been made by Kefauver. In the House Democratic delegation from Pennsylvania, for example, there were only 2 Congressmen who voted the Democratic pattern. On the final vote there was only one. The Republicans were intact throughout. Two of the Ohio Democrats in the House voted the Republican pattern, 3 of the 4 Maryland Democrats did the same, although of these 2 went Democratic in the final vote, and 6 of the Illinois Democrats voted the Republican pattern throughout. In all of these states Republican support of S. 1008 was constant.

While Kefauver was counseling the delegations of other

---

of S. 1008. Five votes provide the elements of the design in the House, and three in the Senate. As the Appendix shows, the Democratic pattern in the House was "aye, nay, nay, nay, aye," while the Republican pattern was "nay, aye, aye, aye, nay." Later in this chapter when it is stated that a Democrat voted in the Republican pattern or a Republican voted in the Democratic pattern, it means that the Congressman cast three or more votes which fitted into the pattern of the opposite party. In the Senate, the Democratic pattern was "aye, nay, nay," and the Republican pattern was "nay, aye, aye." It may be noted that some legislators in the House started to vote the Democratic pattern in the First Session but switched to the Republican pattern in the Second. See, for example, Byrne of New York, Celler of New York, Clemente of New York, Delaney of New York, Fugate of Virginia, Hobbs of Alabama, Magee of Missouri, Quinn of New York, and Ribicoff of Connecticut. The only Republicans to change from the Republican pattern in the First Session to the Democratic pattern in the Second were Engel of Michigan, Mack of Washington, O'Konski of Wisconsin, and Tollefson of Washington. The five Republicans who voted the Democratic pattern in both Sessions were: Gross of Iowa, Hagen of Minnesota, Hull of Wisconsin, Javits of New York, and Withrow of Wisconsin. Many Democrats voted the Republican pattern throughout. One Republican, Mason of Illinois, voted the Democratic pattern in the First Session and the Republican in the Second. The foregoing observations all concern only those legislators who voted the complete pattern of five roll calls, except Delaney and Quinn of New York with four votes. The figures would be higher in each tabulation if voting records of less than five roll calls were counted.

states, he had some trouble with the Congressional delegation from his own state. The voting pattern was a mixed
one. Of the 8 Tennessee Democrats in the House, 2 voted
in the Republican pattern, and 2 clearly voted in the Democratic pattern. The voting of the other Democrats was
confused. On the final vote only 1 of the 2 Republican
members of Congress from Tennessee voted in the Republican pattern.

Douglas of Illinois made special appeals to the West, the
South, and New England, on the ground that they had most
to lose by passage of S. 1008 and the least to gain. The appeal to New England was fruitless. Of the 6 Connecticut
representatives in the House (3 from each party) 5 voted in
the Republican pattern. Only Chase Going Woodhouse
opposed this trend. The 3 Maine Republicans voted the
Republican Party line. Of the 6 Massachusetts Democrats,
4 were, for the most part, in the Republican pattern, and
only 2 were clearly in the Democratic pattern. New Hampshire's 2 Republicans were in the pattern of their party, and
Rhode Island's 2 Democrats were in the pattern of their
party. Vermont's Republican Plumley voted Republican.
Of 28 Congressmen from New England, the Democrats had
a delegation of 11. Of these 11, 6 voted the Republican side.
The Republican votes (except those of Heselton of Massachusetts) were a solid block in support of S. 1008, with the
result that 22 of the 28 New England representatives voted
for S. 1008.

The South, the traditional bulwark of the Democratic
Party, split on the basing-point bill. Four of the 6 Florida
Democrats (no Republican representation) voted in the
Republican pattern. Four of the 7 Mississippi Democrats
voted in the Republican pattern. Tennessee has already
been mentioned. Seven of Virginia's 9 Democratic votes in
the House (no Republican representation) were cast in the
Republican pattern. There was no record of voting for one,

and the ninth was unclear. These four southern states had a total of 32 representatives in Congress, all Democrats, save 2 in Tennessee. Seventeen of these 30 Democrats voted in the Republican pattern.

The record in Alabama, Arkansas, Georgia, Kentucky, Louisiana, North Carolina, and South Carolina was considerably more in the Democratic pattern. Of the 59 Democratic representatives from these seven states, 16 voted in the Republican pattern. No Louisiana Democrats voted with the Republicans, however. In sum, a total of 33 out of 89 Democratic votes in the South were cast in the Republican pattern.

Douglas made a special appeal to the West also. In particular, he sought to persuade O'Mahoney that his often expressed concern about the state of the law on basing-point pricing was without foundation. Wyoming in the House has only one representative (a Republican in the Eighty-first Congress), and he voted in the Republican pattern.

From the midwestern states of Illinois, Iowa, Indiana, Kansas, Michigan, Minnesota, Missouri, Nebraska, North and South Dakota, and Wisconsin came House delegations totaling 108 representatives, of whom the Democrats had 43 and the Republicans 65. Of the 43 Democrats, 7 voted in the Republican pattern, 6 from Illinois and 1 from Missouri. Of the Republicans, 8 voted in the Democratic pattern: Gross of Iowa, Engel of Michigan, Hagen of Minnesota, Burdick and Lemke of North Dakota, and Hull, O'Konski, and Withrow of Wisconsin. It may be said of the Midwest, as it could not be said of the South, that the party lines were substantially unimpaired. Indeed, had it not been for the Illinois Democrats, the opponents of S. 1008 would have picked up strength from the Republicans in the Midwest.

The Southwest—Arizona, New Mexico, Oklahoma, and

Texas—had a representation in the House of 33 Congressmen, all of whom were of the Democratic Party. Of this number 16 voted in the Republican pattern.

The mountain states excluding Wyoming—Colorado, Idaho, Montana, Nevada, and Utah—had a House representation of 11 Congressmen, of whom 8 were Democrats and 3 were Republicans. The party lines held here. All 8 Democrats voted in the Democratic or antirevisionist pattern, and the three Republicans voted in the Republican or revisionist pattern. Wyoming, which has already been mentioned, did not change this alignment. The Pacific Coast states—California, Oregon, and Washington—were represented in the House by 33 Congressmen, of whom 13 were Democrats and 20 were Republicans. One of the 10 California Democrats voted in the Republican pattern and 2 of the Washington Republicans voted in the Democratic pattern. Otherwise the party alignments held.

The Balance of Power

This voting record reveals which blocs were decisive in making majorities for S. 1008. The total Democratic representation in the House for the Eighty-first Congress ranged from 261 to 258. The Republican representation ranged from 171 to 169 in the House. In the House votes of the delegations from New England, the South, and the states west of the Mississippi, 56 Democrats voted in the Republican pattern on S. 1008, and 49 of these came from states below the Mason-Dixon line. Among the New England, southern, midwestern, and western delegations, Republicans yielded only 9 votes to the opponents of S. 1008, none of which came from the South or the Southwest. It is clear then that the South and the Southwest had the balance of power in the voting, and that there was enough defection from the Democrats in these two areas to give to the supporters of S. 1008 a clear majority. When to this is added the strength which was picked up from the Democrats in Illinois, Maryland, Ohio, and Pennsylvania—a total of 24 Democratic votes in the Republican pattern out of a possible 42 Democratic votes—the balance was decisively swung to the supporters of S. 1008. The four steel states plus the South and the Southwest drew enough Democrats out of the Democratic working majority of 90 in the House to carry the day for revision of S. 1008. Indeed, the total number of Democrats in all states who voted in the Republican pattern was 86, or almost equivalent to the entire nominal party majority which the Democrats had won in the 1948 elections.

The evidence that the defections from the Democratic side were concentrated in the steel and oil states and among the Dixiecrats of the South throws light upon the presidential decision to veto S. 1008. Confronted with a choice between losing his friends among the liberals—Patman, Douglas, Kefauver, Long, Humphrey, and so on—and doing something agreeable for the Southerners, who contributed so many votes to the other side, the President did not need to take even the length of the constitutional period to make up his mind on the matter. As the champion of the "liberal" side of public issues, as the foe of the Dixiecrats who tried in 1948 to throw the national election into the Electoral College so that they could beat him, as one who had acquired national prominence as a friend of small business in the matter of war contracts, Truman could not have failed to read the record of the voting in the House as a justification of the veto.

The Senate voting record did nothing to change the presumption in favor of a veto. On the final vote which sent the bill to the White House, Byrd and Robertson of Virginia both voted in the Republican pattern, as did Hoey of North Carolina and Maybank of South Carolina. Of the states of the Southwest, Hayden and McFarland of Arizona,

Kerr and Thomas of Oklahoma, and Anderson of New Mexico, all Democrats, either voted for S. 1008, or were paired for it. Only the Texas Senators, Connally and Johnson, voted or were paired against the measure, although Chavez of New Mexico expressed a Democratic preference. In all, nine Senators from the South and Southwest supported the Republican side of the controversy, enough to weight the balance of power in the Senate on the side of the Republicans, although the Democrats had a formal total of 53, or 4 more than is necessary for an absolute majority in the Senate. The only Republicans who voted "Democratic" on the decisive ballot were the Senators from Wisconsin as has been noted, though Aiken, Langer, Morse, and Young were paired on the Democratic side, and Schoeppel indicated a Democratic preference. The party line on the Republican side was firm. The only other Democrats in the Senate to vote the Republican side on the final vote were the leaders of the drive to revise the law—O'Conor of Maryland, Johnson of Colorado, McCarran of Nevada, Myers of Pennsylvania, and O'Mahoney of Wyoming—who were joined by Chapman of Kentucky and Tydings of Maryland. Hunt of Wyoming, McMahon of Connecticut, and Thomas of Oklahoma were paired in favor. It is evident, therefore, that in their own party the Democratic sponsors of S. 1008 managed principally to lead Senators from the Southern states and the Southwest. Since it is rare for the voters of these states to fail to support a Democratic presidential candidate, even when they do not like him, Truman had relatively little to lose by vetoing the bill which they had supported.

Politics as Group Stuggle

A summary view of the struggle over S. 1008 shows policy emerging as a by-product of group actions and interactions. The congressional phase was set in motion by the Cement

Case of 1948. In this case, the Federal Trade Commission had successfully appealed to the Supreme Court to sustain the Commission order requiring the Cement Institute to dissolve. The character of the Cement Institute as a structure of power in its internal organization and its external relations was well documented by the Commission in its findings. Industrial groups like the steel and oil companies and the cement interests, believing themselves to be adversely affected by the Cement Case, then turned to Congress to persuade it to rewrite the rules, so as to protect pricing practices said to have been endangered and cast in doubt by the pronouncements of the Supreme Court.

Friendly subgroups of Congress carried forward this campaign in the last session of the Eightieth Congress and in the opening months of the Eighty-first. Thereafter the leadership passed into the hands of O'Mahoney, usually the spokesman for the opposition to any relaxation of the antitrust laws. This anomaly was not fully appreciated at the outset, but when it was the leadership of the deserted opposition in the House passed to another of its established champions, Patman of Texas. In the Senate, Douglas took on O'Mahoney's traditional role. Before the full import of the anomaly was appreciated, however, O'Mahoney had succeeded in obtaining an official consensus in support of his measure, a combination which included the Federal Trade Commission and the Department of Justice, official groups sometimes opposed to each other. The resistance of Douglas and his supporters in the Senate helped to weaken this official consensus, and the Federal Trade Commission then withdrew its support, having previously been put in the embarrassing position of supporting action to repudiate policies it had sought to develop. But the O'Mahoney alliance of private and official groups outside of Congress, joined with Republicans and Dixiecrats within Congress,

was able to push through the measure and send it on its way
to the White House.

The Patman-Douglas coalition was not fully effective
until S. 1008 was out of the Senate and in the White House.
When it became apparent to the White House that O'Mahoney was committing the President to the support of business and other groups to which the Patman-Douglas
combination was opposed, the White House had to decide
whether to seek new friends at the risk of losing old and
established friends. It chose to maintain its reputation and
stand with the latter. The strength of the Patman-Douglas
combination was too diffuse when applied to Congress; it
was in full concentrated strength when applied to the
White House.

It may have appeared to O'Mahoney like a betrayal for
the White House to seem to support him in 1949, only to
withdraw this support in 1950. O'Mahoney was looking
for the combination that would win; Patman and Douglas
were looking for the combination that would defeat O'Mahoney. It is quite possible that the balance of power among
the contending groups was actually in favor of O'Mahoney
in 1949, and that if a final vote could have been had at that
time, the White House would have approved the bill. Extra
force was undoubtedly given to the representations and
pressures of the Patman-Douglas coalition in 1950 by the
fact that it was a year of election.

It has been said that Congress represents minorities,
while the President represents the majority. To the extent
that this is true, the White House had to decide what the
majority view was, or was likely to be. This is one of the most
critical and delicate decisions any democratic politician
makes. Polls to one side, the evidence of what the popular
majority is, or is likely to be on any issue, is sometimes as
intangible and uninforming as the viscera from which the
haruspices of Rome once sought to extract reliable inter-

pretations about events that were as inscrutable to the dead fowl as to its slayers. The fact that Congress had enacted a bill did not necessarily mean that it was an action that the popular majority would approve if informed about it. As the voting record revealed, the enactment of the bill by a Democratic Congress did not necessarily imply that the measure was a "party" measure. Although difficult to ascertain, and although the risks of wrong choices may be grave, democratic politicians constantly search for the elusive majorities on the many public issues which press in upon them for decision. The President believed that the majority view was that professed by the small business groups. Governor Duff thought that the judgment of the White House was wrong on this matter, and that therefore S. 1008 would be an issue in the 1950 campaign. Although the Democratic Party lost strength in Congress in 1950, it does not appear that S. 1008 had anything to do with the loss. In fact, the chief prop and support of S. 1008 in Pennsylvania, Senator Myers, was defeated for re-election, and Congressman Javits of New York, the only New York Republican to vote consistently against S. 1008, was returned to Congress.

Those who scorn the vocation of the politician, those who view the history of S. 1008 as just another example of the perfidy of politicos bent upon perpetuating themselves in office at whatever cost, reckon too low the value of this flexibility of opinion, judgment, and action in the democratic process. There is a jest which says that the politician is the man who can rise above principle. Actually he does not, because he serves the principle of toleration and compromise, without which the democratic process would not function at all. Only authoritarian systems push upon the people bodies of fixed principles without counting the desires of the people. Only totalitarian governments profess to know what is best for the people despite the evident assurances of the people to the contrary.

Democratic politicians must reflect the consensus, and most of the time of legislators and chief executives is spent in determining what the consensus is. There are no infallible signs, and the White House guess on the balance of power could have been wrong. Congressmen are vulnerable to particular pressures brought by powerful groups who hope to identify their particular group interest with the national interest, and the pressures of these groups are acutely felt in the small constituencies at home. Besides this, Congressmen continually seek to forecast the reactions of incipient and unorganized groups which, although not immediately organized and aroused, might conceivably become so. The President is generally less vulnerable to the direct pressures of organized groups because his constituency is national and not local; and for pressure groups to defeat him requires an expenditure of effort and money sometimes out of keeping with the value of the prize which this effort wins. But he is not less responsive than the Congressman in his anticipation of the reactions of incipient and unorganized groups.

While we may view the legislature as a vast and intricate apparatus for simplifying complicated questions so that Congressmen may say "aye" or "nay," the history of S. 1008 makes it clear that this engine for the conciliation of differences is not impersonal, and that a shrewd knowledge of the inner workings of the mechanism may speed or slow it to the advantage of those who understand its secrets, may cause it to run more favorably for one side than another, and so may prejudice the final result. Thus, O'Mahoney got Congress to enact a bill on which there had been no formal hearings, indeed no hearings at all, in the procedural sense. It was all very well for the revisionists to display in the record an asserted tally of the time spent on S. 1008 and the number and length of the hearings devoted to it. But the hearings counted were on another measure entirely, and the only formal committee consideration given to O'Mahoney's version of S. 1008 was that of the House Judiciary Committee in executive session in 1949, when the Wyoming Senator appeared to have the Kefauver amendment stricken from the bill.

And yet, without formal committee hearings, the measure did in fact get a full review because of the zeal and watchfulness of Douglas, Long, and Kefauver in the Senate. The debate in 1949 and 1950 in the Senate provided the detailed examination that had not been given to the measure in committee. The traditional liberality of the Senate in debate made this result possible, for the same degree of consideration was denied in the House of Representatives, where stricter discipline prevails. All that Patman could wring from a reluctant leadership in the House was a little time out of the regular schedule. But even in the Senate, the hearing which the Douglas group managed to get might have been stultified by the stratagem of McCarran, who almost managed to slip the first conference report through the Senate without any discussion at all. At critical points, therefore, a knowledge of the workings of the legislative machinery helped to make it fulfill its function as a device for developing and recording the opinions of Congressmen and prevented it from being used as a contrivance for defeating this purpose. On the alert, the Douglas group was supported by the Senate tradition of unlimited debate, and the matter that Myers of Pennsylvania had told Lucas would take an hour took a year. Congressman Jennings of Tennessee expressed the feeling of haste and hurry which the House rules beget when he refused to be interrupted, at one point, saying that he was "like a mummy, pressed for time."

An awareness of the nature of the group struggle, ubiquitous and constant, is basic to an understanding of what went on in the Eightieth and Eighty-first Congresses. But, at the same time, it is impossible to witness the process in

Congress without admiration for the strength of this vital institution of a free people in a democracy. Congressmen looked and sounded inept, and even silly and confused, in various stages of the passage of S. 1008 from committee consideration to final enactment. And many would have disagreed with the way in which Congress finally acted on this particular issue. But when so much is said, the fact remains that a fantastically complicated question of public policy was refined and sifted as it went through the mechanism of legislative procedure, at each stage reducing the number of alternatives to be decided, until the final stage was reached, and it was then possible for Congressmen to say "aye" or "nay" to a specific and simplified, even oversimplified, choice about which they could make up their minds.

Appendix A

VOTING RECORD OF HOUSE OF REPRESENTATIVES ON S. 1008

Explanation of Table

1. Motion to recommit conference report, instructing House managers to insist on House amendments. Rejected, 178 to 138, October 14, 1949.
2. Motion to agree to conference report. Accepted 200 to 104, October 14, 1949.
3. Motion to send to further conference. Passed 240 to 144, February 28, 1950.
4. Motion to table motion to instruct House conferees to insist on House amendments. Passed 210 to 162, February 28, 1950.
5. Motion to recommit to conference. Rejected 204 to 175, March 14, 1950.

Symbols Used for Votes

Y—for	(Y)—paired for
N—against	(N)—paired against

O—absent, general pair, not announced, or not in office

Voting Record

DEMOCRATS	1	2	3	4	5		1	2	3	4	5
						Andrews (Ala.)	N	Y	Y	Y	N
Abbitt (Va.)	O	O	Y	N	Y	Aspinall (Colo.)	Y	N	Y	N	Y
Abernethy (Miss.)	N	Y	Y	Y	Y	Bailey (W. Va.)	N	Y	N	N	Y
Addonizio (N.J.)	Y	N	N	N	Y	Barden (N.C.)	O	O	O	O	Y
Albert (Okla.)	Y	Y	N	N	Y	Baring (Nev.)	O	O	N	N	Y
Allen (La.)	Y	N	(N)	(N)	Y	Barrett (Penn.)	N	Y	Y	Y	N

229

Voting Record (continued)

Bates (Ky.)	Y	N	N	N	Y	Cooley (N.C.)	N	O	Y	Y	Y
Battle (Ala.)	Y	Y	N	N	(Y)	Cooper (Tenn.)	Y	N	Y	N	Y
Beckworth (Tex.)	Y	N	N	N	Y	Cox (Ga.)	N	Y	Y	Y	O
Bennett (Fla.)	Y	N	N	N	Y	Crook (Ind.)	Y	N	N	N	Y
Bentsen (Tex.)	O	O	N	N	Y	Crosser (Ohio)	O	O	N	N	Y
Biemiller (Wisc.)	Y	N	N	N	Y	Davenport (Penn.)	N	Y	Y	Y	N
Bland (Va.)	O	O	O	O	O	Davies (N.Y.)	(Y)	(N)	O	Y	N
Blatnik (Minn.)	O	(N)	N	N	Y	Davis (Tenn.)	Y	Y	O	O	Y
Bloom (N.Y.)	O	O	O	O	O	Davis (Ga.)	N	Y	Y	Y	Y
Boggs (La.)	Y	N	N	N	Y	Dawson (Ill.)	O	O	O	O	(Y)
Bolling (Mo.)	Y	N	N	N	Y	Deane (N.C.)	Y	N	N	N	Y
Bolton (Md.)	N	Y	Y	Y	Y	deGraffenried (Ala.)	O	O	Y	N	O
Bonner (N.C.)	O	O	Y	Y	N	Delaney (N.Y.)	Y	O	Y	Y	N
Bosone (Utah)	Y	N	N	N	Y	Denton (Ind.)	Y	N	N	N	Y
Boykin (Ala.)	N	Y	Y	Y	N	Dingell (Mich.)	Y	N	N	N	(Y)
Breen (Ohio)	Y	Y	N	N	Y	Dollinger (N.Y.)	Y	N	N	N	Y
Brooks (La.)	Y	N	O	O	Y	Donohue (Mass.)	O	O	Y	Y	N
Brown (Ga.)	Y	N	N	O	Y	Doughton (N.C.)	N	Y	N	N	N
Bryson (S.C.)	Y	N	N	N	Y	Douglas (Calif.)	Y	N	(N)	(N)	(Y)
Buchanan (Penn.)	N	Y	Y	Y	N	Doyle (Calif.)	(Y)	(N)	N	N	(Y)
Buckley (N.Y.)	O	(N)	(N)	(N)	(Y)	Durham (N.C.)	O	O	N	N	Y
Buckley (Ill.)	N	Y	Y	Y	N	Eberharter (Penn.)	N	Y	Y	Y	N
Bulwinkle (N.C.)	O	O	O	O	O	Elliott (Ala.)	Y	N	N	N	Y
Burke (Ohio)	Y	N	N	N	Y	Engle (Calif.)	N	Y	Y	O	N
Burleson (Tex.)	N	Y	Y	Y	Y	Evins (Tenn.)	Y	N	N	N	Y
Burnside (W. Va.)	Y	O	N	N	N	Fallon (Md.)	N	Y	Y	Y	N
Burton (Va.)	N	Y	Y	Y	N	Feighan (Ohio)	Y	N	N	N	Y
Byrne (N.Y.)	(Y)	(N)	Y	Y	N	Fernandez (N.M.)	N	Y	Y	Y	N
Camp (Ga.)	O	N	N	N	Y	Fisher (Tex.)	N	Y	Y	Y	N
Cannon (Mo.)	Y	N	O	O	Y	Flood (Penn.)	O	O	Y	Y	N
Carlyle (N.C.)	Y	Y	N	N	Y	Fogarty (R.I.)	Y	N	N	(N)	(Y)
Carnahan (Mo.)	Y	N	N	N	Y	Forand (R.I.)	Y	N	Y	N	Y
Carroll (Colo.)	Y	N	N	N	Y	Frazier (Tenn.)	N	Y	Y	Y	Y
Cavalcante (Penn.)	Y	N	N	N	N	Fugate (Va.)	Y	N	Y	Y	N
Celler (N.Y.)	Y	N	Y	Y	N	Furcolo (Mass.)	Y	N	O	O	Y
Chatham (N.C.)	O	O	Y	N	O	Garmatz (Md.)	(Y)	(Y)	N	N	Y
Chelf (Ky.)	N	Y	Y	Y	N	Gary (Va.)	O	O	Y	Y	N
Chesney (Ill.)	N	Y	Y	Y	N	Gathings (Ark.)	Y	Y	N	N	Y
Christopher (Mo.)	O	O	N	N	Y	Gilmer (Okla.)	N	Y	(Y)	(Y)	(N)
Chudoff (Penn.)	Y	N	(N)	(N)	Y	Gordon (Ill.)	N	Y	Y	Y	N
Clemente (N.Y.)	Y	N	Y	Y	(N)	Gore (Tenn.)	Y	Y	Y	N	O
Coffey (Penn.)	O	O	O	O	O	Gorski (N.Y.)	Y	N	N	N	Y
Colmer (Miss.)	N	Y	Y	O	N	Gorski (Ill.)	(N)	(Y)	O	O	O
Combs (Tex.)	Y	N	N	N	Y	Gossett (Tex.)	N	Y	Y	Y	O

Voting Record (continued)

Granahan (Penn.)	N	Y	Y	Y	N	Lesinski (Mich.)	Y	N	N	N	Y
Granger (Utah)	Y	N	Y	N	Y	Lind (Penn.)	N	Y	Y	Y	N
Grant (Ala.)	Y	O	N	Y	Y	Linehan (Ill.)	N	Y	Y	Y	N
Green (Penn.)	O	O	Y	Y	N	Lucas (Tex.)	O	O	Y	Y	N
Gregory (Ky.)	O	O	N	N	Y	Lyle (Tex.)	Y	O	O	O	Y
Hardy (Va.)	N	Y	Y	Y	N	Lynch (N.Y.)	O	O	N	N	Y
Hare (S.C.)	Y	Y	Y	Y	Y	McCarthy (Minn.)	Y	N	N	N	Y
Harris (Ark.)	N	Y	Y	Y	N	McCormack (Mass.)	Y	Y	Y	N	N
Harrison (Va.)	Y	Y	Y	Y	O	McGrath (N.Y.)	Y	N	(N)	(N)	(Y)
Hart (N.J.)	Y	N	N	N	Y	McGuire (Conn.)	N	Y	Y	Y	Y
Havenner (Calif.)	Y	N	N	N	Y	McKinnon (Calif.)	(Y)	(N)	N	N	Y
Hays (Ark.)	Y	Y	N	N	Y	McMillan (S.C.)	O	O	Y	Y	Y
Hays (Ohio)	(Y)	(Y)	N	N	Y	McSweeney (Ohio)	(Y)	(N)	N	N	N
Hébert (La.)	O	O	Y	N	Y	Mack (Ill.)	O	O	N	N	Y
Hedrick (W. Va.)	N	Y	(N)	(N)	N	Madden (Ind.)	Y	Y	N	N	Y
Heffernan (N.Y.)	(Y)	(N)	N	(N)	Y	Magee (Mo.)	Y	N	Y	Y	(N)
Heller (N.Y.)	(Y)	(N)	N	N	(Y)	Mahon (Tex.)	Y	Y	Y	Y	N
Herlong (Fla.)	N	O	Y	Y	N	Mansfield (Mont.)	O	O	N	N	Y
Hobbs (Ala.)	Y	N	Y	Y	N	Marsalis (Colo.)	Y	N	Y	N	Y
Holifield (Calif.)	Y	N	N	N	Y	Marshall (Minn.)	Y	N	N	N	Y
Howell (N.J.)	Y	Y	N	N	Y	Miles (N.M.)	Y	Y	Y	Y	N
Huber (Ohio)	Y	N	N	N	Y	Miller (Calif.)	Y	N	N	N	Y
Irving (Mo.)	Y	N	N	N	Y	Mills (Ark.)	Y	N	N	N	Y
Jackson (Wash.)	Y	N	N	N	Y	Mitchell (Wash.)	Y	N	N	N	Y
Jacobs (Ind.)	Y	N	N	N	Y	Monroney (Okla.)	Y	Y	N	N	(Y)
Jones (N.C.)	Y	Y	N	N	Y	Morgan (Penn.)	O	O	N	N	N
Jones (Mo.)	Y	N	Y	Y	Y	Morris (Okla.)	Y	Y	N	N	Y
Jones (Ala.)	Y	N	N	N	Y	Morrison (La.)	Y	N	(N)	(N)	Y
Karst (Mo.)	Y	N	N	N	Y	Moulder (Nev.)	Y	N	N	N	Y
Karsten (Mo.)	Y	N	N	N	Y	Multer (N.Y.)	(Y)	(N)	N	N	Y
Kee (W. Va.)	O	O	N	N	Y	Murdock (Ariz.)	Y	Y	N	N	Y
Kelley (Penn.)	N	Y	(Y)	(Y)	N	Murphy (N.Y.)	(Y)	(N)	N	N	Y
Kelly (N.Y.)	O	O	N	N	Y	Murray (Tenn.)	Y	Y	Y	N	Y
Kennedy (Mass.)	Y	Y	Y	(Y)	N	Noland (Ind.)	Y	N	N	N	Y
Keogh (N.Y.)	(Y)	(N)	N	N	N	Norrell (Ark.)	N	Y	Y	O	N
Kerr (N.C.)	Y	Y	N	N	(Y)	Norton (N.J.)	Y	Y	N	N	(Y)
Kilday (Tex.)	N	Y	Y	Y	N	O'Brien (Mich.)	Y	N	(N)	(N)	Y
King (Calif.)	Y	N	N	N	Y	O'Brien (Ill.)	N	Y	Y	Y	N
Kirwan (Ohio)	N	Y	Y	Y	N	O'Hara (Ill.)	N	Y	Y	Y	N
Klein (N.Y.)	Y	N	N	N	Y	O'Neill (Penn.)	N	Y	O	Y	N
Kruse (Ind.)	N	Y	N	N	Y	O'Sullivan (Neb.)	Y	N	N	N	Y
Lane (Mass.)	Y	N	N	N	Y	O'Toole (N.Y.)	Y	N	N	N	N
Lanham (Ga.)	Y	N	N	N	Y	Pace (Ga.)	O	O	O	O	Y
Larcade (La.)	O	O	N	N	Y	Passman (La.)	Y	N	N	N	Y

Voting Record (continued)

Patman (Tex.)	Y	N	N	N	Y	Sullivan (Mo.)	Y	N	N	N	Y
Patten (Ariz.)	(Y)	O	Y	N	Y	Sutton (Tenn.)	Y	N	N	N	Y
Perkins (Ky.)	(Y)	(N)	N	N	Y	Tackett (Ark.)	N	Y	Y	Y	N
Peterson (Fla.)	N	Y	Y	Y	N	Tauriello (N.Y.)	(Y)	(N)	N	N	Y
Pfeifer (N.Y.)	(Y)	(N)	(N)	(N)	N	Teague (Tex.)	O	Y	(Y)	(Y)	N
Philbin (Mass.)	O	O	Y	Y	(N)	Thomas (Tex.)	Y	N	Y	(Y)	N
Pickett (Tex.)	N	Y	Y	Y	N	Thompson (Tex.)	(Y)	(N)	Y	N	Y
Poage (Tex.)	Y	N	O	O	Y	Thornberry (Tex.)	O	O	N	N	Y
Polk (Ohio)	Y	N	N	N	Y	Trimble (Ark.)	Y	N	N	N	Y
Powell (N.Y)	(Y)	(N)	N	N	Y	Underwood (Ky.)	O	O	N	N	Y
Preston (Ga.)	Y	N	N	N	Y	Vinson (Ga.)	O	O	N	N	Y
Price (Ill.)	Y	N	N	N	Y	Wagner (Ohio)	Y	N	N	N	Y
Priest (Tenn.)	Y	Y	Y	N	Y	Walsh (Ind.)	Y	N	N	N	Y
Quinn (N.Y.)	Y	O	Y	Y	(N)	Walter (Penn.)	O	O	Y	Y	N
Rabaut (Mich.)	Y	N	N	N	(Y)	Welch (Mo.)	Y	N	Y	N	Y
Rains (Ala.)	O	O	N	N	Y	Wheeler (Ga.)	N	N	Y	N	Y
Ramsay (W. Va.)	Y	O	Y	O	N	Whitaker (Ky.)	N	Y	(Y)	(Y)	(N)
Rankin (Miss.)	Y	N	N	N	Y	White (Calif.)	Y	O	N	Y	Y
Rayburn (Tex.)	O	O	O	O	O	White (Idaho)	O	O	N	N	Y
Redden (N.C.)	N	Y	O	O	Y	Whitten (Miss.)	N	Y	Y	Y	N
Regan (Tex.)	(N)	(Y)	O	O	N	Whittington					
Rhodes (Penn.)	O	Y	Y	Y	N	(Miss.)	N	Y	Y	Y	N
Ribicoff (Conn.)	(Y)	(N)	Y	Y	N	Wickersham (Okla.)	Y	N	N	N	Y
Richards (S.C.)	O	O	N	N	Y	Wier (Minn.)	Y	N	N	N	Y
Rivers (S.C.)	N	Y	Y	Y	O	Williams (Miss.)	N	Y	N	N	Y
Rodino (N.J.)	Y	N	N	N	Y	Willis (La.)	Y	N	N	N	Y
Rogers (Fla.)	N	Y	N	Y	N	Wilson (Okla.)	Y	N	N	N	Y
Rooney (N.Y.)	Y	N	N	N	Y	Wilson (Tex.)	N	Y	Y	Y	N
Sabath (Ill.)	O	O	O	O	O	Winstead (Miss.)	N	Y	N	N	Y
Sadowski (Mich.)	O	(N)	O	O	(Y)	Wood (Ga.)	O	O	Y	Y	Y
Sasscer (Md.)	N	Y	Y	Y	Y	Woodhouse (Conn.)	(Y)	O	N	N	Y
Secrest (Ohio)	N	Y	(Y)	(Y)	N	Worley (Tex.)	O	O	O	O	Y
Shelley (Calif.)	O	O	(N)	(N)	Y	Yates (Ill.)	Y	N	(N)	(N)	Y
Sheppard (Calif.)	Y	O	N	O	(Y)	Young (Ohio)	Y	N	N	N	Y
Sikes (Fla.)	N	Y	Y	Y	N	Zablocki (Wisc.)	Y	N	N	N	Y
Sims (S.C.)	Y	N	N	N	Y						
Smathers (Fla.)	(N)	(Y)	O	O	O	**REPUBLICANS**					
Smith (Va.)	O	O	Y	Y	(N)	Allen (Calif.)	N	Y	Y	Y	N
Somers (N.Y.)	O	O	O	O	O	Allen (Ill.)	O	O	Y	Y	N
Spence (Ky.)	N	Y	Y	Y	N	Andersen (Minn.)	N	Y	Y	Y	Y
Staggers (W. Va.)	Y	N	N	N	O	Anderson (Calif.)	N	Y	O	O	N
Stanley (Va.)	N	Y	Y	Y	N	Andresen (Minn.)	N	Y	Y	Y	N
Steed (Okla.)	N	Y	Y	Y	Y	Angell (Oregon)	O	O	Y	Y	N
Stigler (Okla.)	Y	Y	Y	Y	Y	Arends (Ill.)	N	Y	Y	Y	N

Voting Record (continued)

Auchincloss (N.J.)	(N)	(Y)	Y	Y	N	Gillette (Penn.)	N	Y	Y	Y	N
Barrett (Wyo.)	(N)	(Y)	Y	Y	N	Golden (Ky.)	O	O	O	O	Y
Bates (Mass.)	N	Y	Y	Y	N	Goodwin (Mass.)	N	Y	Y	Y	N
Beall (Md.)	N	Y	Y	Y	N	Graham (Penn.)	N	Y	Y	Y	N
Bennett (Mich.)	N	Y	Y	Y	N	Gross (Iowa)	Y	N	N	N	Y
Bishop (Ill.)	N	Y	Y	Y	N	Gwinn (N.Y.)	O	O	Y	Y	N
Blackney (Mich.)	N	Y	Y	Y	N	Hagen (Minn.)	Y	N	N	N	Y
Boggs (Del.)	N	Y	O	O	N	Hale (Me.)	N	Y	Y	O	N
Bolton (Ohio)	N	Y	Y	Y	N	Hall, E. A. (N.Y.)	O	O	Y	N	N
Bramblett (Calif.)	N	Y	Y	Y	Y	Hall, L. W. (N.Y.)	N	Y	Y	Y	N
Brehm (Ohio)	N	Y	Y	Y	N	Halleck (Ind.)	N	Y	Y	Y	N
Brown (Ohio)	N	Y	Y	Y	N	Hand (N.J.)	N	Y	Y	N	Y
Burdick (N.D.)	Y	N	N	N	O	Harden (Ind.)	O	O	Y	Y	N
Byrnes (Wisc.)	N	Y	Y	Y	N	Harvey (Ind.)	O	O	Y	Y	N
Canfield (N.J.)	Y	N	N	N	Y	Herter (Mass.)	N	Y	(Y)	(Y)	N
Case (N.J.)	N	Y	Y	Y	N	Heselton (Mass.)	Y	Y	Y	N	Y
Case (S.D.)	N	Y	Y	Y	N	Hill (Colo.)	N	Y	Y	Y	N
Chiperfield (Ill.)	N	Y	Y	Y	(N)	Hinshaw (Calif.)	N	Y	Y	Y	N
Church (Ill.)	N	Y	Y	Y	N	Hoeven (Iowa)	N	Y	Y	Y	N
Clevenger (Ohio)	N	Y	Y	O	O	Hoffman (Mich.)	(N)	(Y)	Y	Y	N
Cole (Kan.)	N	Y	Y	Y	N	Hoffman (Ill.)	O	O	(Y)	(Y)	O
Cole (N.Y.)	O	O	Y	O	N	Holmes (Wash.)	N	Y	Y	Y	N
Colton (N.H.)	N	Y	Y	Y	N	Hope (Kan.)	N	Y	Y	Y	N
Corbett (Penn.)	N	Y	Y	Y	N	Horan (Wash.)	N	Y	Y	Y	N
Coudert (N.Y.)	O	O	(Y)	(Y)	N	Hull (Wisc.)	Y	N	N	N	Y
Crawford (Mich)	O	O	Y	Y	N	Jackson (Calif.)	N	Y	(Y)	(Y)	N
Cunningham						James (Penn.)	N	Y	Y	Y	N
(Iowa)	N	Y	O	Y	N	Javits (N.Y.)	Y	N	N	N	Y
Curtis (Neb.)	N	Y	Y	Y	N	Jenison (Ill.)	N	Y	Y	Y	N
Dague (Penn.)	N	Y	Y	Y	N	Jenkins (Ohio)	(N)	(Y)	Y	Y	(N)
Davis (Wisc.)	N	Y	Y	Y	N	Jennings (Tenn.)	(N)	(Y)	O	Y	N
D'Ewart (Mont.)	N	Y	Y	Y	Y	Jensen (Iowa)	N	Y	Y	Y	N
Dolliver (Iowa)	N	Y	Y	Y	(N)	Johnson (Calif.)	N	Y	Y	Y	(N)
Dondero (Mich.)	(N)	(Y)	Y	O	N	Jonas (Ill.)	O	O	Y	Y	N
Eaton (N.J.)	(N)	O	Y	Y	N	Judd (Minn.)	O	O	Y	Y	N
Ellsworth (Ore.)	(N)	(Y)	Y	Y	(N)	Kean (N.J.)	(N)	(Y)	Y	Y	(N)
Elston (Ohio)	(N)	(Y)	Y	Y	N	Kearney (N.Y.)	O	O	Y	Y	N
Engel (Mich.)	N	Y	N	N	Y	Kearns (Penn.)	N	Y	Y	Y	N
Fellows (Me.)	O	O	Y	Y	N	Keating (N.Y.)	O	O	Y	N	Y
Fenton (Penn.)	N	Y	Y	Y	N	Keefe (Wisc.)	N	Y	Y	Y	N
Ford (Mich.)	N	Y	Y	Y	N	Kilburn (N.Y.)	O	O	Y	Y	N
Fulton (Penn.)	N	Y	Y	Y	N	Kunkel (Penn.)	N	Y	(Y)	(Y)	N
Gamble (N.Y.)	N	Y	Y	Y	N	Latham (N.Y.)	N	Y	Y	Y	N
Gavin (Penn.)	N	Y	Y	Y	N	LeCompte (Iowa)	N	Y	Y	Y	N

Voting Record (continued)

Name					
LeFevre (N.Y.)	N	Y	Y	Y	N
Lemke (N.D.)	Y	O	N	N	Y
Lichtenwalter (Penn.)	N	Y	Y	Y	N
Lodge (Conn.)	N	Y	Y	N	N
Lovre (S.D.)	N	Y	Y	Y	N
McConnell (Penn.)	N	Y	Y	Y	N
McCulloch (Ohio)	N	Y	Y	Y	N
McDonough (Calif.)	N	Y	Y	Y	N
McGregor (Ohio)	N	Y	Y	Y	N
McMillen (Ill.)	N	Y	Y	Y	N
Mack (Wash.)	N	Y	N	N	Y
Macy (N.Y.)	(N)	O	Y	Y	O
Martin (Mass.)	N	Y	Y	Y	N
Martin (Iowa)	N	Y	Y	Y	N
Mason (Ill.)	(Y)	(N)	Y	Y	N
Merrow (N.H.)	N	Y	Y	Y	O
Meyer (Kan.)	N	O	Y	Y	N
Michener (Mich.)	N	Y	Y	Y	(N)
Miller (Neb.)	(N)	(Y)	Y	Y	N
Miller (Md.)	N	Y	Y	Y	N
Morton (Ky.)	O	O	Y	O	N
Murray (Wisc.)	N	O	O	O	N
Nelson (Me.)	N	Y	Y	Y	N
Nicholson (Mass.)	N	Y	Y	Y	N
Nixon (Calif.)	(N)	(Y)	Y	O	N
Norblad (Ore.)	N	Y	Y	Y	N
O'Hara (Minn.)	N	Y	Y	Y	O
O'Konski (Wisc.)	N	Y	N	N	Y
Patterson (Conn.)	N	Y	Y	Y	N
Pfeiffer (N.Y.)	(N)	(Y)	Y	Y	(N)
Phillips (Tenn.)	O	O	N	N	Y
Phillips (Calif.)	O	O	Y	Y	N
Plumley (Vt.)	(N)	O	(Y)	Y	N
Potter (Mich.)	N	Y	Y	Y	N
Poulson (Calif.)	O	O	Y	N	O
Reed (Ill.)	(N)	O	Y	Y	N
Reed (N.Y.)	O	O	Y	Y	O
Rees (Kan.)	N	Y	Y	Y	Y
Rich (Penn.)	N	Y	Y	Y	N
Riehlman (N.Y.)	N	(Y)	Y	Y	N
Rogers (Mass.)	N	Y	Y	Y	N
Sadlak (Conn.)	O	O	Y	Y	N
St. George (N.Y.)	(N)	(Y)	Y	Y	N
Sanborn (Idaho)	O	O	Y	Y	N
Saylor (Penn.)	N	Y	Y	Y	N
Scott, Hardie (Penn.)	N	Y	Y	Y	N
Scott, Hugh D. (Penn.)	N	Y	Y	Y	N
Scrivner (Kan.)	N	Y	Y	Y	N
Scudder (Calif.)	N	Y	Y	Y	N
Shafer (Mich.)	N	Y	Y	O	O
Short (Mo.)	N	Y	Y	Y	N
Simpson (Pa.)	N	Y	Y	Y	N
Simpson (Ill.)	N	Y	Y	Y	N
Smith (Ohio)	(N)	(Y)	O	O	O
Smith (Wisc.)	N	Y	Y	Y	N
Smith (Kan.)	N	Y	Y	Y	N
Stefan (Neb.)	N	Y	Y	Y	N
Stockman (Ore.)	N	Y	Y	Y	N
Taber (N.Y.)	N	Y	Y	Y	N
Talle (Iowa)	N	Y	Y	Y	N
Taylor (N.Y.)	O	O	(Y)	(Y)	N
Thomas (N.J.)	O	O	O	O	O
Tollefson (Wash.)	N	Y	N	N	Y
Towe (N.J.)	(N)	(Y)	Y	(Y)	N
Van Zandt (Penn.)	N	Y	Y	Y	N
Velde (Ill.)	N	Y	Y	Y	N
Vorys (Ohio)	N	Y	Y	Y	N
Vursell (Ill.)	N	Y	Y	Y	N
Wadsworth (N.Y.)	N	O	Y	Y	N
Weichel (Ohio)	N	Y	Y	Y	N
Welch (Calif.)	O	O	O	O	O
Werdel (Calif.)	N	Y	Y	Y	N
Widnall (N.J.)	O	O	Y	Y	N
Wigglesworth (Mass.)	N	Y	Y	Y	N
Wilson (Ind.)	N	Y	Y	Y	N
Withrow (Wisc.)	Y	N	N	N	Y
Wolcott (Mich.)	N	Y	Y	Y	N
Wolverton (N.J.)	N	Y	Y	Y	(N)
Woodruff (Mich.)	N	Y	Y	Y	N

ALP

Marcantonio (N.Y.)	(Y)	(N)	(N)	(N)	Y

DEMOCRAT-LIBERAL

Roosevelt (N.Y.)	Y	N	N	N	(Y)

Appendix B

Explanation of Table

1. Motion to reconsider sending to conference. Rejected 49 to 28, August 12, 1949.
2. Motion to table motion that consideration be postponed until 1950. Rejected 29 to 29 with Chair voting in the negative, October 18, 1949.
3. Motion to accept conference report. Passed 43 to 27, June 2, 1950.

Symbols Used for Votes

Y—for   (Y)—paired for
N—against   (N)—paired against
    Y, N—not voting, unpaired, but expressed preference
   O—absent, general pair, not announced, or not in office

Voting Record

DEMOCRATS	1	2	3		1	2	3
Anderson (N.M.)	Y	N	(Y)	Downey (Calif.)	O	N	O
Benton (Conn.)	O	O	*N*	Eastland (Miss.)	O	O	(N)
Broughton (N.C.)	O	O	O	Ellender (La.)	Y	N	N
Byrd (Va.)	N	O	Y	Frear (Del.)	O	O	N
Chapman (Ky.)	(Y)	Y	Y	Fulbright (Ark.)	Y	N	N
Chavez (N.M.)	N	O	*N*	George (Ga.)	N	N	N
Connally (Tex.)	Y	N	N	Gillette (Iowa)	N	O	N
Douglas (Ill.)	Y	N	N	Graham (N.C.)	Y	N	*N*
				Green (R.I.)	Y	N	O

235

Voting Record (continued)

Hayden (Ariz.)	N	N	Y	Baldwin (Conn.)	(Y)	Y	O
Hill (Ala.)	Y	N	N	Brewster (Me.)	N	(Y)	Y
Hoey (N.C.)	N	O	Y	Bricker (Ohio)	(N)	(Y)	Y
Holland (Fla.)	Y	N	N	Bridges (N.H.)	N	Y	Y
Humphrey (Minn.)	Y	(N)	(N)	Butler (Neb.)	N	O	Y
Hunt (Wyo.)	N	O	(Y)	Cain (Wash.)	N	Y	Y
Johnson (Colo.)	N	Y	Y	Capehart (Ind.)	N	Y	Y
Johnson (Tex.)	(Y)	(N)	(N)	Cordon (Ore.)	N	Y	Y
Johnston (S.C.)	Y	N	(N)	Darby (Kan.)	O	O	Y
Kefauver (Tenn.)	Y	(N)	N	Donnell (Mo.)	N	Y	Y
Kerr (Okla.)	N	Y	Y	Dulles (N.Y.)	N	O	O
Kilgore (W. Va.)	N	N	N	Dworshak (Idaho)	O	Y	Y
Leahy (R.I.)	O	N	N	Ecton (Mont.)	N	Y	Y
Lehman (N.Y.)	O	O	N	Ferguson (Mich.)	N	N	Y
Long (La.)	Y	N	N	Flanders (Vt.)	O	O	Y
Lucas (Ill.)	Y	Y	N	Gurney (S.D.)	N	(Y)	(Y)
McCarran (Nev.)	N	O	Y	Hendrickson (N.J.)	(Y)	(N)	Y
McClellan (Ark.)	N	O	N	Hickenlooper (Iowa)	N	Y	(Y)
McFarland (Ariz.)	N	Y	(Y)	Ives (N.Y.)	N	N	Y
McGrath (R.I.)	Y	O	O	Jenner (Ind.)	N	Y	Y
McKellar (Tenn.)	N	N	O	Kem (Mo.)	N	Y	Y
McMahon (Conn.)	N	Y	(Y)	Knowland (Calif.)	N	Y	Y
Magnuson (Wash.)	Y	N	N	Langer (N.D.)	Y	N	(N)
Maybank (S.C.)	Y	O	Y	Lodge (Mass.)	N	Y	O
Miller (Idaho)	O	O	O	McCarthy (Wisc.)	N	Y	N
Murray (Mont.)	Y	O	N	Malone (Nev.)	N	N	Y
Myers (Penn.)	(N)	Y	Y	Martin (Penn.)	N	Y	Y
Neely (W. Va.)	O	N	N	Millikin (Colo.)	N	Y	Y
O'Conor (Md.)	N	Y	Y	Morse (Ore.)	Y	N	(N)
O'Mahoney (Wyo.)	N	N	Y	Mundt (S.D.)	N	O	Y
Pepper (Fla.)	Y	N	N	Reed (Kan.)	(N)	(Y)	O
Robertson (Va.)	N	O	Y	Saltonstall (Mass.)	(N)	Y	(Y)
Russell (Ga.)	Y	N	N	Schoeppel (Kan.)	N	Y	N
Sparkman (Ala.)	Y	(N)	N	Smith (N.J.)	N	Y	Y
Stennis (Miss.)	Y	O	(N)	Smith (Me.)	N	(N)	(Y)
Taylor (Idaho)	Y	O	N	Taft (Ohio)	(N)	(Y)	Y
Thomas (Utah)	N	N	N	Thye (Minn.)	N	(Y)	Y
Thomas (Okla.)	Y	O	(Y)	Tobey (N.H.)	(Y)	O	Y
Tydings (Md.)	N	O	Y	Vandenberg (Mich.)	N	O	Y
Wagner (N.Y.)	O	O	O	Watkins (Utah)	N	Y	Y
Withers (Ky.)	O	O	N	Wherry (Neb.)	N	Y	Y
				Wiley (Wisc.)	Y	O	N
REPUBLICANS				Williams (Del.)	N	Y	Y
Aiken (Vt.)	Y	N	(N)	Young (N.D.)	N	O	(N)

Index